Coaching to Empower Teachers

Learn how to make instructional coaching more empowering and effective by supporting teachers as learners and leaders in their own classrooms. This unique book offers a powerful assets-based coaching framework that capitalizes on teachers' strengths, internal motivation, and professional goals. The authors provide a useful analysis of popular theories and models that ground coaching and support intentional planning; tools and strategies to help you enact the framework through ongoing coaching cycles; and examples, vignettes, and transcripts to illustrate coaching in practice. Each chapter also includes opportunities for reflection and practice to guide you along the way.

Appropriate for school- and district-based coaches of all levels of experience, this book will enable you to provide a more targeted, proactive learning experience for ongoing teacher growth. With an instructional framework designed to empower teachers, increased teacher professional capacity can be expected for lasting impact on students, classrooms, schools, and communities.

Catherine Pendleton Hart, MEd and **Fredrica M. Nash, MAT** collectively have 18 years of experience as teachers and 16 years of experience as instructional coaches and education consultants. Currently an Education Consultant at RTI International, Catherine is a former high school English teacher. Her current instructional coaching work focuses on topics such as integrating SEL and rigor, planning for inquiry-based learning, and using competency-based assessments. Her work also includes developing teacher leaders and instructional coaches and supporting RTI's Aspire Teacher Preparation Program, an alternative program for teacher licensure. Fredrica is also currently an Education Consultant at RTI and is a former high school science teacher. Her coaching work covers a variety of topics and audiences—from developing instructional coaching programs, to coaching teachers, to supporting executive coaches in schools, districts, and state agencies. Her coaching is driven by her work in social and emotional learning, social justice pedagogies, and teacher empowerment.

Follow the authors on Twitter at @CatherinePHart and @Teach2Empower.

RTI Press Past Titles in Education Research

Cultivating Dynamic Educators:
Case Studies in Teacher Behavior Change in Africa and Asia
Sarah R. Pouezevara (Ed.)
(https://doi.org/10.3768/rtipress.2018.bk.0022.1809)

Leveraging Data for Student Success:
Improving Education Through Data-Driven Decisions
Laura G. Knapp, Elizabeth Glennie, Karen J. Charles
(https://doi.org/10.3768/rtipress.2016.bk.0018.1609)

The Early Grade Reading Assessment:
Applications and Interventions to Improve Basic Literacy
Amber Gove, Anna Wetterberg (Eds.)
(https://doi.org/10.3768/rtipress.2011.bk.0007.1109)

Noncognitive Skills in the Classroom:
New Perspectives on Educational Research
Jeffrey A. Rosen, Elizabeth J. Glennie, Ben W. Dalton,
Jean M. Lennon, Robert N. Bozick
(https://doi.org/10.3768/rtipress.2010.bk.0004.1009)

Coaching to Empower Teachers

A Framework for Improving Instruction and Well-Being

Catherine Pendleton Hart and Fredrica M. Nash

First published 2022
by Routledge
605 Third Avenue, New York, NY 10158

and by Routledge
2 Park Square, Milton Park, Abingdon, Oxon, OX14 4RN

Routledge is an imprint of the Taylor & Francis Group, an informa business

© 2022 RTI Press/RTI International. RTI International is a trade name of Research Triangle Institute. RTI and the RTI logo are U.S. registered trademarks of Research Triangle Institute.

The right of Catherine Pendleton Hart and Fredrica M. Nash to be identified as authors of this work has been asserted by them in accordance with sections 77 and 78 of the Copyright, Designs and Patents Act 1988.

All rights reserved. No part of this book may be reprinted or reproduced or utilised in any form or by any electronic, mechanical, or other means, now known or hereafter invented, including photocopying and recording, or in any information storage or retrieval system, without permission in writing from the publishers.

Trademark notice: Product or corporate names may be trademarks or registered trademarks, and are used only for identification and explanation without intent to infringe.

Library of Congress Cataloging-in-Publication Data
A catalog record for this book has been requested

ISBN: 978-1-032-02965-8 (hbk)
ISBN: 978-1-032-02366-3 (pbk)
ISBN: 978-1-003-18604-5 (ebk)

DOI: 10.4324/9781003186045

Typeset in Palatino
by Apex CoVantage, LLC

Dedication

For my mom and in loving memory of my dad (who would've called this book outstanding—whether it is or isn't). Thank you for empowering me.
—Catherine

For my parents, my ancestors, and my forever students, I am humbled and empowered by you.
—Fredrica

Contents

Preface	*xiv*
Authors' Gratitude	*xxiii*
About the Authors	*xxiv*

PART I
Foundations of Coaching — 1

1 Addressing Teacher Well-Being — 3
   Introduction to Teacher Well-Being — 3
   Factors That Impact Teacher Well-Being — 4
      Disempowerment — 4
      Secondary Traumatic Stress — 5
      Burnout — 5
   Impact of Stress and Burnout on Classroom Outcomes — 6
   Coaching as a Mitigating Factor — 7
   Conclusion — 9

2 Principles of Coaching — 10
   The Role of a Coach — 10
   Who Needs a Coach? — 12
   The Qualities of a Coach — 14
   The CoachED Principles of Coaching — 15
      Teachers Are Professional, Passionate, and Autonomous Individuals — 15
      Empowered Teachers Are Leaders in Their Classrooms Who Create Environments in Which Students Thrive — 15
      Teacher Beliefs (Including Beliefs About Personal Efficacy) Are Malleable — 17
      Teachers' Reflective Thinking Is Essential to Building Instructional and Leadership Capacity — 17
   Revisiting Context — 19
   Conclusion — 20

3 Research-Based Coaching — 21
   Approaches, Models, and Theories — 21
      Engage Teachers as Learners — 23
          Self-Determination Theory — 23

Theory of Andragogy	24
Asset-Based Approach	24
Understand Change	25
Conscious Competence Model	25
Transtheoretical Change Model (TTM)	25
Leveraging Learning Experiences	26
Transformative Learning Theory	26
Experiential Learning Theory	27
Conclusion	27
4 Foundational Techniques of Coaching	**30**
Opening Vignette: Jolie and Mr. Parsons	30
Building Foundations for Coaching	32
The Purpose of Coaching	32
The Process of Coaching	34
Macrocoaching	34
Visioning	35
Goal Setting	36
Planning	37
Microcoaching	38
Planning	38
Implementation	39
Reflective Thinking	39
Microcycles in Action: Classroom Data Collection	40
Pre-Visit	40
Visit	41
Post-Visit	42
The Role of Data in Microcycles	42
Components of Microcoaching Conversations	43
Opening and Relationship Building	43
Implementation Check-In	44
Next Steps	44
Other Work	44
Foundational Coaching Skills	45
Building Relationships	45
Providing Effective Feedback	47
Types of Feedback	47
Purpose of Feedback	49
Foundational Questioning Techniques	51
Clarifying vs. Probing vs. Suggestive Questions (NSRF and SRI)	52
Asset-Based Questioning	55

Active Listening	56
Nonjudgment and Body Language	57
Reflective Listening Statements	57
Silence	61
Addressing Equity through Foundations of Coaching	62
Conclusion	62

PART II
The CoachED Framework   65

5 An Introduction to the CoachED Framework   67

Opening Vignette: Jonathon and Ms. Varghese	67
Getting Started	69
Not Action-Ready vs. Action-Ready Coaching	69
Not Action-Ready	69
Action-Ready Coaching	70
The Four CoachED Approaches	71
Defining the Levers	73
Knowledge (About Teaching and Learning)	73
Application (Of Research-Based Practices That Engage Students and Lead to Equitable and Rigorous Student Outcomes)	74
Engagement (In Teaching and Continuous Learning)	74
Awareness (Of a Need for Change)	74
The Approaches in Detail	75
Coaching Values	76
The Example	76
The Levers	76
The Approach	77
The Reason	77
The Goal	78
Coaching Beliefs	78
The Example	78
The Levers	78
The Approach	80
The Reason	80
The Goal	80
Coaching Thinking	80
The Example	80
The Levers	81
The Approach	82

The Reason	82
The Goal	82
Coaching Behaviors	82
The Example	82
The Levers	82
The Approach	83
The Reason	84
The Goal	84
Bringing the Pieces Together	84
Conclusion	85

6 Coaching Values — 87

Opening Vignette: Jolie and Mr. Martinez	87
The Levers	89
Goals of the Approach	90
Stages of a Values-Based Approach	90
Stage 1: Exploring Values	90
Stage 2: Identifying Focus	92
Techniques for Identifying Focus	92
Stage 3: Setting SMARTE Goals and Action Steps	94
Challenges and Barriers	96
Stage 4: Executing and Reflecting	96
Outcome #1: Success!	97
Outcome #2: Partial Success	98
Outcome #3: No Action Taken	98
Techniques for Coaching Values	98
Visioning	99
Step 1: Future State	99
Step 2: Current State	100
Step 3: Goal-Setting and Action Steps (Notice How These Questions Begin to Address Spheres of Control, Impact, and Importance)	100
Advanced Listening Techniques	100
DARN-CAT	100
Ability to Change	102
Reason for Change	102
Need to Change	102
Commitment to Change	103
Activation of Change	103
Taking Steps Toward Change	103
Double-Sided Reflective Listening Statement	103
Complex Reflective Listening	104
The Importance Ruler	105

	Why Helpful Suggestions Don't Help	108
	Addressing Equity through Coaching Values	109
	Conclusion	110
7	**Coaching Beliefs**	**112**
	Opening Vignette: Jonathon and Ms. Harris	112
	The Levers	113
	Goal of the Approach	116
	Realigning a Teacher's Practices with Their Beliefs	116
	Realigning a Teacher's Beliefs with Their Values	117
	Techniques for Coaching External Beliefs	117
	Classroom Data Collection	118
	Coaching Goal	118
	What Data Were Collected?	118
	How Were the Data Collected?	118
	How Were the Data Used?	119
	Data Conversations	119
	Step 1: Teacher Perception	120
	Step 2: Data-Based Reflective Thinking	120
	Step 3: Data-Based Next Steps	120
	Focusing on Specifics	121
	Modeling, Co-Teaching, and Co-Planning	124
	Modeling	124
	Co-Teaching and Co-Planning	124
	Techniques for Coaching Internal Beliefs	124
	The Confidence Ruler	125
	Metaphorical Thinking	126
	Step 1: Identify Current State	126
	Step 2: Explore Current State	127
	Step 3: Identify Desired Future State	127
	Step 4: Explore Desired Future State	127
	Step 5: Shift to Action	127
	Addressing Equity through Coaching Beliefs	130
	Conclusion	131
8	**Coaching Thinking**	**133**
	Opening Vignette: Jolie and Mr. Dudley	133
	The Levers	135
	Goals of the Approach	136
	Facilitating Reflective Thinking	138
	Reflective Thinking: Focusing on Knowledge	138
	Reflective Thinking: Focusing on Skills	139
	Reflective Thinking: Focusing on Experience	140

	Techniques for Coaching Thinking	142
	Three-Stage Problem-Solving Technique	142
	Identifying a Single Layer Inquiry Question	144
	Progress Monitoring	146
	Conduct Classroom Visits	146
	Assess Student Work	146
	Advanced Questioning Techniques	147
	Exploring Emotional Responses	150
	Addressing Equity through Coaching Thinking	152
	Conclusion	152
9	**Coaching Behaviors**	**154**
	Opening Vignette: Jonathon and Ms. Shah	154
	The Levers	156
	Goals of the Approach	157
	Techniques for Coaching Behaviors	158
	Elicit-Provide-Elicit	158
	Step 1: Elicit	159
	Step 2: Provide	159
	Step 3: Elicit	160
	Co-Planning	161
	Brainstorming Technique	161
	Using Past Experiences	161
	Considerations for Early-Career and Alternative-Entry Teachers	162
	Addressing Equity through Coaching Behaviors	163
	Conclusion	164
10	**Integration of Approaches**	**165**
	Priority Approaches	165
	Putting It All Together: Integrating the Approaches	170
	Ms. West—Priority Approach: Coaching Beliefs	171
	Ms. Torres—Priority Approach: Coaching Thinking	172
	Mr. King—Priority Approach: Coaching Values	173
	Mr. Bell—Priority Approach: Coaching Behaviors	173
	Flexible and Responsive Coaching	174
	Remembering Mr. Parsons	175
	Coaching Shifts	178
	Conclusion	179
11	**Getting Started**	**181**
	Identifying a Priority Approach	181
	The Coaching Wheel	183

How to Use a Coaching Wheel	185
Stage 1: Explore the Self-Assessment	186
Stage 2: Examine the Ratings	186
Stage 3: Focus on Values and Beliefs	187
Planning the Coaching Approach	188
Planning Step 1: Plan the Priority Approach	188
Planning Step 2: Consider and Explore Additional Approaches	188
Planning for Powerful Questions	189
Hypothetical Situations	190
Perspectives	190
Beliefs and Feelings	190
Past Experiences	191
Comparisons	191
Reflections	192
Conclusion	192
Appendix A. Tools for Coaching	**194**
The Coaching Wheel	194
Coaching Wheel: High Quality Teaching and Learning	194
Coaching Wheel: Culture of Project-Based Learning	194
Planning and Reflection Tools	195
Planning the Approach	195
Planning for a Coaching Conversation	197
Reflecting on Coaching	199
Data Tools	199
Data Tool 1: Tallies and Symbols	199
Data Tool 2: Scripting	202
Data Tool 3: Visual Representation	203
Appendix B. Coaching Transcripts	**206**
Transcript 1: Coaching Values—Exploring Values	206
Transcript 2: Coaching Beliefs—The Confidence Ruler	208
Transcript 3: Coaching Thinking—Problem-Solving Technique	211
Transcript 4: Coaching Behavior—Elicit-Provide-Elicit	214
Appendix C. Key Terms	**217**
References	**219**

Preface

Coaching is important and powerful work, and *Coaching to Empower Teachers: A Framework for Improving Instruction and Well-Being* is intended to be your partner—as a tool and a guide—in the coaching work that you do with teachers. When coached successfully, teachers feel empowered to make a difference in the lives of their students, schools, and communities. The CoachED framework provided in these pages will help you to think about the teachers with whom you work as individuals with the capacity and energy to impact students in an empowering way. By considering each teacher individually and with an asset-based approach that identifies and capitalizes on teachers' strengths instead of focusing on their deficits, coaches provide a unique, targeted, and proactive learning experience for ongoing teacher growth.

The Goals of This Book

This book provides a framework for coaching that treats teachers as individual learners and leaders in their classrooms. We visit foundational approaches, theories, and models of adult learning and motivation (e.g., self-determination theory, transformative learning theory, transtheoretical change model) in order to identify, understand, and empower teachers as leaders of their own learning. Although we ground our approach in research and cite references where applicable, our intent is to create a practitioner's guide that provides foundational tools of coaching and introduces a concrete framework for making intentional coaching decisions. As such, we write from our own experiences to share specific tools and techniques that support coaching teacher values, beliefs, thinking, and behaviors and illustrate these through vignettes and transcripts that portray specific coaching examples, which have been created from a compilation of true experiences although no real names have been used.

Our primary audiences for this coaching book are school- and district-based coaches (e.g., math coach, literacy coach, project-based learning coach) who work with teachers to improve and refine instruction on a regular basis through reflective conversation and innovative practices. Although we write specifically for instructional coaches, the CoachED framework, the tools, and the techniques we describe can be useful to anyone who works with teachers to build their professional capacity by focusing on the teacher's own goals and intentions for student learning. Therefore, this book can also benefit mentors, principals, and other school and district leaders willing to engage in empowering teachers in pursuit of their own growth and learning.

In this book, we provide coaches with:

1. the CoachED framework for instructional coaching;
2. theories, models, and approaches to support intentional planning for and thinking about coaching;
3. specific tools, strategies, and techniques to enact this framework with individual teachers through ongoing coaching cycles; and
4. examples, vignettes, and transcripts to illustrate coaching in practice.

A variety of approaches to instructional coaching focus on changing teacher behavior and practice. However, many of these approaches also rely heavily on coaches as experts to "improve" teacher practice. In these models, coaches identify problems of practice *for* teachers, decide on strategies that teachers *must* use in order to fix their problems, and then engage in cycles of observation and feedback to hold teachers accountable for improved practice. In these coaching cycles, an individual teacher's needs for improvement are prioritized by their coach, and strategies for "fixing" the teacher come from the top down. This provides little opportunity for a teacher to discuss their own goals for instruction and strips them of the autonomy to lead in their own classroom. Although some might argue that this is exactly the approach necessary for new teachers or those who have entered teaching through alternative routes, we believe that when a teacher is removed from the process of learning by a coach with an expert and directive stance, they are disempowered. Restricting a teacher's role in the coaching process not only disempowers them but also neglects to build their capacity to meet the needs of all of their students. This is true even for new and alternative entry teachers. In a sense, coaches who take an expert and directive stance are perpetuating negative perceptions of teachers that are communicated through media—that "those who can't do, teach." The CoachED instructional coaching framework in this book differs from other coaching methods in our asset-based stance to coaching, our intentional focus on teachers' values and beliefs, and our emphasis on supporting teachers in reaching their own personal goals. Through the framework, we aim to empower teachers and increase teacher professional capacity, student learning, and teacher retention.

About the Authors

The authors of this book, Catherine Pendleton Hart and Fredrica M. Nash, collectively have 18 years of experience as teachers and 16 years of experience as instructional coaches and education consultants. They write this book to share their experiences and the knowledge they have gained as coaches from being in schools and working with teachers for many years. Catherine is a former high school English teacher whose interests include personalized learning and competency-based education, inquiry-based learning, content literacy, the integration of social and emotional learning and rigor, teacher and coach development, and student and teacher agency. She has a Master of Arts in Education. Fredrica is a former high school science teacher whose interests include social and emotional learning, social justice education and pedagogy, social context of education, science education, and teacher development. She is currently finishing an EdD in Curriculum and Instruction.

About Our Context

Coaching takes many forms around the world and each coach approaches coaching from their own expertise, experience, and expectations. Our own backgrounds inform our thinking and writing about coaching in a number of ways. For example, our experiences are based on the context of the United States where we live and work. As a result, the ways in which we think about coaching to a great extent rely on the interworking of the U.S. education system and the values and beliefs of the Western world. While all of our experiences as coaches have been in this context and the examples we provide reflect systems of coaching within the United States, there are many skills, strategies, and conversations that may have application elsewhere. Specifically, we write for an audience that is dedicated to allowing teachers to give voice to their own strengths and areas for growth—no matter where in the world they may be or the system within which they work. Throughout this book, readers will notice an emphasis on teacher voice and choice within a system of coaching that supports teachers to reach their own professional goals to improve student learning. No matter how or how much teachers need to change for improved student outcomes, coaches cannot build a teacher's capacity or support sustained behavioral changes in classroom practice if the teacher is not aware of a need to change or motivated to engage in change. As a result, it is imperative for coaches to bring teachers into their own learning process.

Our collective coaching context further includes experiences as job-embedded coaches as well as outside coaching consultants; coaching in rural and urban districts; and coaching in traditional and alternative schools. Although most of our teaching experiences have occurred in high schools, we have coached across the U.S. K-12 educational context and have attempted to include a broad spectrum of examples to support coaches in thinking about their own craft within the K-12 grade span.

No matter a coach's context, whether it be rural or urban, third grade or tenth, virtual or face-to-face, monthly or daily touchpoints, high performing or underperforming schools, resourced or under resourced environments, United States or other global locations, empowering teachers through the coaching process is important. While we provide a framework that is agnostic of context and grounded in principles of adult learning and theories of motivation and change that cross contexts, individual coaching context is important and certainly impacts the boundaries, structures, and systems within which a coach works. As such, each reader will determine how the framework and underlying principles apply to their own work. We hope that each reader will find something of value within these pages.

COVID-19

Most of our past coaching experiences have been face to face; however, at the time of this writing we have fully transitioned to navigating coaching conversations, classroom visits, and even classroom data collection virtually due to the COVID-19 pandemic. While virtual coaching is not new, the extent to which we are engaging in virtual coaching has increased and has given us the opportunity to see that our coaching framework works within the remote context as it does in face-to-face contexts. The vignettes and examples throughout the book depict face-to-face coaching as they were written prior to school closures, but we have found that the approaches and tools described can be implemented within a virtual context to support teachers providing remote and hybrid instruction as well as to support teachers virtually who may still be engaged in traditional face-to-face instruction. Adaptation of coaching to a remote setting is important as coaches work to support teachers during this time of unprecedented challenge and rapid innovation. Many teachers with whom we have worked during this time have expressed frustration with a lack of student engagement, feelings of inefficacy as they work to create lessons within a new context and feel like first-year teachers all over again, and a sense of exhaustion as preparation times have increased and the boundaries between work life and home life have disappeared. Increasing teacher empowerment through coaching that emphasizes asset-based thinking and locus of control is especially important at this time to maintain teacher well-being. Furthermore, given the role of coaching in supporting teachers to meet the needs of all of their students regardless from where each student begins, the value of coaching will increase in the coming years as we seek to recover from the pandemic. As we recover from the impact of the pandemic on learning across the nation and the world, teachers will need to fill the learning gaps of students whose experiences of remote teaching and learning have been and continue to be widely varied. Coaches can provide additional insight, support, and guidance to help teachers meet the needs of all students intentionally and equitably.

More on Addressing Equity

Educational equity—regardless of gender, race, ethnicity, disability, or other background—is paramount, and although we provide coaches with ways to build and strengthen equitable learning throughout this book, the tools and tips we provide merely scratch the surface. While we do not claim that coaching is the solution to educational equity, we do believe that coaching has a role in impacting teacher awareness, knowledge, and opportunities to address equity by raising consciousness and increasing teacher capacity to mitigate the impact of oppression and inequity in their classroom and across their schools. We recommend that readers further explore issues of equity in learning and coaching through additional resources (Box 0.1).

Box 0.1 Recommended Reading: Equity

For further reading and development regarding equity, consider these resources (for full references, see references list):

Equity Visits—A New Approach to Supporting Equity-Focused School and District Leadership—Rachel Roegman, David Allen, Larry Leverett, Scott Thompson, and Thomas Hatch (2019)

Excellence Through Equity—Alan Blankstein, Pedro Noguera, and Lorena Kelly (2016)

Indigenous Children's Survivance in Public Schools—Leilani Sabzalian (2019)

Interrupting Hate: Homophobia in Schools and What Literacy Can Do About It—Mollie V. Blackburn and Katherine Schultz (2015)

More Courageous Conversations About Race—Glenn E. Singleton (2012)

Pedagogy of the Oppressed—Paulo Freire (1993)

Savage Inequalities—Jonathon Kozol (1991)

The History of "Zero Tolerance" in American Public Schools—Judith Kafka (2011)

Your Students, My Students, Our Students: Rethinking Equitable and Inclusive Classrooms—Lee Ann Jung, Nancy Frey, Douglas Fisher, and Julie Kroener (2019)

*Note: these are simply a few of the many options that we have read and found useful. This list is certainly not intended to be exhaustive or prescriptive.

Decisions We Made

We have designed this book so that it can be read cover to cover or in sections. Coaches who have more experience in coaching and already feel comfortable with the foundations of coaching, for example, may elect to skim the foundational chapter. Likewise, coaches who are new to coaching may want to spend additional time practicing foundational techniques before moving into the chapters on the CoachED framework. To facilitate intentional use of the book, we have divided the book into two parts. Part I: Foundations of Coaching focuses on the foundations of coaching, including principles of coaching, theories and models that support coaching, and foundational coaching skills. Part II: The CoachED Framework introduces the CoachED framework and provides a more complex way of making intentional coaching decisions based on the needs of individual teachers. At the beginning of Part II, readers will find a "Stop and Assess" activity to facilitate decisions about whether to pause reading to practice foundational techniques or continue on to more complex ideas. Each coach should read the book in the manner that best meets their needs. Readers will also find opportunities for reflection and practice throughout the book that can be used in a manner that supports individual learning preferences. To help coaches make decisions about how to read the book, we offer an overview of the content and book structure in the next sections.

Structure of the Book

The empowerment of teachers is critical to their well-being, the educational outcomes of students, and the effectiveness of schools. Therefore, our book begins with an orientation to the importance of teacher empowerment. Because teaching as a caring profession is a complex and emotional endeavor and because the context of the educational system is complicated and can disempower teachers, teachers are highly susceptible to symptoms of stress, secondary trauma, and burnout. Chapter 1 explains the importance of teacher well-being and sets the stage for the CoachED framework of coaching, which emphasizes teacher empowerment.

Chapters 2 through 4 present and explore principles; underlying approaches, models, and theories; and foundational techniques of coaching. One chapter is devoted to each of these to introduce our beliefs about coaching, to highlight the importance of grounding our work in research, and to provide an introduction to coaching. In our experience, some school and district leaders assume that good teachers automatically make good coaches, and teachers are thrust into the coaching role without any formal training or support. Because we intend to meet the needs of instructional coaches no matter their level of experience, Chapter 4 is included to orient both new and veteran coaches to what we classify as the foundational techniques of coaching. Use of these techniques is necessary in any coaching conversation with teachers, and identifying and naming these techniques supports intentional implementation of a coaching practice. Beginning with foundational techniques establishes a common understanding of coaching from which to start.

Chapter 5 presents the CoachED framework, the structure that we use to identify coaching priorities related to values, beliefs, thinking, and behaviors. In this chapter, coaches will consider their own approach to coaching and how they make intentional choices to ensure effective and impactful work. Then, we present our framework of four priority approaches and the defining levers—knowledge, application, engagement, and awareness—a coach uses to prioritize a specific approach to each coaching partnership.

Chapters 6 through 9 provide in-depth explanations, descriptions, examples, and activities for engaging in each of the priority approaches included in the CoachED framework. During coaching conversations and cycles, coaches will likely move between the various approaches within the framework; however, having a clear understanding of each approach separately helps coaches know when to access and apply each approach during a coaching session or cycle.

Chapters 10 and 11 provide support in putting everything together. Chapter 10 provides a glimpse into what coaching looks like when the approaches are integrated, and Chapter 11—the concluding chapter—provides tools and ideas for getting started.

Final Notes

Effective coaches use multiple approaches, tools, and strategies to fit the individual teacher with whom they are working at any given moment. The question is often how to best approach each teacher and which tools and strategies will be most effective given a specific context, personality, or scenario. This book provides a framework for thinking about intentional coaching decisions based on individual teachers and specific levers. The CoachED framework is designed around four coaching approaches, each of which draws on and incorporates models and strategies from many coaching traditions—both within the instructional coaching field and beyond. Techniques and strategies within each approach are examples of tools that might fit within a certain approach but are by no means the only tools that fit that approach. We encourage you to consider the tools you already have in your toolbox to identify where they fit within the framework and to reflect on your own values and beliefs about coaching before you move forward. Box 0.2 provides a starting point for reflecting on your values and beliefs as a coach.

One final but important note: Because of the long history associated with and many branches of coaching (health and wellness coaching, cognitive coaching, transformational coaching, life coaching, career coaching, mindfulness coaching, business coaching, and leadership coaching to name a few), it is sometimes difficult to identify the original creator of various tools, techniques, and ideas and to determine exactly from where our own strategies, techniques, and understandings have emerged; however, to the extent possible, we have given credit for specific tools and techniques to the traditions and experts through which each one has been developed. We strongly encourage you to review the foundational resources listed in Box 0.3 that have informed our work and have contributed greatly to our own understanding of the tools and techniques that support effective coaching.

Box 0.2 On Your Own: Values and Beliefs

Before reading further, take a minute to engage in reflective thinking.

- What is most important to you about your work as a coach (or, if you are not yet a coach, what interests you most about coaching)?
- What do you believe is the impact of coaching on teachers, schools, and districts?

Box 0.3 Recommended Reading: Instructional Coaching

For further reading and development, consider these resources (for full references, see references list):

Agents of Change: How Content Coaching Transforms Teaching & Learning—Lucy West and Antonia Cameron (2013)

Coaching Questions: A Coach's Guide to Powerful Asking Skills—Tony Stoltzfus (2008)

Co-Active Coaching (4th ed.)—Henry Kimsey-House, Karen Kimsey-House, Phillip Sandhal, and Laura Whitworth (2018)

Cognitive Coaching: Developing Self-Directed Leaders and Learners—Arthur L. Costa and Robert J. Garmston (2016)

Cognitive Coaching: A Foundation for Renaissance Schools—Arthur L. Costa, Robert J. Garmston, Robert H. Anderson, and Carl D. Glickman (2002)

Differentiated Coaching: A Framework for Helping Teachers Change—Jane A.G. Kise (2006)

Instructional Coaching: A Partnership Approach to Improving Instruction—Jim Knight (2007)

The Art of Coaching—Elena Aguilar (2014)

The Impact Cycle—Jim Knight (2018)

*Note: again, these are simply a few of the many options that we have read and found useful. This list is certainly not intended to be exhaustive or prescriptive.

Authors' Gratitude

From Catherine

First and foremost, I am grateful to my parents for giving me voice and for empowering me to reach my goals. They have been my first and best teachers and coaches. Speaking of coaching, most of what I know about coaching has come from long discussions with three amazing friends and colleagues: Jason Dudley, Mia Pumo, and my co-author Fredrica M. Nash. Thank you to each of you individually for your wisdom, friendship, and support. I would also like to thank Angela Quick, Joe Edney, Laurie Baker, Stacy Costello, and the rest of the Center for Educational Services team for making this possible. You are all empowering and inspiring leaders and coaches, and I am grateful to be a part of your team. To the team of trainers that allowed me to audit the VA's Whole Health Coaching Training, thank you for allowing me to learn from you, to understand the connections between health coaching and instructional coaching, and to deepen my knowledge of coaching as a practice. Finally, to the coaches, teachers, and other educators with whom I have learned, thank you for teaching me and for your dedication to teachers and students.

From Fredrica

This book would not have been possible without my faith and the unwavering belief that my mom and dad have in me that I deserve the goals and dreams I pursue. It also would not have been possible without Sofi Frankowksi and Pauline Younts who gave me the first opportunity to become a full-time coach, or Dr. Danielle Durham, my forever friend, who is an epidemiologist and allows me to practice coaching techniques with her, and of course to my co-author Catherine Pendleton Hart who believed that I could co-write a book—while also writing a dissertation! Thank you to each of you for your friendship, encouragement, and trust. I would also like to thank every student that I have ever taught, tutored, or worked alongside for teaching and coaching me. To every coach that I've had, teacher that I have coached, and every coach that I have coached, this is for you. It is with gratitude that I thank the entire Center for Education Services Team at RTI International for embarking on this journey with Catherine and me in 2018; your smiling faces, encouragement, critical feedback, and insight helped us to write a better book.

About the Authors

Catherine Pendleton Hart

Catherine Pendleton Hart is an Education Consultant with 13 years of classroom experience at the high school level. She received National Boards certification in 2004 and re-certified in 2013. During her tenure as a teacher, Hart served as a mentor, department chair, School Improvement Team co-chair, National Boards Coach, and Kenan Fellow. Her professional development work emphasized differentiated instruction, implementing the Common Core in the ELA classroom, and co-teaching. Hart has written ELA curriculum with an emphasis on literacy and complex texts both locally and nationally. She has been an education consultant and instructional coach for six years and has served comprehensive high schools and early college high schools in both rural and urban settings. Her work as a coach has included implementation of inquiry-based and project-based learning, the integration of social and emotional learning with rigorous instructional practices, competency-based education, reading in the content areas, effective PLC practices, and development of teacher leaders and instructional coaches. Hart also works with RTI International's Aspire Teacher Preparation Program, an alternative program for teacher licensure in which Hart is a course developer, instructor, and coach. Hart's Masters work focused on developing teacher leaders, and she works to empower teachers in their classrooms and their schools so that they, in turn, will work to empower their students. In addition to her background in education, Hart also has experience as a corporate trainer.

Education:

M.Ed., Culture, Curriculum, and Change, University of North Carolina at Chapel Hill
BA, English, Davidson College

Fredrica M. Nash

Fredrica M. Nash began her path toward education when selected to participate in the prestigious N.C. Teaching Fellow program. She spent the early years of her career teaching science in Durham Public Schools and facilitating professional learning experiences for teachers on project-based learning for the New Tech Network and serving as an NCSU Kenan Fellow for Teacher Leadership. Ms. Nash's specialty is education coaching and she is the chief architect of the Coach Development program and Social Emotional Learning services offered by RTI International. She has designed and delivered presentations at state and national conferences on project-based learning, instructional coaching, instructional best practices, equity, and academic, social, and emotional learning. Prior to joining RTI, Ms. Nash served as an instructional coach, curriculum writer, vice-president of a nonprofit community outreach program, and a director of coaching services. She has coached new, veteran, and alternative entry teachers throughout her educational career focusing on the development of instructional capacity. Her research interests include teacher agency and learning through professional learning, teacher effect on marginalized student learning with attention to equity and social justice, and program evaluation using a multi-method approach.

Education:

EdD (in process), Curriculum and Instruction, The George Washington University
MAT, Secondary Education and Teaching, University of North Carolina at Chapel Hill
BS, Biology, University of North Carolina at Chapel Hill

Part I
Foundations of Coaching

1

Addressing Teacher Well-Being

Introduction to Teacher Well-Being

Teachers *make a difference* in the lives of students. Teachers who engage in instructional practices that contribute to the development of critical and curious thinkers and who value a students' social and emotional states and foster their social and emotional competence support long-term success in life. Teachers contribute to the joy and achievement—both personal and professional—of children by cultivating caring classroom environments, facilitating rigorous instruction, and emphasizing student perseverance and agency. Teachers help children find their purpose and their passion and help them create pathways to achieve their goals. Because of the difference they make, it is critical to promote the well-being of all teachers.

While the well-being of teachers is critical, the intensity of caring for students and meeting the demands of the job leads to a sometimes overwhelming list of responsibilities that can impact teacher well-being. Results from the American Federation of Teachers' 2017 Quality of Teacher Work Life survey reveal this impact: 61% of respondents found their work always or often stressful—double that of the general population. Further, 58% of educators reported seven or more days of poor mental health in the month prior to completing the survey. Teachers *make a difference* in the lives of students, and yet this difference is taking a toll on their own well-being.

Every student deserves not only a technically competent teacher but also a wholly engaged teacher. Until all students are taught by engaged teachers, we will continue to have inequities in education.

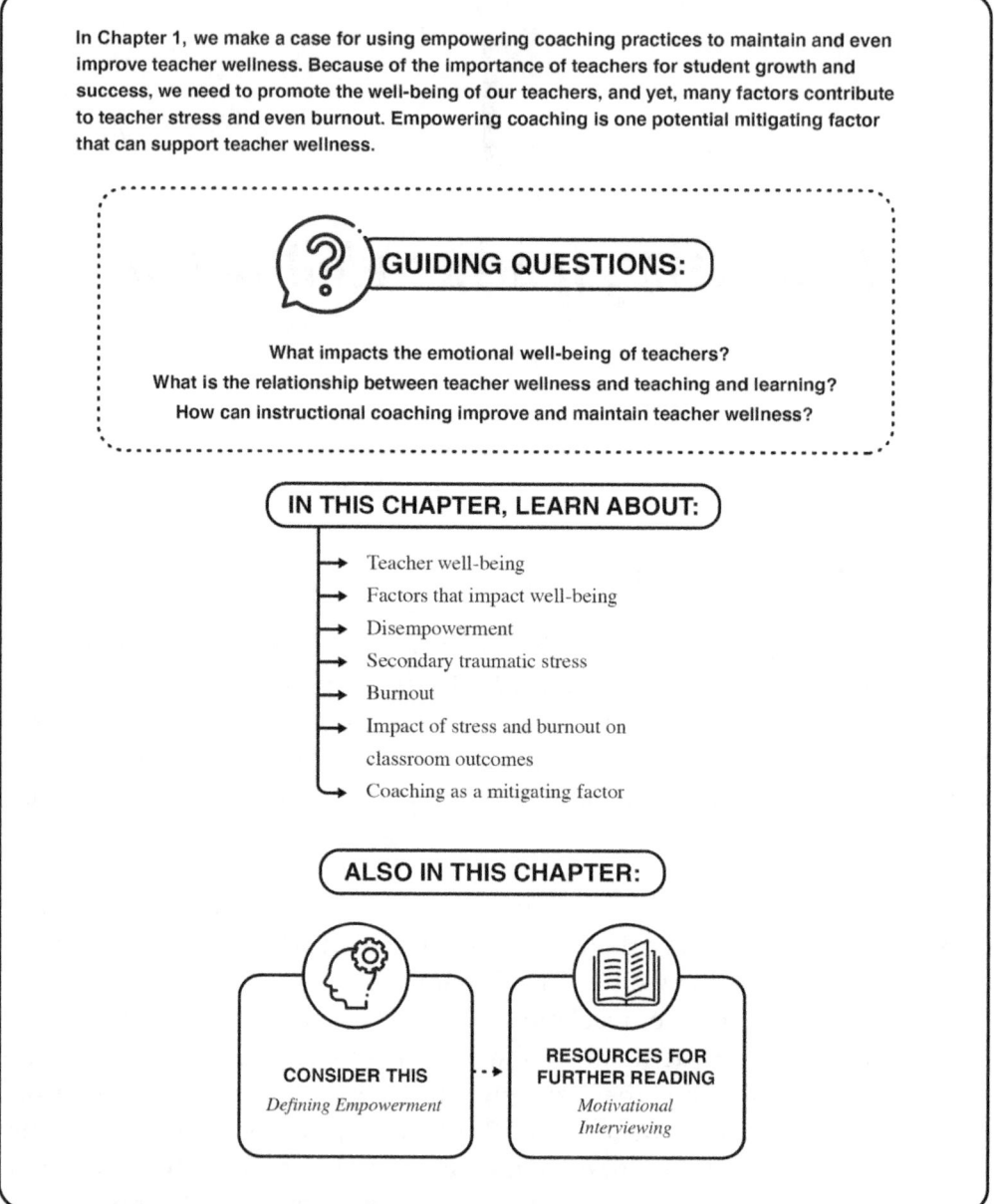

Figure 1.1 Chapter 1 Overview

Factors That Impact Teacher Well-Being

Disempowerment

Disempowering factors in schools include a revolving door of school reforms that sometimes ignore teacher voice (Fullan, 2007), external decision-making that devalues teacher expertise (Meier, 2002), increased emphasis on testing and accountability that limits teacher autonomy in the classroom (Smith & Kovacs, 2011), and negative public perception about teachers that can be demoralizing (Day, Kington, Stobart, & Sammons, 2006). These disempowering factors in schools decrease teacher well-being as they increase stress and erode a teacher's self-image and feelings of self-efficacy.

Secondary Traumatic Stress

In addition to disempowerment in schools, teachers are exposed to secondary traumatic stress daily. The National Child Trauma Stress Network (NCTSN, 2020) defines secondary traumatic stress as "the emotional duress that results when an individual hears about the firsthand trauma experiences of another." Teachers, who work with students from various backgrounds, experience secondary trauma when students with whom they have built strong, trusting relationships share individual, first-hand experiences of trauma—and this occurs day after day and year after year. Traumatic experiences students share might include abuse at home, food or shelter insecurity, exposure to unsafe neighborhoods, and even divorce. These adverse childhood experiences, or ACEs, can result in chronic toxic stress for students without mitigating or buffering support. Students' stress is then taken on by the teacher who cares for and teaches these students. A data brief by the Health Resources and Services Administration (HRSA) in 2020, showed that one in three children ages 0–17 (33.3%) had experienced at least one ACE in their lifetimes and 14.1% had experienced 2 or more. As teachers demonstrate care for their students, their stress begins to increase as their ability to buffer their attachment decreases, leading to diminished emotional capacity to effectively teach their students.

Burnout

Burnout differs from secondary traumatic stress in that it does not occur because of specific trauma but as a result of ongoing work-related stress. Christina Maslach has studied and written about burnout, especially burnout in the caring professions, since the 1970s (Maslach, 1978, 2003). According to her work, people in the caring professions—education and health care, for example—are susceptible to burnout because of the high level of emotional engagement between workers and their clients (e.g., teacher and students) and the "prevailing norms" in these professions of selflessness, going the extra mile, and working long hours (Maslach & Leiter, 2016). Nel Noddings (2002) further underscores the impact of caring on teachers. She writes about the ethic of care in education, especially relational care, which describes how people are deeply affected by the experience of caring for others. This deep care for others is the reason many teachers do the work they do and yet it can be emotionally exhausting.

Impact of Stress and Burnout on Classroom Outcomes

Travis and Ryan (2004) in Wellness Workbook identify three concepts of wellness: wellness exists along a continuum; illness and health have a number of causes; and the ways individuals manage energy impacts and transforms wellness. They state that "even though people often lack physical symptoms, they may still be bored, depressed, tense, anxious or simply unhappy with their lives" (p. xviii-xix). Emotional states like these in turn contribute to decreased wellness. Travis and Ryan further describe overall health as only the "tip of the iceberg." Not only do motivation, values, and behaviors also contribute to an individual's wellness, the authors of the Wellness Workbook share that humans take energy from the sources around them, "organize it, transform it, and return (dissipate) it to their environment" (p. xxiv). These ideas are illustrated by the impact of secondary traumatic stress on teachers and the trickle-down impact on their students.

Stress, secondary traumatic stress, and burnout can deeply affect teachers. Secondary traumatic stress, for example, leads to fatigue, increased anxiety, self-doubt, and an overall lack of energy (Treatment and Services Adaptation Center, 2020). Symptoms of burnout include "overwhelming exhaustion, feelings of cynicism and detachment from the job, and a sense of ineffectiveness and lack of accomplishment" (Maslach & Leiter, 2016).

Further, teachers who are tired, anxious, and detached and who feel ineffective in their work pass the impact of these symptoms on to their students. A low sense of teacher self-efficacy, for example, has been correlated with lower student achievement (Hargreaves & Fullan, 1996). Teachers who are emotionally exhausted can be more critical of students which in turn leads students to feel less competent themselves (Klusmann, Richter, & Lüdtke, 2016). Notably, it is not just academic achievement that is impacted by teachers who are not at their optimal level of well-being; students' social and emotional well-being is impacted as well.

Finally, stress and burnout exacerbate equity issues because they contribute to high levels of teacher attrition in our most vulnerable schools. Teachers shift from one school to another, one district to another, or leave the profession entirely in part due to the caring nature of the profession and impacts on teacher well-being (Hughes, 2012; Ryan et al., 2017). Often, schools that are most vulnerable have the highest numbers of novice teachers. These teachers come into the profession with care to give but face challenges that impact their well-being, their students' well-being, and student learning (Berry, Daughtrey, & Wieder, 2009).

We've seen this cycle of stress and burnout recently during the COVID-19 pandemic. Teachers are spending more time planning lessons for their students only to anxiously await as no students arrive for their synchronous lessons. The barriers of time have been dissolved as teachers try to meet their students' every need whenever they are not asleep and yet many of the teachers with whom we have worked no longer feel that they are making a difference in their students' lives. Teachers who believe in the powerful role of relationships in the classroom have struggled to connect with students whom they have never met in person. Exacerbating already emotionally draining conditions, we have seen and heard teachers looking for solidarity in the loneliness, limiting beliefs, and negative energy brought about by the pandemic—thereby allowing their own energy to impact and be impacted by the energy of others.

Coaching as a Mitigating Factor

Improved student outcomes are the primary goal of coaching, and coaching for this purpose has been shown to be effective. Kraft, Blazar, and Hogan (2018) found that when teachers were engaged in coaching, their instructional practices changed and the effects of their instruction on students' academic performance and achievement increased. In fact, coaching had a larger effect on achievement than almost all other school-based interventions. The ongoing relationship between a teacher and a coach, however, has the potential to provide supports that can also improve or maintain teacher well-being, especially when a coach understands the factors that contribute to teacher stress, poor mental health, and burnout as well as how their own empowering coaching stance can mitigate those factors through increasing teacher agency.

If teachers feel they do not have a voice in their schools or autonomy in their classrooms, empowering coaching practices can provide them with voice and autonomy. If teachers have lost a sense of self-efficacy, empowering coaching practices can rebuild self-efficacy by supporting teachers in identifying targeted goals and providing concrete evidence of progress. If teachers feel isolated in their classrooms—one specific cause of stress and burnout (Hock, 1988)—empowering coaches can provide a partner with whom teachers can learn and grow. Furthermore, practices that empower teachers further improve academic, social, and emotional outcomes for students because empowered teachers are more likely to empower their students, more likely to be innovative in the classroom, and less likely to simply "cover" the curriculum (Bandura, 1989; Elmore, 2005; Lopez & Louis, 2009; Ryan & Deci, 2000). Supportive and empowering coaches meet teachers where they are and partner with them to make a difference in the lives of students. Ultimately, when teachers know and are able to see the difference they make for students, they are more likely to remain engaged in the classroom. For more on our definition of empowerment, see Box 1.1.

>
> **Box 1.1 Consider This: Defining Empowerment**
>
> Empowerment has been a buzzword in education for years and, like other buzzwords, can be used without intentional definition.
>
> In an attempt to "move the debate beyond the rhetoric of empowerment" (Short, 1992, p. 8), Paula Short defined six dimensions of this construct: decision-making, professional growth, status, self-efficacy, autonomy, and impact. We use this definition to understand the meaning of empowerment. As such, you will see that the CoachED framework, including approaches and suggested techniques, addresses these dimensions.

We recognize, of course, that not all teachers experience a sustained negative sense of well-being. Many teachers are resilient and have found their own strategies to decrease the effect of stress on themselves and their students. Whether a coach is working with a teacher who is experiencing symptoms of stress and burnout that need to be improved or a fully engaged teacher whose engagement needs to be maintained, empowering teachers by giving them voice, autonomy, and agency is good for students and good for schools.

To address teacher well-being, the CoachED framework draws upon practices from health coaching. Additionally, we incorporate effective instructional coaching frameworks and techniques from coaches who have come before us (Aguilar, 2013; Joyce & Showers, 2002; Knight, 2007, 2009; Killion & Bryan, 2012; West & Cameron, 2013) to provide a comprehensive, capacity-building approach to instructional coaching. Because we draw on previous coaching work, there may be techniques and strategies within this book that coaches are already familiar with and use. Our framework is not designed to share earth-shattering, new techniques to coaching but to support coaches in making intentional decisions about how and when to use effective techniques.

Box 1.2 provides further reading on motivational interviewing—a specific approach often used in the health field.

>
> **Box 1.2 Consider This: Motivational Interviewing**
>
> Because of the emphasis throughout this book on coaching to maintain or improve teacher wellness as well as the emphasis on teacher empowerment and internal motivation, we draw heavily

> on the ideas of Motivational Interviewing. Motivational Interviewing is a method, often used in health care, designed to elicit intrinsic motivation for change. Applying the idea of Motivational Interviewing to education, the method relies on the idea that the only person in the coaching partnership who can enact change is the teacher, and therefore, the motivation for change must come from the teacher. In other words, a coach cannot force a teacher to change. Motivational Interviewing techniques encourage teachers to evoke and activate internal motivations for change through techniques that connect change to values and help a teacher explore their own interests and their confidence to change.
>
> For additional information about motivational interviewing, including tools and techniques not described in this book, read *Motivational Interviewing in Health Care* (Rollnick, Miller, & Butler, 2008) or *Motivational Interviewing: Helping People Change* (Miller & Rollnick, 2013).

Conclusion

Our framework is designed with the belief that coaching with an empowering stance is one avenue toward maintaining the well-being of teachers. *When teachers are healthy and energized, when they feel competent and autonomous, and when they are confident in taking risks, they are in a position to facilitate positive outcomes for their students.* We believe that the CoachED framework with its four specific approaches to coaching provides a road map to support coaches as they improve and maintain teacher well-being and engage, reengage, and reenergize teachers in their profession.

Every student deserves not only a technically competent teacher but also a wholly engaged teacher. Until all students are taught by engaged teachers, we will continue to have inequities in education.

2

Principles of Coaching

The Role of a Coach

While traditional images of coaching are likely to include athletes, competition, and sporting equipment, the explosion of coaching as a profession outside sports has expanded the definition of coaching. We now have life coaches, business coaches, executive coaches, health coaches, and others. Inside schools, we have data coaches, digital teaching and learning coaches, math coaches, peer coaches, MTSS coaches, SEL coaches, beginning teacher coaches, and instructional coaches. Coaches in schools support teachers individually in their classrooms, guide small groups or professional learning communities, and provide school- or district-wide professional learning.

Although many types of coaching take place in schools, in this book we focus on instructional coaching and specifically on one-on-one coaching conversations between a coach and a teacher about instruction and student learning outcomes.

To begin to understand our vision of instructional coaching, it is important to differentiate the work of a coach from work performed by other instructional leaders in schools. While there is an important place for each of the feedback and support activities given later on, understanding the differences between each helps to define the work of a coach. Box 2.1 can help you reflect on your own coaching philosophy.

DOI: 10.4324/9781003186045-3

Principles of Coaching ◆ 11

Coaching is for those teachers who never want to stop improving, no matter where they begin.

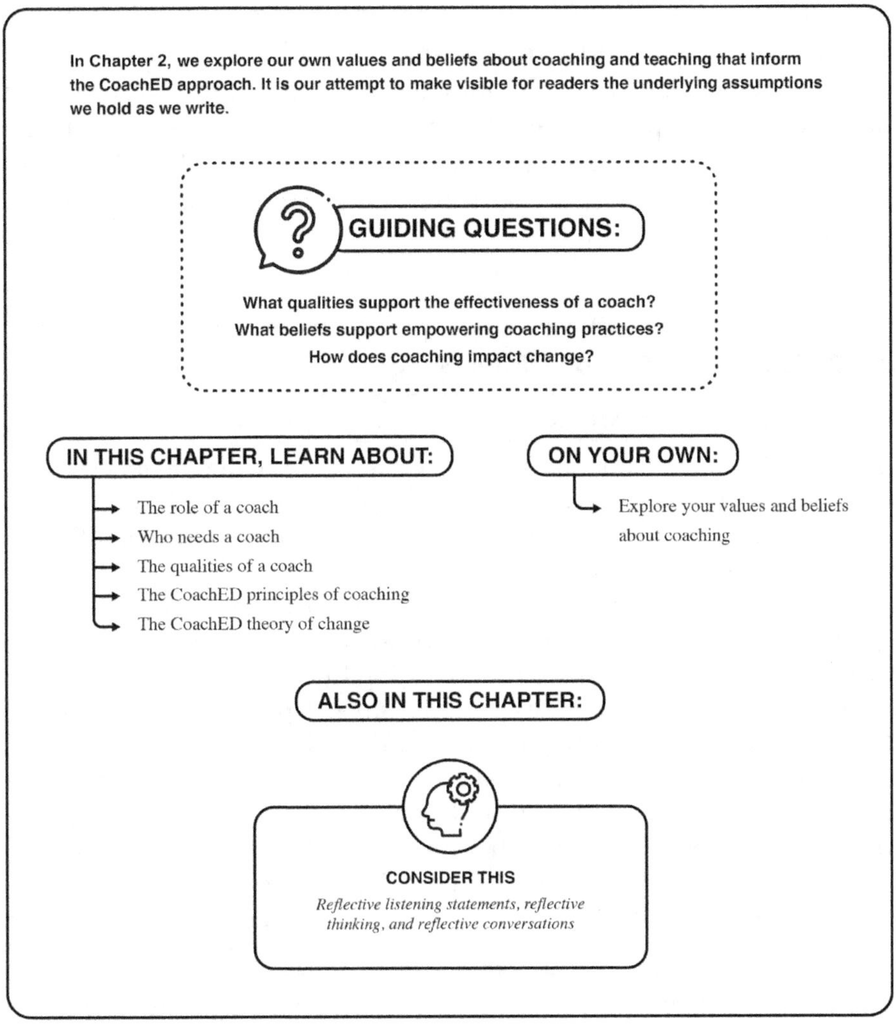

In Chapter 2, we explore our own values and beliefs about coaching and teaching that inform the CoachED approach. It is our attempt to make visible for readers the underlying assumptions we hold as we write.

GUIDING QUESTIONS:

What qualities support the effectiveness of a coach?
What beliefs support empowering coaching practices?
How does coaching impact change?

IN THIS CHAPTER, LEARN ABOUT:
- The role of a coach
- Who needs a coach
- The qualities of a coach
- The CoachED principles of coaching
- The CoachED theory of change

ON YOUR OWN:
- Explore your values and beliefs about coaching

ALSO IN THIS CHAPTER:

CONSIDER THIS
Reflective listening statements, reflective thinking, and reflective conversations

Figure 2.1 Chapter 2 Overview

Box 2.1 On Your Own: My Coaching Philosophy

Before you read this chapter, take a few minutes to consider your coaching philosophy. Reflect on your beliefs about coaching by answering the questions listed here.

- What do you believe about coaching?
- Based on your beliefs, what do you think coaches do?
- Based on your beliefs, how do you think coaches interact with others?

While it is true that evaluators and mentors may find themselves embracing a coaching approach, we believe that the role of a coach differs from the role of an evaluator and a mentor most specifically through the coach's empowering stance. Unlike evaluators and mentors, coaches are not evaluative and are not primarily engaged in providing expert advice. Rather, they take on a support role to facilitate a teacher's own goals. Box 2.2 shows the continuum of feedback and support that differentiates coaching from other forms of feedback and support.

Box 2.2 Continuum of Feedback and Support

Evaluating	Mentoring	Coaching
Providing feedback related to specific indicators on an evaluation instrument designed to show areas of strength and growth for the teacher using a common framework and common language for feedback (Kraft & Gilmour, 2016)	Engaging in observation and feedback cycles focused on instructional practice with the purpose of improving pedagogical or content knowledge according to expert experience, supporting personal and professional development and understanding of school context and norms (Lai, 2005)	Facilitating reflective thinking, fostering agency, and building empowerment through intentional conversation and purposeful design. Focusing on the pursuit of instructional excellence and equitable outcomes for all students. Empowering all teachers toward continuous growth and innovative practice (see p. 14).

Who Needs a Coach?

We have encountered districts, schools, and individuals who believe that coaching is for teachers who are struggling—new teachers or veteran teachers who have never quite become "good" at teaching. This approach emphasizes a deficit model of coaching and perpetuates the perception that coaching is for teachers who are on action plans or about to be! In deficit-based environments like this, there is a resulting stigma attached to teachers seen engaging with a coach, and the coaching process is often ill-explained. In these schools, coaching is not valued despite the powerful transformations that can result from coaching partnerships.

Yet, even in districts and schools like this, we have found teachers who voluntarily seek out coaching and who are excited to work with coaches. Often, these teachers are the most innovative and empowered teachers in the school. They are risk-takers and career-long learners who are willing to look critically at their practice and find opportunities for improvement. They are teachers who want to stay current in their work, build upon their strengths, and be the most effective teachers they can be. They also are the teachers who aren't afraid to be vulnerable and who see their coach as a partner who will empower them with coaching support aligned to their own goals for learning and growth.

According to Atul Gawande, a surgeon who has used coaching to improve the complication rates of his surgeries, everybody needs a coach (2011, 2017). Gawande based his thinking on a sports model, where even the greatest athletes in every sport have coaches throughout their careers. In his 2017 TED Talk, Gawande said:

> Turns out, there are numerous problems to trying to make it on your own. You don't recognize the issues that are standing in your way, or if you do, you don't necessarily know how to fix them. And the result is that somewhere along the way, you stop improving.

For Gawande, a coach provides a new perspective that increases personal awareness and leads to improvement, no matter how "good" someone already is.

Instructional coaching, then, is not for those teachers who need to be "fixed" but rather for all teachers—for those who are new to the profession, for veterans who may be finding challenge in the profession, *and* for those who already believe they are "good" teachers and want to aim ever higher. Coaching is for those teachers who need foundational support *and* for those teachers who, rather than reaching a plateau of "good enough" teaching, want to continuously improve, refine, and enhance their practice throughout their career. *Coaching is for those teachers who never want to stop improving, no matter where they begin.*

We believe coaching is a collaborative approach that facilitates reflective thinking, fosters agency, and builds empowerment through intentional conversation and purposeful design. Instructional coaching pursues excellence and equitable outcomes for all students (Bandura, 1997, 2001; Costa & Garmston, 2016; Knight, 2007; Short, 1992) and empowers all teachers in the pursuit of continuous growth and innovative practice.

To achieve educational equity, all students deserve not only technically capable, highly qualified teachers but also teachers who are passionate about their work, find daily joy in their work, and are curious about their practice and about improving student learning outcomes. All students deserve teachers who seek out challenges and opportunities to learn and grow, are willing to take healthy risks to try innovative practices with students, and advocate not only for their students but also for their colleagues, their schools, and the system of education as a whole.

The Qualities of a Coach

Essential qualities of effective coaches include a history of strong instructional practice (we recommend 5+ years) and strong skills in active listening and effective questioning, communication, building relationships, and leadership (Killion & Bryan, 2012). In addition to these basic skills, we believe that effective coaches:

- **Believe in teacher capacity.** Coaches believe that each and every teacher has or can build the capacity to positively impact student learning. They recognize that teachers come to the coaching conversation with their own expertise and have the capacity to solve their own problems. Coaches treat all teachers as professionals and are skilled at ensuring equity of voice during coaching conversations and using conversation to build teacher capacity.
- **Understand and catalyze change.** Coaches are aware of the factors that influence change and leverage this understanding to increase internal motivation for a teacher's change. Coaches also understand that change is about more than behavior. Change can occur in attitudes, beliefs about oneself and others, mindsets, and knowledge, among other things.
- **Respond flexibly to teacher needs.** Coaches are nimble and adjust to match their coaching practice to a teacher's needs. Coaches meet teachers where they are.
- **Focus on equity and classroom culture**. Coaches take action against educational inequities by building their own knowledge and skill and by engaging teachers in conversations about equity. Coaches promote and help create safe, positive, joyful, and loving classroom environments for students and teachers.
- **Focus on student learning.** Coaches never lose sight of the ultimate goal of successful academic, social, and emotional outcomes for students. Although many coaches only work directly with teachers, their conversations and goals are focused on instruction that is best for students.

- **Engage in continuous improvement and reflective practice.** Coaches engage in ongoing professional learning to continue to improve their coaching practice and to continue to learn about effective instructional practices. Coaches also engage in reflective practice as they continue to refine their skills and develop into more effective coaches for all teachers.

The CoachED Principles of Coaching

According to Opper (2019), teachers matter most when it comes to student performance, and it is the *practice* of teachers, not their background or experience, that makes them effective. Intentional and purposeful coaching impacts practice to improve equitable outcomes for all through an emphasis on teacher capacity and empowerment (for more on our change theory see Figure 2.2). Therefore, the model you will read about in this book was designed and is intended to be used with the guiding principles in Figure 2.3.

Teachers Are Professional, Passionate, and Autonomous Individuals

Teaching is as critical a profession as medicine, law, or accounting. We believe that teachers are dedicated to the purpose of ensuring that all students achieve and succeed as evidenced not only by academic achievement outcomes but also by the development of student voice, agency, and autonomy. As professionals, teachers constantly refine their knowledge, expertise, and advocacy efforts over the course of their careers. Several core strengths of the teaching profession include expert knowledge, autonomous thought and judgment, responsibility to stakeholders, collaboration, personal reflection, and a commitment to continuous learning and individual improvement. Central to our beliefs about the professionalism of teachers is our belief in teacher agency to control their own motivation and action (Bandura, 1989). Additionally, teachers effect change in themselves and in their environments because their judgments and actions are self-determined (Day, Sammons, & Gu, 2007; Luttenberg, Imants, & van Veen, 2013).

Empowered Teachers Are Leaders in Their Classrooms Who Create Environments in Which Students Thrive

Empowered teachers set high expectations for all students, pairing and scaffolding academically rigorous content with the development of students' social and emotional skills. Teachers who feel a sense of empowerment,

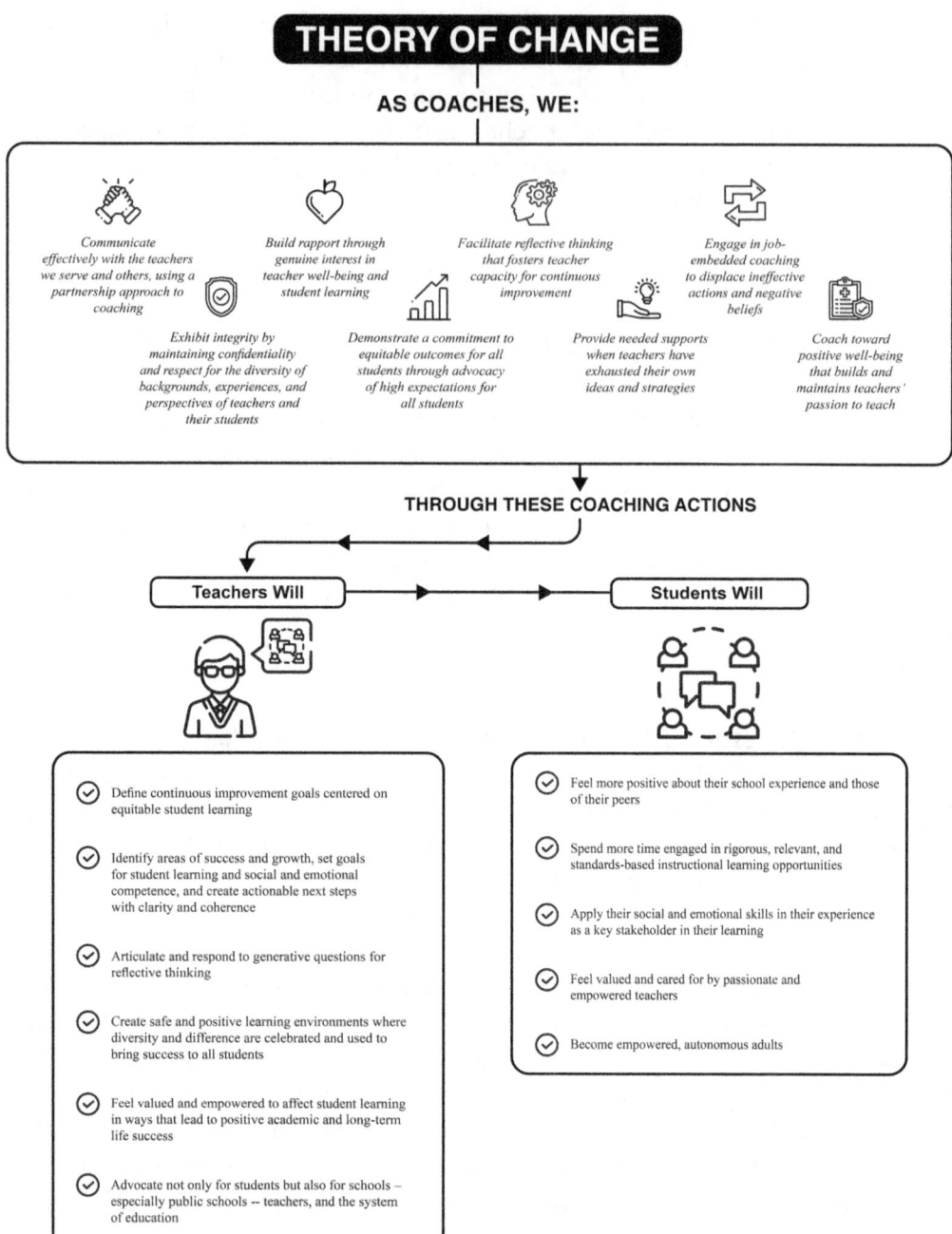

Figure 2.2 The CoachED Theory of Change

agency, and autonomy not only model these dispositions for students but also are more likely to provide students with tasks that increase their own sense of agency and autonomy (Elmore, 2005). Empowered teachers intentionally design lessons that engage students in student-centered instruction

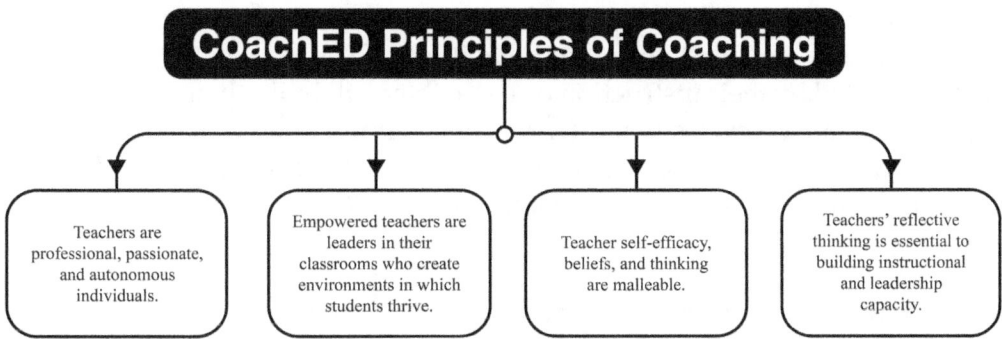

Figure 2.3 CoachED Principles of Coaching

that provides voice and choice, relevance, and multiple entry points and tasks that support students in building their own self-efficacy and ability to lead their own learning. These teachers do not anticipate student failure but rather show all students that they believe in their ability to achieve. They seek to understand the motivations of their students, and they build authentic relationships that allow for genuine conversations about growth and learning. Empowered teachers celebrate diversity and bring students and their families' backgrounds and experiences into the classroom, providing all students with the opportunity to learn and to support the learning of others.

Teacher Beliefs (Including Beliefs About Personal Efficacy) Are Malleable

Over time, unexamined beliefs can lead to assumptions about students and learning that can impact outcomes for students in a variety of ways, and unexamined instructional practices may become misaligned with a teacher's core beliefs. Likewise, a teacher's teaching identity and self-efficacy is also shaped and reshaped over time by their experiences, interactions, and context. Coaches understand when to help teachers uncover limiting beliefs that may be impacting their practice, student learning, and equitable outcomes in their classrooms and when to use conversations about beliefs in conjunction with classroom data to help teachers transform their teaching practices to align with their core beliefs. While teacher beliefs are malleable, examining beliefs, changing beliefs, and aligning classroom practices to a teacher's best beliefs takes time (Shirrell, Hopkins, & Spillane, 2019; Stephens et al., 2011).

Teachers' Reflective Thinking Is Essential to Building Instructional and Leadership Capacity

Thoughtful action comes through reflective thinking. In order for teachers to grow and build instructional and leadership capacity, they must engage in critical thinking about their practice. Empowered teachers often naturally self-reflect on their teaching actions and yet, when immersed in a conversation with their coach, they feel a sense of even deeper thinking about their work. When teachers are able to engage in habitual reflective thinking with structures provided by their instructional coach, they will build their own capacity to engage in action cycles that intentionally examine their practices and lead to growth and improvement. For more on the distinctions between the way the term "reflective" is used in this book, see Box 2.3.

> **Box 2.3 Consider This: Reflective Listening Statements, Reflective Thinking, and Reflective Conversations**
>
> The importance of reflection in education—that is thinking about and analyzing one's own thoughts, assumptions, and experiences to learn and become a stronger educator—has been around for years. In fact, reflection as an important skill for educators dates as far back as Dewey (Dewey, 1938; Adler, 1990, 1991; Marzano, Boogren, Heflebower, Kanold-McIntyre, & Pickering, 2012).
>
> Reflection is a powerful technique used in coaching. Unfortunately, there are multiple definitions of *reflection* and multiple ways that reflection is used in coaching, which can make the term confusing. We will use the idea of reflection in four ways throughout this book and define each here for clarity.
>
> **Reflective listening statements** (Rollnick et al., 2008; Miller & Rollnick, 2013) are a *technique* a coach uses to support a teacher's thinking. Using reflective listening statements requires that a coach repeat what a teacher has said through parroting, paraphrasing, summarizing, etc. (for more detail, see Chapter 4). Through reflective listening statements, a coach both ensures they understand what a teacher has said and provides the teacher the opportunity to hear their own words in a new way. Reflective listening statements can bring awareness to a teacher about their own way of thinking and can also provide an opportunity to consider new perspectives.
>
> For example:
>> Teacher: I was hoping that during the collaborative time students would have conversations about what they were discovering in their research about suicide prevention.
>>
>> Coach's reflective listening statement: You were expecting to hear more dialogue between students as they worked together.
>
> **Reflective thinking** is a *process* both **the teacher and the coach** engage in to intentionally consider plans, implementation, and results.
>
> A **teacher's reflective thinking** may include considerations about a past lesson and/or predictions about a future lesson. When working with a teacher, a coach prompts reflective thinking with a powerful question.

For example:
> Coach's powerful question: What is the relationship between your lesson plan and student collaboration during this lesson?
>
> Teacher's reflective thinking: I expected that students would talk to each other on their own without my guidance, so I didn't plan for any structured conversation. Next time maybe I need to add structured dialogue to support student conversation.

A **coach's reflective thinking** may include considerations about the results of a past coaching session with a teacher, what they might do differently next time, or specific plans for an upcoming coaching session. Typically, a coach reflects on their own immediately after or right before a coaching session through journaling or other methods of personal reflection, but coaches can also support one another through peer coaching.

Each of the earlier examples provides a snippet of a reflective conversation between a teacher and a coach. Based on these snippets, a coach might reflect that their question about the relationship between the teacher's lesson and student collaboration helped the teacher identify a next step. The coach might also reflect, though, that they did not provide an opportunity for the teacher to examine how the lesson plan provided *equitable* opportunities for student collaboration. Perhaps based on this reflection, the coach will make a plan to address equity in the next coaching session with the teacher.

Reflective conversations are a *strategy* **a coach** uses to engage a teacher in purposeful conversation. Reflective conversations between teachers and coaches include reflective listening statements and powerful questions to facilitate reflective thinking.

For further reading about the role of reflection in professional growth, consider these resources:

The Reflective Practitioner—Donald Schon (1983)

Reflective Teaching: An Introduction—Kenneth M. Zeichner and Daniel P. Liston (1996)

Becoming a Reflective Teacher—Robert J. Marzano, Tina Boogren, Tammy Heflebower, Jessica Kanold-McIntyre, and Debra Pickering (2012)

Revisiting Context

The principles of coaching that we have presented here and that support our framework are derived from our experiences as coaches for the past 16 years and underscored by the research literature about what supports adults in learning and change. While this book is not a review of the coaching literature, it does incorporate a variety of scholarly voices, as well as well-known coaching researchers and scholars from the United States. This book is not meant to be a review of coaching literature, a metanalysis, an autoethnography, or anything of the sort. We understand the power of turning coaching knowledge into coaching practices that empower teachers and, therefore, have written this book to present a framework—the CoachED framework—to help coaches make intentional choices about their practice that are grounded in the building blocks of adult learning and change theory. Our framework expands coaching mindsets to consider not only the practical teaching skills of a teacher but also their readiness to change and provides tools, techniques, and approaches to empower teachers and impact the culture of classrooms and school systems.

Conclusion

A teacher's strengths and creative abilities are critical in meeting the needs of all learners and impacting the system of education in powerful ways. By grounding our approach to coaching in principles of equity and empowerment and by emphasizing the relationship between the role of the teacher and the outcome of their practice on students, we emphasize the power of teachers to make a difference not only for students in their classrooms but also for their schools and districts and even for the world in which we all live.

3

Research-Based Coaching

Approaches, Models, and Theories

The role of coaching in schools is sometimes misunderstood, and coaches can find themselves explaining their work to principals and teachers alike. At times, coaches are simply asked to describe their role to teachers, principals and others who wish to know more about their work. At other times, uncomfortable situations may arise when a principal asks a coach to "fix" a particular teacher or shares that a teacher is on an action plan and the principal expects the coach to enforce the plan. Likewise, coaches can experience discomfort when teachers resist coaching or even actively denounce coaching.

While it is a coach's role to support teachers in strengthening their practice and making improvements, understanding why and how coaching works will arm coaches with language to fully explain to teachers and principals why the coaching role is NOT designed to "fix" someone and why coaches do not and should not be used to tell teachers what to do in their classrooms.

The approaches, models, and theories presented in this chapter (Figure 3.2) provide insight into why coaching with an empowering stance works to change teacher practice in schools. We share this information to reiterate and underscore the importance of partnering with teachers, engaging from a capacity building stance, and treating teachers as the experts of their own classrooms. We do not expect coaches to memorize the information presented

Understanding why and how coaching works will arm coaches with language to fully explain to teachers and principals why the coaching role is NOT designed to "fix" someone and why coaches do not and should not be used to tell teachers what to do in their classrooms.

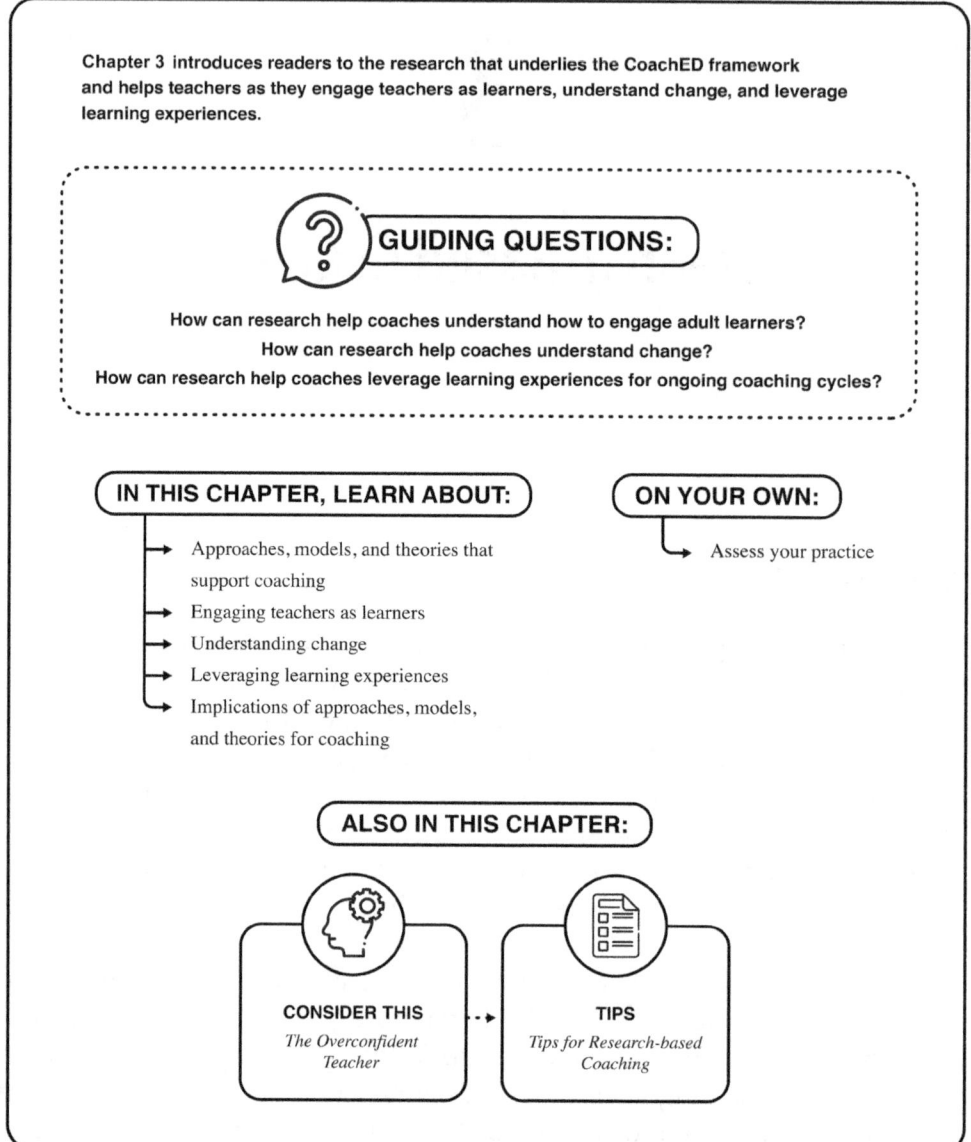

Figure 3.1 Chapter 3 Overview

here but that they will come to see commonalities among the approaches, models, and theories that help to inform their overall philosophy of coaching and to later understand the CoachED framework. We will provide a brief summary of each approach, model, and theory to orient coaches to this research and then provide brief implications of each for coaching practices.

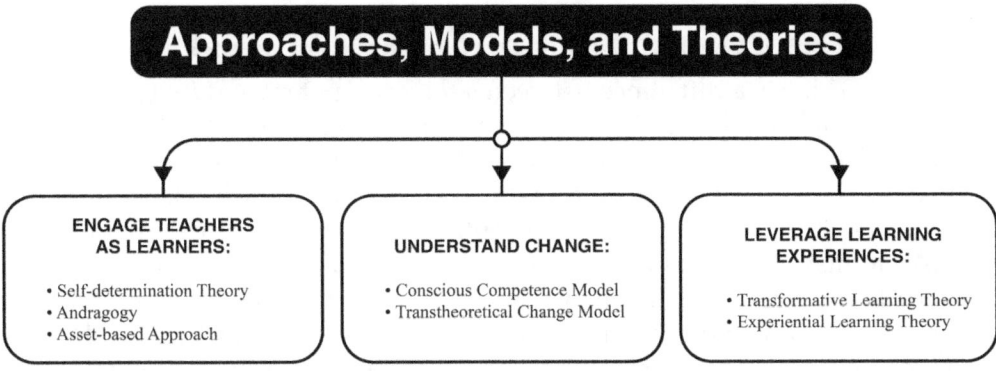

Figure 3.2 Approaches, Models, and Theories

Overall, the theories help coaches to engage teachers as learners, understand change, and leverage learning experiences.

Engage Teachers as Learners

Self-Determination theory, the theory of andragogy, and the asset-based approach all provide insights into how coaches should build relationships with teachers and engage them in the learning process. Incorporating these ideas into a coaching approach will help teachers prepare for and be open to the coaching relationship.

Self-Determination Theory

Self-determination theory is based on three foundational human needs: relatedness, autonomy, and competence (Ryan & Deci, 2000).

- Relatedness: a connection to others in the learning experience
- Autonomy: choice in what and how one learns; control of decisions that affect one's own life and experiences
- Competence: a sense of ability and skill to achieve one's goals

According to this theory, these three basic needs affect an individual's intrinsic motivation—that is, their engagement in an activity without need of an external reward. Teachers who feel relatedness, autonomy, and competence are more likely to embrace learning and to follow through on actions that support their growth than teachers who do not. Coaches who understand this theory prioritize relationships with teachers and engage in the coaching process as co-learners, ensure that teachers make the final decisions about their students, their classrooms, and their practice, and build confidence in the teachers with whom they work (see Box 3.1 for how to approach overconfident teachers).

> **Box 3.1 Coach's Dilemma: The Overconfident Teacher**
>
> There is a difference between *feeling* competent and *being* competent. Sometimes, in coaching, you may encounter a teacher who is overconfident in their own competence. In other words, they are unable to see their own opportunities for growth and learning. Overconfidence might be the result of the teacher's misperception or it might be a coping mechanism to mask fear of and discomfort with change. In case the overconfidence is a coping mechanism, a coach should always engage the teacher nonjudgmentally and empathetically. At the same time, however, to help the teacher recognize their own opportunities for growth and learning, the coach should emphasize evidence-based coaching conversations.

Theory of Andragogy

Andragogy is the practice of teaching adults. Malcolm Knowles' theory of andragogy (1990; Knowles, Elwood, Holton, & Swanson, 1998) describes adults as self-directed learners who come to learning with an awareness of their own strengths, weaknesses, interests, and ways of learning. Because adults are aware of their own needs, the best learning experiences involve them in solving problems of practice related to their current professional responsibilities. Additionally, effective learning experiences elicit and acknowledge the expertise adults bring with them and provide adults with resources and ideas that can be implemented in their work right away. Adults learn best when they understand the purpose behind the learning and when they can participate in collaborative ways with other learners as well as with the facilitator. Coaches who base their work on this theory empower teachers to bring their own experiences and ways of knowing to the collaborative process.

Asset-Based Approach

When teachers begin from a place of confidence, they are more willing to be vulnerable. Coaches who understand this idea use an asset-based approach to coaching. This approach focuses on beginning with teachers' strengths instead of their deficits. As this approach builds feelings of competence and self-efficacy in teachers, they are increasingly willing to take healthy risks for innovation in their classrooms. Although increasing a teacher's confidence and sense of competence is beneficial in and of itself, there are benefits for students as well. Teachers who lack a sense of competence and self-efficacy are more likely to impose control on their students and less likely to create a classroom environment that empowers students as agents of their own learning (Lopez & Louis, 2009).

Understand Change

Two models help coaches understand change and the power of the change process. Understanding change allows a coach to make informed decisions about how and when to engage teachers in active change activities.

Conscious Competence Model

The conscious competence model is often attributed to Noel Burch, who reportedly developed it in the 1970s; however, it may have even earlier roots (see Broadwell, 1969). This model portrays learning as a series of stages: unconscious incompetence, conscious incompetence, conscious competence, and unconscious competence.

- **Unconscious incompetence:** the learner is not yet aware of a new skill and may also be unaware of the need to learn the skill. For example, a teacher who relies on a teacher-centered, lectured-based approach may be unaware of student-centered instruction as a pedagogical approach. They may also be unaware of a need to change their current practice.
- **Conscious incompetence:** the learner has become aware of the new skill or approach they need to learn and understands the need for learning it. For example, the lecture-based teacher has become aware that student-centered instruction may lead to more student engagement. The teacher is now aware that their approach may not be as effective as another approach.
- **Conscious competence:** the learner now knows how to implement a new skill or approach but must do so with intentionality. For example, the teacher who has traditionally used a lecture-based approach may find that student-centered instruction takes more time, planning, and focus to implement effectively.
- **Unconscious competence:** After supports and multiple trial-and-error opportunities, the learner now naturally implements the change without explicit consideration or specific focus; it occurs naturally. The lecture-based teacher is now able to implement student-centered instruction quickly and without additional planning or extra effort.

Transtheoretical Change Model (TTM)

Prochaska and DiClemente's (1982, 1983; Prochaska, Redding, & Kerry, 2008; Prochaska & Velicer, 1997) transtheoretical change model, also called TTM or stages of change, identifies change as a *process* and not a single event. This model is often used in the context of health professions in which professionals, including health coaches, work with clients to change health-related behaviors. In our CoachED framework we draw on all six stages of TTM: precontemplation, contemplation, preparation, action, maintenance, and termination.

1. **Precontemplation:** an individual is not aware of a specific practice (or other behavior) or the *impact* of the practice (or behavior) on others; they are **not considering a change**.
2. **Contemplation:** an individual is aware that a change might be beneficial for themselves or others and is considering whether or not to make the change. This consideration includes **weighing pros and cons of the change**.
3. **Preparation:** an individual **decides** to make a change and **commits** to creating an action plan.
4. **Action:** an individual **takes** action to make the change a reality.
5. **Maintenance:** an individual has fully made the change and is **maintaining** the change without relapse. Relapse is a deterioration in use of the practice or behavior identified as the "change" that has happened.
6. **Termination:** The change is now a **habitual action**, and the cycle is completed. (*Note: this is not a required part of the model. Some argue that some changes are never terminated because they require too much effort, awareness, and intentionality to be considered final. We include it here because it has specific implications for coaching.*)

Coaches who understand this model know that any change a teacher implements is unlikely to be linear. There will be multiple cycles of learning, potentially including cycles of determination, action, and even relapse before a teacher reaches maintenance.

Leveraging Learning Experiences

Two learning theories—transformative learning theory and experiential learning theory—highlight the role of experience in learning and growth. Coaches support learning by guiding reflective thinking and engaging in reflective conversations with teachers, but they also support learning by creating and facilitating experiences that catalyze the learning process.

Transformative Learning Theory

Individual views and assumptions develop from an early age and often go unquestioned; however, new experiences have the potential to bring about new thinking. Transformative Learning Theory (Mezirow, 1997) suggests that personal growth occurs when an experience challenges an individual's personal views of and assumptions about the world. New experiences can create "disorienting dilemmas" that lead to cognitive dissonance, or the discomfort that occurs when evidence does not fit into an existing mental schema. This discomfort can be a catalyst for self-reflection and prompt questions such as, "How did this come to be?" "How is this true?" or, "Should I be thinking about this differently?" (Mezirow & Associates, 1990; Mezirow, 1991). Disorienting dilemmas may be sudden or gradual, resulting from an accumulation of a progressive sequence of insights (Mezirow, 2009).

Experiential Learning Theory

David Kolb's experiential learning theory illustrates a cycle of learning occurring in four stages: a concrete experience, reflective observation, abstract conceptualization, and active experimentation (Kolb & Kolb, 2005, 2009). In other words, an individual has an experience (concrete experience), which is followed by review and analysis of the experience (reflective observation). From this analysis, an individual learns new ideas (abstract conceptualization) and applies new ideas to new experiences (active experimentation). This cycle then begins again as a cycle of learning based on the resulting active experiment.

Table 3.1 shows implications for coaching based on each theory, model, or approach.

Conclusion

In this chapter, we have identified specific research-based approaches, models, and theories that serve as a foundation for the CoachED framework. Collectively these research-based approaches help us understand:

- ◆ Teachers deserve to have voice and choice over their goals and actions to meet their needs for relatedness, autonomy, and competence.
- ◆ When teachers can identify their own goals, they understand that their experiences are valued. Knowing their experiences are valued encourages them to become self-directed learners of their practice.
- ◆ Drawing on teachers' strengths promotes change in practice and innovation in the classroom.
- ◆ Teachers may be at different levels of awareness and competence in their practices. Additionally, they may be more or less aware or competent in one strategy, tool, or technique than others.

Table 3.1 Implications for Coaching

Theory Model Approach	Self-Determination Theory	Theory of Andragogy	Asset-Based Approach	Conscious Competence Model	Transtheoretical Change Model	Transformative Learning Theory	Experiential Learning Theory
Key Word	◆ Relatedness ◆ Autonomy ◆ Competence	Self-directed learners	◆ Strengths ◆ Competence ◆ Self-efficacy	◆ Unconscious competence ◆ Conscious incompetence ◆ Conscious competence ◆ Unconscious competence	Stages of change	◆ Disorienting dilemmas ◆ Cognitive dissonance	◆ Experience ◆ Analysis of experience ◆ Lessons learned
(Some) Implications for coaching	◆ Build trusting relationships ◆ Give teachers voice and control over their goals, action steps, and decisions ◆ Build from teachers' strengths	◆ Engage in inquiries into practices related to teachers' own professional responsibilities ◆ Recognize and honor the experiences teachers bring to the partnership ◆ Be clear about the purpose behind the need to learn	◆ Highlight teachers' observable strengths, ◆ Begin with the positive ◆ Focus on capacity building	◆ Engage teachers in micro cycles to support new learning ◆ Support teachers with intentional plans for and reflection on implementation ◆ Utilize protocols to encourage teachers to identify new goals for continued growth and learning	◆ Increase teacher's awareness that change may be beneficial ◆ Help teacher consider the impact of change on their overall well-being and practice ◆ Support the teacher in identifying an end goal and design coaching cycles to support teachers' action	◆ Collect data based on goal ◆ Allow teachers to review and analyze data collected prior to coach analysis ◆ Model practices in classrooms to support vicarious experiences for teachers ◆ Use video for teachers to see themselves in practice	◆ Set up concrete experiences for teachers through model teaching, collecting data, co-teaching, facilitating peer rounds ◆ Ground coaching conversations in observable data and experiences

- Change is a process and not all teachers are ready for immediate change or even aware of a need for change.
- Supporting teachers through concrete experiences, which may include disorienting dilemmas, can help a teacher identify a need for change.
- Grounding coaching conversations in concrete experiences supports teachers in using observable data to create meaningful and intentional actionable next steps.

In reading this book, implications for the use of these theories will surface in anecdotes, transcripts, coaches' dilemmas, tips, tools, and approaches for coaching. Again, we are not providing the research for coaches to memorize but to make connections and demonstrate alignment between the work that coaches do and the importance of coaching that empowers teachers and supports positive changes in practice. Boxes 3.2 and 3.3 provide tips and a self-assessment for navigating research-based coaching.

Box 3.2 Tips for Research-Based Coaching

- Emphasize and focus on teacher strengths and successes to build confidence and self-efficacy.
- Prioritize the teacher's goals, interests, and ideas.
- Build relationships with the teachers you are coaching.
- Give voice to the teacher's experience, expertise, and context.
- Plan for transformative learning experiences and engage teachers in reflective thinking.
- Use ongoing cycles of learning to achieve coaching goals.
- Be empathetic and patient, especially with a teacher who is not aware of a need for change.
- Watch for signs that a teacher is ready for a change; it is often in these moments that teachers are most open to the coaching process.

Box 3.3 On Your Own: Assess Your Practice

- How do these approaches, models, and theories currently play out in your practice?
- Which of the ideas described in this chapter would you like to pay more attention to for improved practice?

4

Foundational Techniques of Coaching

Opening Vignette: Jolie and Mr. Parsons

Jolie, a new coach, was ecstatic the first time she was asked by a teacher to visit his classroom. During the class—a health and PE class—students were working in teams to develop presentations on suicide prevention. At Mr. Parsons's request, Jolie was collecting evidence of student interactions with one another so that Mr. Parsons could work on his goal to more effectively implement collaborative group work. This is what Jolie saw:

Although this school was 1:1 with every student in possession of a working and networked computer, groups of four left just one or two group members to do the work while the others chatted about their weekend plans or played on their

Foundational Techniques of Coaching ◆ 31

Put simply, the purpose of instructional coaching is to support teachers in continuous improvement and personal growth, no matter the teacher's level of experience or expertise.

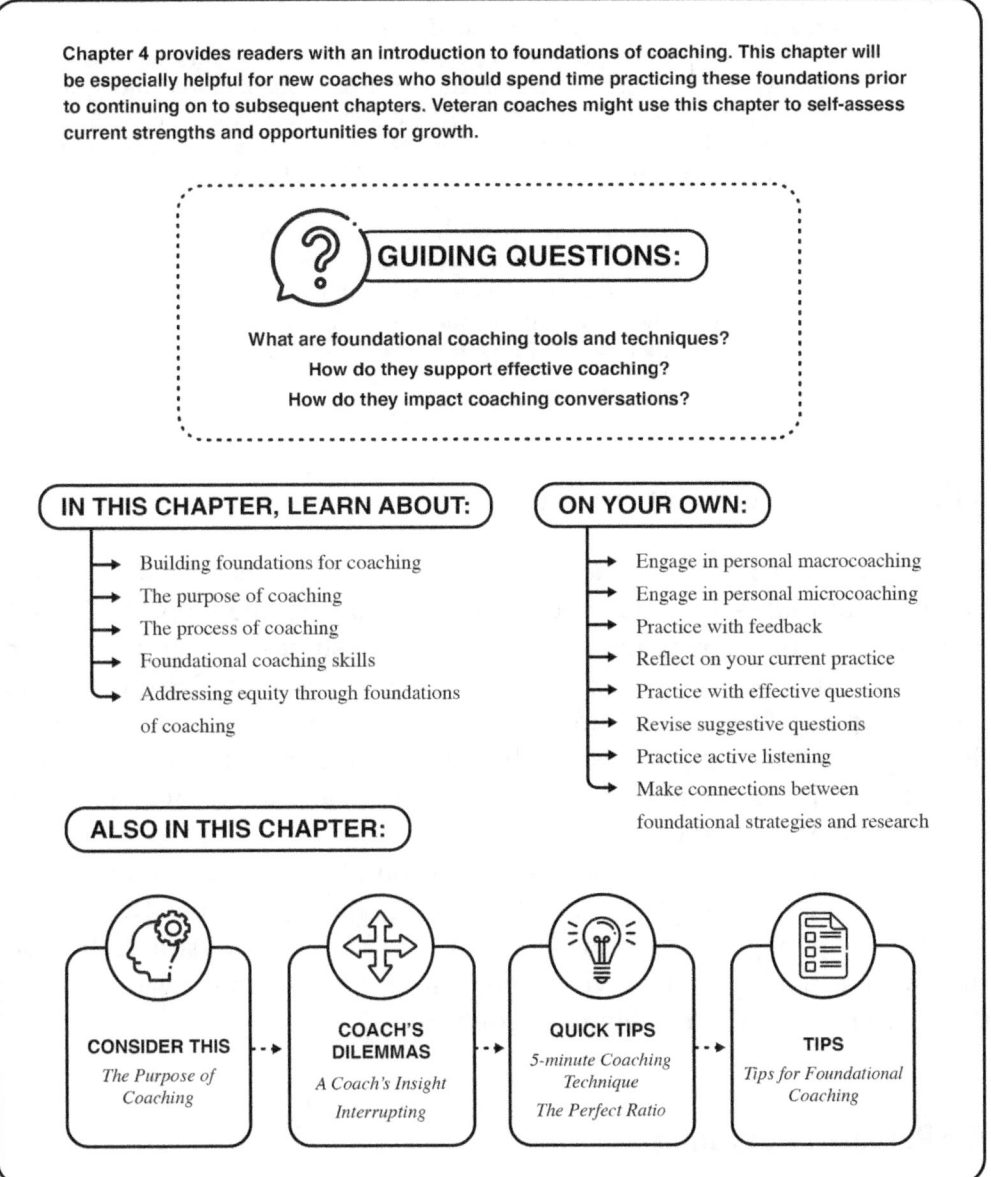

Figure 4.1 Chapter 4 Overview

cell phones. The students who were engaged in working on the presentations were searching the Internet—googling "suicide prevention"—and cutting and pasting content they found on websites. Jolie did not see students engaging one another in conversations about the task, nor did she hear conversations evaluating content of websites or coming to group consensus. The data began to show a trend:

the only content-based interactions between students in the groups occurred when the student working on the PowerPoint wanted approval of a slide. The interaction included turning the computer to a classmate who silently read the slide and nodded or grunted their assent.

Using the data she collected, Jolie intended to plan for a post-visit conversation with Mr. Parsons by intentionally crafting questions to help Mr. Parsons consider how he might want to change the assignment to increase collaboration among students. However, she was not prepared for what happened as the class ended. At the end of the lesson, Jolie handed Mr. Parsons his data and anticipated scheduling a post-visit meeting, but he surprised her by asking, "What did you think? How did it go?"

As a newly trained coach, Jolie knew she was not supposed to answer this question or to fix Mr. Parsons's "problems" in the classroom—the thinking was supposed to come from him! She stuttered awkwardly and, in a state of confusion and with extreme hesitation, she answered his question, "I . . . well . . . I think it went well." In that moment, Jolie forgot to implement the most foundational of coaching techniques.

Building Foundations for Coaching

By answering Mr. Parsons's question (in the Opening Vignette)—and answering it untruthfully—Jolie did not build trust, nor did she help Mr. Parsons become aware of his own understanding of what success looked like for him in his classroom or his own ability to measure that success. She did not support his capacity to self-assess, make course corrections, or engage in reflective thinking about his decisions. Not only did Jolie take away the opportunity to engage Mr. Parsons in a real coaching conversation, but she also reinforced his ineffective teaching practices.

A powerful coaching practice rests on foundational skills that support someone else in reaching their potential through their own capacity. Coaching is not about giving someone the answers but rather about using techniques such as questioning and active listening to guide someone else in solving their own problems or reaching their own goals.

The Purpose of Coaching

Our vision of instructional coaching, as evidenced through our coaching principles (outlined in Chapter 2), includes the transformation of individual teachers to become more innovative and more empowered. However, a simpler explanation of the fundamental goals of day-to-day coaching can illuminate the basic concept and tenets of coaching and help a coach—especially a new coach—understand both their role and the process of coaching.

Put simply, the purpose of instructional coaching is to support teachers in continuous improvement and personal growth, no matter the teacher's level of experience or expertise. Through coaching conversations that emphasize intentionality and reflective thinking, a coach elicits a teacher's vision for change in their classroom. This change may be a large-scale revisioning of classroom practice or a subtle yet impactful refinement of existing practice. It may be the adoption of an entirely new approach to teaching or a simple yet explicit awareness of a nuanced strategy and its impact on diverse learners.

No matter how big the innovation or how small the adjustment, a coach's role is to help clarify a teacher's vision, values, and beliefs; define a plan for success; and support follow-through and accountability (see Boxes 4.1 and 4.2 for further reflections on the purpose of coaching and the role of a coach).

Box 4.1 Consider This: The Purpose of Coaching

Another way to think about the purpose of coaching is to consider the importance of time and space for reflective thinking and planning intentional action steps during a change process. Have you ever made a New Year's resolution only to fail at that resolution because you simply didn't have time for follow-through? Have you ever made a New Year's resolution and failed because you never told anyone about the resolution and so it was easy to let it go?

A coach provides a structure for follow-through simply by holding time and space for intentional work on a goal and by acting as an external accountability partner to help a teacher maintain consistent focus and effort on a goal. How would your resolution have fared if you had structured, weekly time for focusing on and engaging in reflective thinking about the change? What would have happened if you had someone to share successes and challenges with? How might an external accountability partner have impacted your motivation, your focus, and your approach?

Box 4.2 Coach's Dilemma: A Coach's Insight

As practicing coaches, we know that there are times when a teacher chooses to work on one goal and, based on your observations in the classroom and your expertise in teaching and learning, you think that the teacher should focus on something else for a more equitable and effective practice. We are not suggesting that you ignore opportunities to address needed changes in the classroom; however, we are suggesting that you find ways to do so within the context of the teacher's goal.

> For example, perhaps a teacher would like to use more technology in their classroom. They invite you to observe a student activity so you can work together to determine how more technology might be integrated. What you observe in the classroom leads you to think the teacher might also benefit from more intentional planning of lessons *without* technology! There isn't much structure to the activity you observe, students are unclear about expectations, and there is no time limit set.
>
> Each of these aspects of planning can be addressed *as* the teacher works toward their personal goal of infusing technology into the classroom. Without suggesting the teacher needs better structure to their lessons, the coach can support stronger structure by working with the teacher on lesson plans that infuse technology. Further, the coach can ask reflective questions about how the teacher's insights into teaching with technology might impact other areas of teaching. As a coach develops strong, trusting relationships with a teacher, they will also have more opportunity to provide input on the teacher's goals.

The Process of Coaching

At a high level, coaching is a process in which a coach partners with a teacher in setting, following through with, and learning from a goal. Although every coaching relationship and every coaching encounter is different, coaching typically follows a standard structure to support change. Coaches should always be prepared to be flexible and meet each teacher where they are in the moment; however, having a basic understanding of the process will provide guidance to frame coaching in most cases.

The coaching process includes both macro- and microcoaching phases (Figure 4.2) and engages teachers in envisioning a change, setting a goal, planning for change, implementing change, and engaging in reflective thinking about change.

Macrocoaching

The macrocoaching process begins with big-picture conversations that often begin with a teacher's exploration of their own values; and, in addition, these conversations engage a teacher in envisioning a change, setting goals, identifying measures of success, and creating an action plan. Although it is possible to complete all of these steps in one conversation—and this may in fact be the norm once a coach and teacher have a strong working partnership in which they know one another well—in the beginning stages of a relationship with a teacher, this process may take more than one meeting. No matter

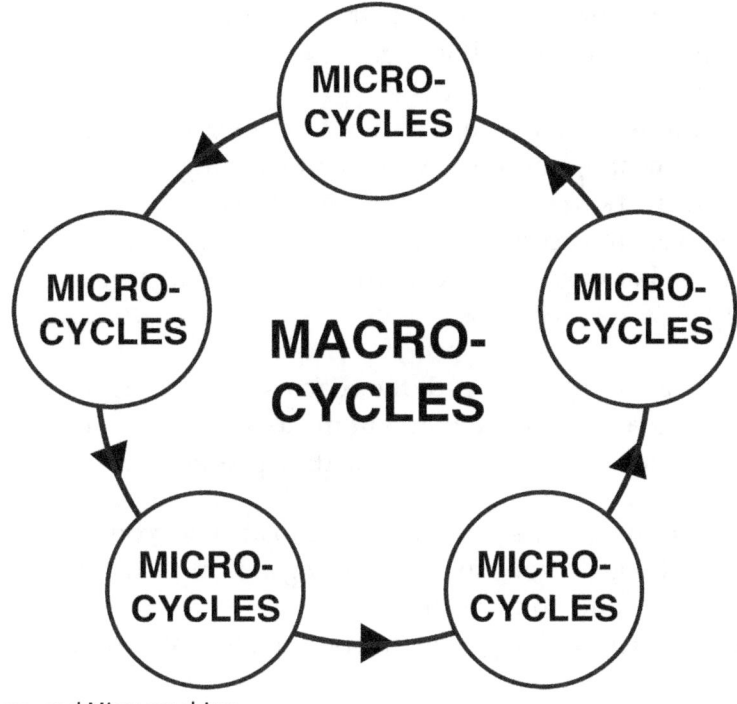

Figure 4.2 Macro- and Microcoaching

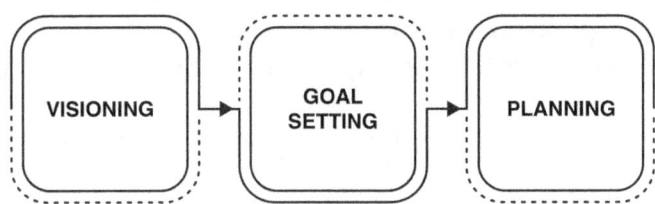

Figure 4.3 Macrocoaching Process

the structure or number of conversations, the first three stages—envisioning change, setting a goal, and making a plan—make up the macrocoaching—or big picture—phase of the coaching process (Figure 4.3).

Visioning

To make a change, one must first know what that change might be. The first task of a coach is to help a teacher identify a goal for change and to ensure that the goal is aligned with the teacher's values. Identifying a goal for change focuses the coaching relationship; ensuring that the change is important to the teacher and aligned with their values enhances motivation and perseverance throughout the change process. To this end, conversations in the macrocoaching phase often start with a visioning conversation. Visioning questions might include the following:

- If there were no constraints, what would your ideal classroom look like?
- What is most important to you about teaching? What would it take for your work to more closely align with your values?
- If you were to successfully implement change aligned with your values, what would your classroom look like in X years?

Goal Setting

After a vision has been developed, the coach supports the teacher in identifying a specific goal for change that will make their reality a closer match to their vision. Questions to begin the goal setting process include the following:

- What are some steps you might take to achieve your vision?
- What options do you have for making a change that will better align your reality and your vision?
- What big-picture changes might you need to make to succeed in your plan?

During these goal-setting conversations, the coach should also ensure that the change the teacher is planning to make is wholly within their control. Attempting to make a change that is outside one's locus of control will only bring frustration. The following questions engage the teacher in an exploration of control:

- How much control do you have over this decision or action? How do you know?
- Who are stakeholders who might impact this decision or action?
- What is the relationship between stakeholders and your goal?
- Is anyone else likely to derail your efforts? If so, how?

Based on a vision of success and an understanding of control, the teacher determines a concrete goal for coaching (macrogoal). This goal might be to increase student voice in the classroom, to equitably provide all students with opportunities to answer higher-order thinking questions, or to start using a new approach such as project-based learning. This portion of the coaching conversation could include the following questions:

- Based on what we have discussed, what one change would make the most difference for you and your students?
- What is the first step you will need to take to better align your work with your values?
- How would you like to begin to implement your vision?

It is important for a teacher not only to identify a specific goal for the coaching process but also to consider what success will look like. Discussing success from the start helps both the coach and teacher know when a coaching cycle has reached completion and when it is time to set new goals.

Once a final goal within the teacher's control is selected by the teacher, the coach supports the teacher in understanding how they will measure success. Without a clear understanding of what success looks like and how it will be measured, the coach and teacher can get caught in an unproductive cycle of coaching that becomes unfocused as the target for change begins to shift from day to day. Questions to drive this conversation include the following:

- How will you know when you are successful?
- How might you measure impact of the change on student outcomes?

Planning

Finally, once a goal has been determined and measurements of success have been identified, it is time to break the big-picture goal into smaller action steps. No goal worth setting and working toward with a coach can happen overnight. At this point, it might be possible to set out a complete timeline of work toward the overall goal or the teacher may need to identify and take only one step at a time. As always, the coach should adjust and align their approach with the teacher's needs and preferences.

When identifying action steps—either one single step at a time or many steps all at once—the coach should also engage the teacher in a conversation about potential pitfalls and obstacles. This conversation is not intended to deflate or overwhelm the teacher but, instead, to help the teacher proactively plan for anything that might get in the way of their success. Armed in advance with a plan for facing challenges head on, the teacher is more likely to succeed.

This macrocoaching cycle, which notably is guided by the coach through powerful questioning and not suggesting, occurs each time the teacher is ready to set a new goal for change. Try a macrocoaching cycle in the exercise in Box 4.3.

Box 4.3 On Your Own: Macrocoaching

Let's try a macrocoaching cycle based on your own vision for coaching. Reflect on each of these questions in order.

1. What do you value most about coaching?
2. How does your practice currently align with your values?

> 3. What is one aspect of your coaching skills you'd like to improve or change in order to better align with your values?
> 4. If you successfully made this change, how would your coaching practice change?
> 5. How would you know when you were successful in your change?
> 6. What are some specific ways *within your control* to begin to make this change?
>
> That's macrocoaching! The cycle is complete when your coaching practice aligns with your answers to the first four questions.

Microcoaching

Once the big-picture goal has been set, coaching shifts to microcycles focused from session to session on implementing this one change. Short-cycle, microcoaching rounds (microcycles) support follow-through on the goal set during the macrocoaching phase. Microcycles emphasize deep and ongoing reflective thinking and learning in a continuous and intentional process. Microcycles generally include planning, implementation, and reflective thinking (Figure 4.4). While a coach facilitates this process, it is the teacher's planning, implementation, and reflective thinking that compose a microcoaching cycle.

Planning

The planning stage of a microcycle involves identifying and planning for an action step that will move a teacher closer to reaching their macrogoal. Planning conversations to identify next steps might include the following:

- identification of potential resources and supports;
- ongoing discussion of potential pitfalls and obstacles; and
- consideration of impact on students.

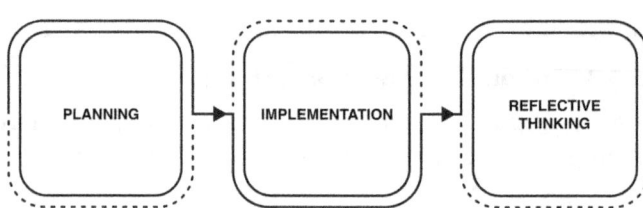

Figure 4.4 Microcoaching Process

Once the next step is determined, the coach may also be involved in the planning process. For example, a coach may help co-plan

- a classroom visit for data collection, and
- a lesson or activity for students.

During this stage, a coach guides a teacher in determining what the right next step will be. Depending on the action step, the coach may be involved in creating a plan for implementation as well.

Implementation

As suggested in Kolb's experiential learning theory, experiences provide the opportunity for reflective thinking, which is the catalyst for new learning. In the case of microcycles, the implementation stage involves enacting the action step in order to provide the experience that informs new thinking. Typically, though not always, this stage involves the teacher trying something new in the classroom with or without coach support. Possible action steps for implementation include the following:

- modeling (the coach models a lesson for the teacher);
- co-teaching (the coach and teacher teach together);
- classroom data collection (the coach collects student data during a lesson for later analysis); and
- peer classroom visit (the teacher observes another teacher in action).

Note: More on classroom data collection following this and in Chapter 7. Details on modeling and co-teaching follow in Chapter 7.

Reflective Thinking

The final stage in a microcycle involves reflective thinking on the results of the implementation phase. Topics for reflective thinking might include the following:

- lessons learned through implementation of action steps,
- analysis of classroom visit data,
- celebration of successes,
- exploration of challenges, and
- application of lessons learned to next steps.

A microcoaching cycle ends by applying lessons learned to a plan for a next step; hence, the ending of one microcoaching cycle is often the beginning of the next cycle. Practice a microcoaching cycle in Box 4.4.

> **Box 4.4 On Your Own: Microcoaching**
>
> Now, let's try a microcoaching cycle. Complete these steps.
>
> 1. Considering the specific ways *within your control* you might begin to achieve your macrogoal, what's the best first step? Make a plan to take that step.
> 2. Implement the step.
> 3. Engage in reflective thinking about the step. You might write about the experience or discuss it with a fellow coach. Questions to guide your reflection include the following:
>   a. What were the results of the step you took? What successes did you achieve? What challenges did you face?
>   b. What did you learn from this step? How might you use what you learned to continue moving forward?
>   c. What is your next step?
>
> Granted, this is a very simplified version of a microcoaching cycle and you didn't have a coach to guide you with follow-up questions to deepen your thinking, but you get the idea.

Microcycles in Action: Classroom Data Collection

Although some classroom visits, especially early in a coaching relationship, may be informal to provide an opportunity for a coach to better understand a teacher and his context, most classroom visits will be more intentional and will focus on classroom data collection. These classroom visits represent one typical example of a microcycle of instructional coaching. Applied to classroom visits for data collection, the stages of the microcycle are the pre-visit (planning), the classroom visit (implementation), and the post-visit (reflective thinking).

Pre-Visit

When a coach visits a classroom for data collection, they should always have a specific focus; this focus is typically on the students and their learning. We call this focus a student learning data collection question. The student learning data collection question should align with the teacher's current action step and/or overall coaching goal and should be *co-developed* by the coach and teacher to ensure that the question meets the teacher's interests and learning needs. For example, remember Mr. Parsons? His coaching goal was to more effectively implement collaborative group work in his classroom. Jolie's student learning data collection question during her visit to Mr. Parsons's classroom was, "How are students interacting with one another?"

Other sample student learning data collection questions include the following:

- Whose voice is heard in the classroom?
- What evidence is there that all students are able to answer higher-order thinking questions?
- What evidence shows students collaborating with one another to build understanding?
- What evidence shows students understanding and/or misunderstanding the lesson?
- What evidence shows students understanding the relevance of the learning?

Once a student learning data collection question has been determined, the coach and teacher again *co-develop* a data collection tool that will guide the coach in collecting the data. To ensure common expectations, the coach and teacher should discuss the structure of the tool, the meaning of related terms, and the method of data collection. The tool should be specific so the coach and teacher have common expectations about how it will be used and how data will be captured. For examples of data collection tools, see Appendix A.

During the pre-visit, the coach also gathers information about what they can expect to see in the classroom as well as logistics and expectations for their presence. Questions a coach might ask during the pre-visit include the following:

- What will the students learn during this class?
- What activities will the students be engaged in?
- Are there any specific modifications I should be aware of?
- On what day would you like me to collect this data?
- What time would you like me to arrive? How long would you like me to stay?
- Would it be OK if I moved around the room?
- Would it be OK if I spoke to the students?
- How do you define X [participation, voice, leadership, etc.] in the context of this class?

Visit

During the visit, the coach should adhere to decisions made during the pre-visit conversation. These include whether or not the coach is welcome to walk around the room, whether or not they should interact with the students, and how long they should stay. The length of a classroom visit will vary according to the purpose of and method for data collection. If, for example, a teacher wants specific data on a 10-minute warm-up activity, the coach need only stay for the 10 minutes. It is not important for a coach to stay an entire class period unless the data desired by the teacher require the coach to stay the whole period. During the visit, the coach maintains focus on the student learning data collection question and collects data as planned.

Post-Visit

The post-visit provides the opportunity for reflective conversation and should take place as soon as possible after the classroom visit—ideally within 24 hours. While this isn't always possible, the coach should do their best to prioritize post-visit conversations to ensure that they happen in a timely fashion. Virtual conferencing platforms provide opportunities for traveling coaches to prioritize post-visit conversations even when they are not on campus.

During a reflective conversation, the coach uses powerful questions and reflective listening statements to support the teacher in learning from and engaging in reflective thinking about the data. During the post-visit, the coach should ask the teacher questions like:

- What do you notice about the data?
- How do the data align with your expectations?
- How might you wish the data looked different?
- What might you do in your classroom to better align the data with your vision?
- What might you do in your classroom next to continue this success?

One other note on classroom data: the absence of data is data and can provide a disorienting dilemma for a teacher's reflective thinking. In the case of Mr. Parsons, the data Jolie collected during student group work in his class showed very few student interactions. This lack of data could have led to a coaching conversation in which Jolie and Mr. Parsons discussed how he planned for student interaction and what more students needed to be successful in interactions with one another.

The Role of Data in Microcycles

Although it is not always necessary for the coach to be involved in data collection, coaching conversations in microcycles typically rely on some type of external data. These data allow the teacher to check their assumptions about teaching, learning, and/or specific students or groups of students; identify gaps in their own thinking; and see their classroom from a new perspective. Sometimes data are collected by the coach as in the example mentioned earlier; at other times, data might include informal student work samples, like exit tickets and other formative assessments, or more formal student work like tests, projects, and formal benchmarking data. These are data that the teacher can bring to a coaching conversation and do not require a classroom visit by the coach. Whether or not the coach is involved in the data collection, the coach's role during a data conversation is to support objective data analysis. Coaches can use the same questions listed earlier for coach-collected data with other types of data the teacher may have.

Components of Microcoaching Conversations

Every coaching conversation is unique, and a coach should remain flexible as they navigate each conversation and respond to individual teachers; however, knowing the components of a typical cadence of coaching conversations can help a coach focus and guide individual sessions. Short-cycle conversations focus on intentional goal-related steps and provide time and space for the teacher to consider and engage in reflective thinking on their progress, examine data, make adjustments as necessary, and celebrate successes. Each microcycle should tie to the teacher's overall vision for success, include opportunities for reflective thinking on action to date, and include a discussion of next steps.

A typical microcoaching conversation might include the components listed in Figure 4.5.

Opening and Relationship Building

Because building trust and vulnerability is so important to the coaching relationship, the coach should set aside time for informal conversation and relationship building. The coach should balance the need for informal conversation with the teacher's personality; some teachers prefer to get down to business right away while others want to spend some time in social conversation. Additionally, the coach will need to keep in mind time constraints

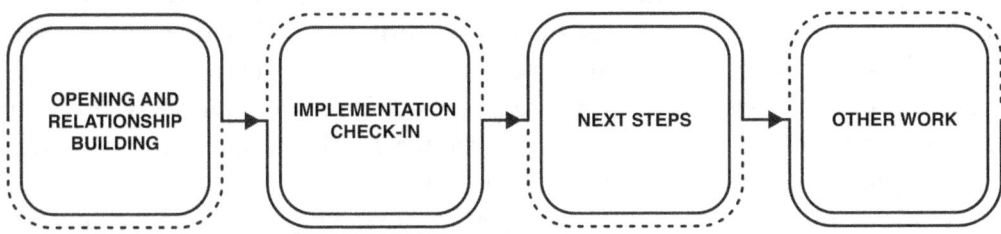

Figure 4.5 Components of a Microcoaching Conversation

as well as any other mitigating factors. As always, the coach should remain flexible and respond to the teacher's needs and preferences.

Implementation Check-In

The implementation check-in allows the coach to ask about progress made since the last conversation. This check-in should begin with successes to align with asset-based coaching and to ensure the teacher feels a sense of progress. In fact, it may be necessary to simply celebrate the initiative and risk a teacher took to try something new, even if the attempt was unsuccessful. Celebrating initiative and risk will help a teacher develop a growth mindset.

After focusing on strengths and celebrating successes, the conversation might move to implementation challenges the teacher has faced since the last visit and lessons learned through these challenges. The implementation check-in often relies on a data source as described earlier.

The overall goal of this check-in is to provide the teacher opportunity and support for deep reflective thinking. To this end, the check-in is not over after the teacher has shared progress to date. Rather, the coach uses powerful questions to help the teacher think more deeply about how their progress and insights can lead to even deeper learning. This opportunity for reflective thinking during the check-in is at the heart of coaching.

Next Steps

After reflective thinking about implementation and progress since the last coaching conversation, the conversation turns to next steps. Based on progress to date, what will the teacher do next to continue moving toward their vision for their classroom? This portion of the coaching conversation includes a discussion of any potential obstacles and plans to proactively address challenges. The coach might also ask the teacher what supports they need that the coach can provide as well as how they would like to be held accountable for progress.

Other Work

Depending on the teacher's specific goals, additional coaching support may also be included during a coaching conversation. This work may include co-planning a lesson and finding resources, co-developing a data collection tool, connecting teachers with colleagues, and revisiting school-wide goals. As the coach considers what additional work might fit into a coaching conversation, they will rely on the guidance of the teacher to inform their supports. A coach should not, for example, offer resources the teacher has not asked for or step in to co-plan a lesson without first being invited.

While we have provided steps for the process of macro- and microcycle coaching, these steps are simply guidelines for the coach within which they should be flexible in their response to the teacher with whom they are working. Steps might be re-arranged, added, or even skipped to meet the needs of the teacher.

Foundational Coaching Skills

In addition to the typical process of coaching represented by macro- and microcoaching cycles, there are a number of foundational skills a coach will use. These include building relationships, providing effective feedback, using foundational question techniques, and active listening (Figure 4.6).

Building Relationships

Relationship building is an ongoing piece of a coaching conversation as described earlier; however, it is also a skill in and of itself with specific strategies used to intentionally focus on building trust. Jolie's response to Mr. Parsons, for example, was intended to make a connection and build a relationship but it did not help build trust—and trust is the foundation of the coaching relationship.

Relationship building begins with meeting the teacher where they are without judgment. This means listening to them in a manner that allows them to feel heard. This does not mean that what the teacher says needs to be validated, and this is an important distinction. For the teacher to feel heard, the coach must simply validate the feelings the teacher has and not the actions they have taken or the beliefs underlying those actions.

For example, if a teacher makes a statement like, "These kids just can't learn," the coach can validate the teacher's frustration without validating the belief by saying, "You sound frustrated." Doing so in a nonjudgmental tone, even when the coach disagrees with the belief, will build trust that will allow the coach to begin transforming the belief through additional coaching sessions. More on Coaching Beliefs follows in Chapter 7.

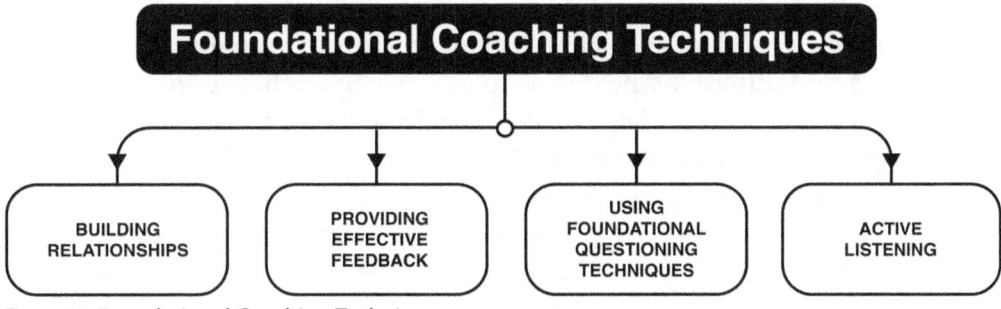

Figure 4.6 Foundational Coaching Techniques

Other relationship-building skills of coaching include the following:

- **Flexibility.** When teachers cancel or reschedule a meeting, coaches should be understanding and as flexible as their schedules allow. Through understanding, coaches assure teachers that they are aware of the demands of the teaching profession and the many unexpected needs teachers must meet on a daily basis. This understanding helps build relationships as teachers feel valued and understood by their coaches.
- **Vulnerability.** Coaches can show vulnerability by sharing their own experiences, challenges, frustrations, questions, and successes. Showing their own vulnerability and sharing their own opportunities for continuous growth and improvement can help make teachers feel safe to share theirs. It is, of course, essential that coaches share appropriately and professionally. This means carefully selecting experiences and remembering not to overshare. Coaches should create a balance and leave space for teachers to be vulnerable in response.
- **Deference.** Coaches should remember the importance of self-determination theory and treat teachers as the experts of their own experiences. A teacher with whom a coach is working likely knows more about their students, their content, and their context than the coach does, even if the coach is site-based. Treating teachers as the experts of their own experiences empowers them by showing them that coaches believe in their competence and respect their autonomy.
- **Support.** Coaches should support teachers' decisions . . . even when a teacher decides to try something the coach believes may fail. Teachers must be allowed to fail forward and learn from their experiences. This support gives teachers a sense of autonomy and control over their own learning, and failure nicely sets up opportunities for rich reflective thinking. If all decisions and changes teachers made worked out perfectly, there would be no need for coaching.
- **Neutral, nonjudgmental positioning.** If and when teachers fail, coaches should remain nonjudgmental and support them in learning from their experiences. This means asking powerful questions to help them understand what did not work as expected and what they might do differently next time to increase their chances of success. This also means celebrating their willingness to take risks and try innovative things. Not everything is going to work, but the coach's role is to ensure that everything adds to a teacher's understanding of what works *for them and their students*, what doesn't work, and why.
- **Respect.** A coach should be respectful of teachers as well as their spaces. This means always thanking teachers for their time before any

coaching engagement, following up by e-mail with written notes of appreciation, and always asking permission to enter their classrooms. If a teacher is not in the classroom when a coach arrives, the coach should wait outside the door until the teacher returns. Following basic rules of etiquette will go a long way in establishing a relationship.

Providing Effective Feedback

One way for coaches to build relationships is to ensure that teachers are prepared for the type of feedback coaches will provide. This means that no matter the data being used in coaching conversations, it is important for coaches to understand what type of feedback they are providing and the impact of that feedback. They should also know how and when to intentionally use each type of feedback.

Types of Feedback

To define and provide examples of various types of feedback, we will refer to data from Mr. Parsons's classroom (Figure 4.7).

Figure 4.7 Mr. Parsons's Classroom Data

Objective feedback. Objective feedback includes specific and measurable data points. These data points are not based on opinion but based on fact. For example:

- There were 14 on-topic interactions between students.
- Out of 6 groups, 5 groups were working on the PowerPoint.
- There were 11 female-to-female interactions, 1 male-to-male interaction, and 2 female-to-male interactions.

Subjective feedback. Two additional types of feedback defined by Carl Rogers (1961) are interpretive and evaluative. Interpretive and evaluative feedback are both subjective; that is, they rely on personal understanding and meaning instead of factual data points.

Subjective interpretive feedback involves analysis and interpretation of the data. The feedback provider sees the data, assigns meaning to the data, and forms an interpretation of what it means. For example:

- The girls were more interested in the topic of this lesson than the boys were.
- Boys are intimidated by the girls in this classroom.
- The students in group 4 don't like each other.

Subjective evaluative feedback involves assigning positive or negative value to the data. For example:

- Group 5 was working together the best out of all the groups.
- Mr. Parsons did a good job engaging female students.
- Mr. Parsons has not done a good job of scaffolding communication between boys and girls in his classroom.

Practice on your own with the exercise in Box 4.5 and the corresponding data in Figure 4.8.

Box 4.5 On Your Own: Practice with Feedback

Practice developing feedback statements in each category using classroom discussion data. The student learning data collection question for the data was, "Who is contributing to classroom discussions?" As indicated by the data collection tool, student desks were placed in a square for the discussion. Check marks indicate student participation in the discussion. A circled checkmark indicates that the student was called on by the teacher and the participation was not voluntary. If the circle has an X over it, the student who was called on chose not to respond to the teacher's invitation to participate.

For more explanation of and context for this classroom data, see explanation in Appendix A, page 200 (Whose Voice Is Being Heard). For an answer key that provides possible statements for each feedback type see Appendix A, Box A.5 (page 202).

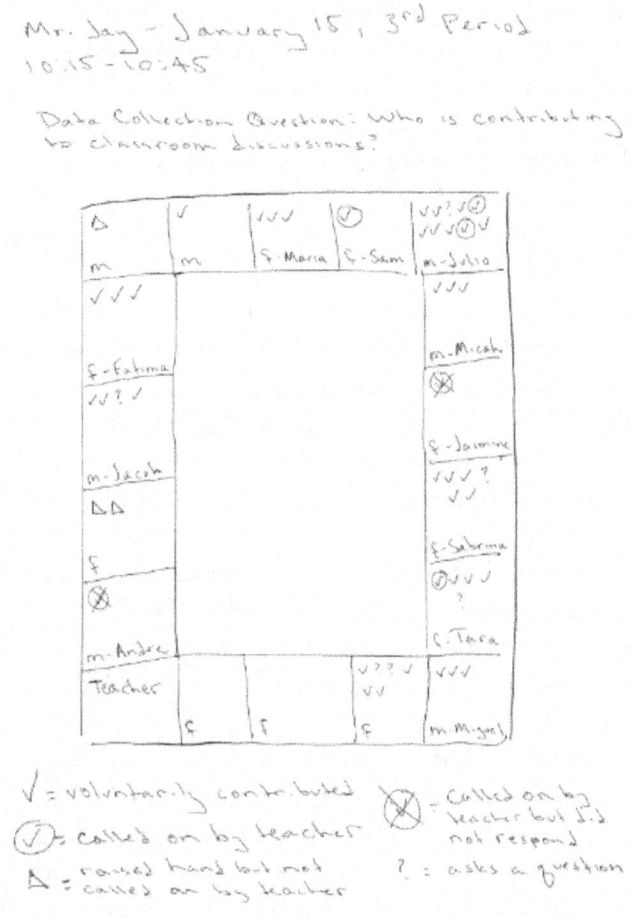

Figure 4.8 Classroom Discussion Data

Purpose of Feedback

Each type of feedback has a different impact on the recipient and each type of feedback has value in its own right as long as it is given at the appropriate time. The important thing is to understand the impact of each type of feedback and to be intentional about using the most appropriate feedback in every coaching situation. We will review the three types of feedback again and consider the impact of each applied to the data collected by Jolie for Mr. Parsons.

Objective feedback. Objective feedback is used to hold a mirror up to classroom practice to allow a teacher to engage in reflective thinking about what occurred during a lesson. Additionally, the data provide an opportunity for a teacher to check their own assumptions and interpretations about how the class went. In providing objective feedback, the coach is an "external set of eyes and ears providing a more accurate picture of . . . reality" (Gawande, 2017).

Sometimes a teacher's perception of a lesson can be inaccurate. Inaccurate perceptions about a lesson can be based on assumptions a teacher makes about their students, their content, or their facilitation. They can also be based on the amount of information a teacher must pay attention to at any one moment in a classroom. Looking at objective data can help a teacher see a more accurate portrayal of what happened during a lesson. Having an accurate idea of what happened allows a teacher to evaluate the data and come to their own conclusions about the outcomes of a lesson. Often, it is objective feedback that provides a disorienting dilemma that requires the teacher to reevaluate their assumptions about their students and their teaching.

Subjective interpretive feedback. Interpretation involves observing objective data and coming to some conclusion about the meaning of that data. It is important for a coach to be wary of interpretive feedback for a number of reasons. First, the coach does not always have all of the information about the students that the teacher has. For example, perhaps there is a student in Mr. Parsons's class who does not engage with any classmates at all during the collaborative group work. In addition, Jolie notes that Mr. Parsons allows the student to sit apart from the rest of his group. Imagine that Jolie makes an interpretation that Mr. Parsons is ignoring this student when, in fact, the student has social anxiety and has asked that all communication and collaboration with peers be in written form. Now, what would happen if Jolie's feedback included a statement that Mr. Parsons had ignored one of his students? Depending on the existing relationship and understanding between coach and teacher, a statement like this could damage a coaching partnership.

To avoid jumping to conclusions, coaches should rely on clarifying questions to ensure that they have all the necessary information before providing interpretations. Additionally, coaches should ask teachers to provide their own interpretations first and only offer interpretation if teachers request they do so.

Although interpretive feedback should generally be avoided for the reasons stated earlier, there are times when it is helpful when used intentionally. For example, if—as a team—the coach and teacher have decided to brainstorm possible interpretations in order to expand their thinking, a coach might provide some insightful interpretations the teacher had not thought of. At these times and in this way, an interpretive comment from a coach might be helpful.

Subjective evaluative feedback. Subjective evaluative statements include the speaker's values in the statement. For example, the statement "I don't think the students were effectively set up for today's collaboration" includes a judgment about how the teacher should have conducted the class. Although evaluative statements are generally avoided by a coach—it is, after all, the teacher's values that matter in the coaching conversation—there are times when a coach may need to use evaluative statements. Evaluative statements made from an asset-based or positive approach can be most useful when a teacher needs a "pick-me-up" but should be used sparingly so that teachers do not come to rely on external evaluations of their work but begin to see value in their own internal judgments.

Although coaches will most often use objective data in conversations with teachers, there are occasions when subjective feedback is called for. Intentional decisions about when, how, and why to use each type of feedback is a foundational coaching skill and decisions should be made deliberately and carefully.

Reflect on your own current practice with the exercise in Box 4.6.

Box 4.6 On Your Own: Reflect on Your Current Practice

Reflect on how you are currently using feedback in your work with teachers.

- What kind of feedback do you rely on most during coaching conversations?
- How do teachers respond to your coaching feedback?
- What if anything do you need to change to provide more effective feedback?

Foundational Questioning Techniques

Questioning is arguably one of the most powerful coaching tools a coach has in their toolbox because powerful questions guide a teacher's reflective thinking and help them identify key insights. This guidance occurs as teachers explore and talk through their own thinking in response to open-ended questions that are often, but not always, focused on data. To be used effectively, questions must be planned and asked intentionally—although coaches must also be flexible and respond to teachers in the moment by asking questions that were not previously planned and disregarding questions that were.

Questioning can become more intentional through an awareness of various question types. The National School Reform Faculty (NSRF) (https://nsrfharmony.org/) and School Reform Initiative (SRI) (www.schoolreforminitiative.org/) both break questions into two types: clarifying and probing. Greater awareness of question types will help a coach with intentional preparation for all components of both macro- and micro-coaching cycles and will help a coach become more adept at revising, refining, and completely changing planned questions as necessary during a coaching conversation.

Clarifying vs. Probing vs. Suggestive Questions (NSRF and SRI)

NSRF and SRI categorize questions by their purpose. Clarifying questions, for example, are intended for coaches to gather more information from teachers to ensure that both parties understand the context of a given situation—for example, a lesson plan, classroom data, or a dilemma. Having a clear understanding of the context allows the coach to provide better feedback and ask more powerful questions during the coaching conversation.

Probing questions, on the other hand, are for the teacher's benefit. These questions should help the teacher think of the situation in a different way. Probing questions are **not** intended to better equip the *coach* to solve or help solve a situation. In fact, in questioning, the coach's role is not to solve the problem at all but rather to help the teacher gain insight through another perspective developed through questioning. Finally, both NSRF and SRI caution against questions that use the tone of a question, often ending with an upward inflection, but actually provide a suggestion or solution to the teacher. Even when the coach doesn't intend to offer a suggestion, asking a question about a specific technique, tool, or idea may be perceived by the teacher as suggestive. So, probing questions should be kept broad and should not direct the teacher toward any particular path.

Let's consider our vignette about Mr. Parsons and the challenges he was having with collaborative group work. Remember that, during this class, students were placed in groups but were not working together. One student was typically taking the lead and doing the work while other students socialized. The students doing the work were often simply googling a topic and cutting and pasting information from the results. Mr. Parsons asked for immediate feedback, but it would have been best for Jolie to delay to provide time for Mr. Parsons to engage in reflective thinking on his own data while she prepared for an intentional coaching conversation. In intentionally planning for a follow-up conversation, Jolie might have planned the following questions:

Clarifying questions. To gather additional information about Mr. Parsons's plans and expectations, Jolie might have asked the following clarifying questions:

- How were students grouped?
- How were the resources designed to support the lesson and student collaboration?
- What expectations did you have for the final product?
- How did you anticipate students would work together?

Probing questions. To help Mr. Parsons consider his plans and the implementation and impact of those plans in a different way, Jolie might have asked the following probing questions:

- What factors did you consider in determining how you would set up the groups?
- How did students' response to the group work compare to your expectations?
- What, if anything, surprised you most about students' responses to today's structure and assignment?
- What is the relationship between your planning for today's activity and the outcomes?

Practice effective questions on your own with the exercise in Box 4.7.

Box 4.7 On Your Own: Practice with Effective Questions

Imagine that you are working with a teacher using the aforementioned data example showing how students engaged in a whole class discussion. Mr. Jay, the teacher whose class is represented by the data, is focusing on improving equity of voice in his classroom. What clarifying and probing questions might you develop to guide Mr. Jay's reflective thinking about his data?

What's the problem with suggestive questions? It is often challenging for coaches to avoid suggestions when asking probing questions. To illustrate, consider one of the probing questions from earlier: How did student response to the group work compare to your expectations? The question structured in this way allows for the teacher to consider their own expectations and evaluate student response—thus, it is probing. A similar question posed another way, however, can easily become suggestive. For example,

> How did you use roles to be sure that all students in each group participated in the activity today?

Notice that the specificity of this question provides Mr. Parsons with a suggestion; the implication is that he should have (or at least could have) used roles to ensure equal participation in collaboration. While assigning roles is one way students can be taught to distribute the workload evenly among group members, it is not the only way to ensure equal distribution. The question effectively blocks Mr. Parsons's opportunity to analyze and revise his own plans or to consider any other way of structuring group work besides using roles. Because the role of coaches is to empower teachers to make their own decisions within their own contexts—thereby building their capacity—coaches should avoid suggestive questions.

There are, of course, times when teachers may need support in brainstorming or identifying resources, and there are ways coaches can address these times in a manner that aligns with our coaching model; however, unsolicited suggestions from coaches can undermine a teacher's autonomy and sense of competence. Based on self-determination theory, decreased autonomy and competence will, in turn, decrease internal motivation for change and growth. Suggestions should be used sparingly with intention and specific techniques (more on suggesting in Chapter 9).

Additional unintended outcomes of suggestions include the following:

- **Universal/singular solutions.** Narrow thinking, whereby the teacher sees only one solution to a potential challenge.
- **Capacity issues.** Reliance on the coach to solve problems, leading ultimately to disempowerment of the teacher.
- **Defensiveness.** A sense of being judged, which harms the coaching relationship and decreases willingness of the teacher to change.

Work on revising suggestive questions with the exercise in Box 4.8.

Box 4.8 On Your Own: Revising Suggestive Questions

Review these suggestive questions. Revise them to create powerful probing questions. Use the examples to guide your thinking.

Suggestive	Probing
Do you think students have too much time for this activity?	How will pacing impact the lesson?
	What is the relationship between the amount of time students are given and your expectations for their work?
Do you think students need a graphic organizer to be successful?	
Are you going to assign the groups?	
Is this lesson too easy for some of your highfliers?	
Can you make this lecture more student centered?	
Can you avoid lecturing?	
Can you make this more exciting and engaging?	
Do you need to add a quiz at the end?	
Is this too hard for your students?	
Did you think about teaching X before moving into this lesson?	
Do you think students should have a break from sitting so long?	

Asset-Based Questioning

Asset-based questioning is a technique coaches use to frame questions with strengths as opposed to deficits and gaps. To use this technique, coaches simply pose their questions from an asset stance. So, for example, even when things don't go as planned, coaches ask what worked before delving into what didn't work. Here are some other examples of asset-based questions in situations where it might be easy to emphasize deficits rather than attributes:

- Instead of, "What was the problem with that lesson?" ask, "While the lesson didn't turn out as planned, what did work for you or your students?"
- Instead of, "What are you struggling with most?" ask, "When you have been faced with a similar challenge in the past, what have you done that worked?"
- Instead of, "Why weren't you [or your students] successful?" ask, "What resources do you have available that would help you [or your students] achieve your goal?"
- Instead of, "What problems do you have that are getting in your way?" ask, "What strengths do you have that would help you solve this problem?"

Maintaining emphasis on assets instead of deficits helps build a teacher's confidence and sense of self-efficacy and aligns to what we know about what motivates adults to learn. Before coaches ask a question, they should pause to see whether it is focused on assets or deficits and revise as necessary.

Box 4.9 provides a quick coaching technique to use when you don't have much time with a teacher.

 **Box 4.9 Quick Tip: 5-minute Coaching Technique**

Coaching does not always have to mean long conversations. Helping a teacher focus in on one specific aspect of a lesson can provide an opportunity for deep reflective thinking. Next time you only have five minutes to talk to a teacher, consider the following series of questions:

- What are you teaching today?
- What are you most excited about?
- What is one thing you are not sure about that you want to pay attention to as you implement your lesson?

These questions help focus a teacher on a positive aspect of the lesson while at the same time highlighting an opportunity for growth. They also prepare the teacher to think intentionally about classroom data.

Active Listening

Active listening, including reflective listening from *Motivational Interviewing* (Rollnick et al., 2008; Miller & Rollnick, 2013), not only supports effective questioning

Figure 4.9 Active Listening Techniques

techniques but can also be a powerful coaching tool. Active listening ensures that the coach understands the situation being discussed and therefore can create appropriate powerful questions and that the teacher feels heard and, therefore, valued. Active listening helps build trust between teachers and coaches and also allows teachers to express frustration, disappointment, anger, and other emotions in a healthy way. Techniques for active listening include nonjudgment and body language, reflective listening statements, and silence (Figure 4.9).

Nonjudgment and Body Language

While we may know—in theory—that a coach's job relies on an ability to remain neutral and nonjudgmental, our faces and our bodies often reveal the truth; hence the expression, "Arrange your face." A coach's awareness of and ability to control their body and facial expressions is essential to building trust with a teacher. If coaches grimace or show surprise at the words of teachers, teachers will know their coaches not only disagree but perhaps even judge them for their thinking. If coaches nod or smile, teachers may quickly realize that their coaches agree—and even judge them positively—for their thinking. Whether coaches agree or disagree, judge to the bad or to the good, the body language of coaches can disempower teachers.

While body language should not be used to judge or to agree or disagree, it should be used to make a teacher feel safe and heard. Body language that supports coaching includes eliminating barriers or power dynamics during conversations, for example, talking across a desk or over a laptop screen, leaning forward toward teachers as they speak and maintaining effective eye contact. Of course, cultural differences affect how individuals feel about appropriate body language and eye contact. Coaches must know the teachers they coach and adjust their methods accordingly.

Reflective Listening Statements

Reflective listening statements are statements that a coach uses to repeat what teachers have said. They affect a coaching conversation in a number of ways.

Not only do reflective listening statements ensure that teachers feel heard but reflective listening statements can also drive the conversation forward just as a powerful question can. Reflective listening statements create the opportunity for teachers to hear their own words from a different perspective. Although a coach is simply returning words to their original speaker during reflective listening, doing so through paraphrasing or summarizing allows the teacher to hear their ideas in a new way. The result can lead a teacher to continue speaking to clarify their own thinking or to identify a powerful insight, all without any additional questions being asked by the coach. Powerful insights can occur when a teacher hears their words and disagrees with themselves or realizes that what they said isn't quite what they meant. Insights can also occur when a teacher hears their words and simply realizes the importance and weight of them.

Just as with questioning, reflective listening statements can be broken into different types and are most powerful when these types are used with intentionality. The first way to categorize these statements is into simple and complex reflective listening statements (Miller & Rollnick, 2013). Simple reflective listening statements include parroting, paraphrasing, and summarizing (Whole Health Coaching Participant Manual, 2018). Simple reflective listening statements are only simple in that they repeat what a teacher has said without making any inferences. We will come back to complex reflective listening statements in Chapter 6 but provide additional information about simple reflective listening statement types (Figure 4.10).

Parroting. Parroting is repetition of a few key words from a teacher's statement using the teacher's exact words. When a coach parrots, they should listen for words that seem particularly powerful or laden with hidden meaning, energy, or emotion. Notice how parroting is used in this

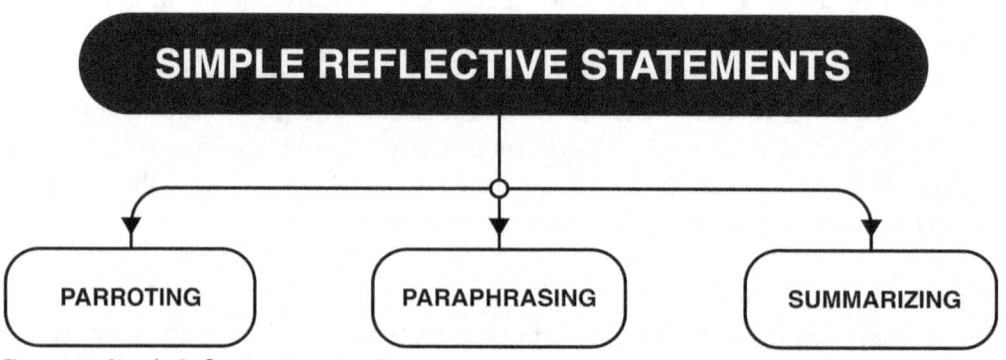

Figure 4.10 Simple Reflective Listening Statements

example of a conversation that might have taken place between Jolie and Mr. Parsons:

Jolie: What surprised you most about today's lesson?
Mr. Parsons: Well, I was hoping that students would be excited about the topic and identify different opportunities for more research. I had hoped that they would research their own interests and come back to synthesize the information as a collaborative group, but they didn't do that at all.
Jolie: "Synthesize." Tell me more.
Mr. Parsons: Well, I had hoped that they would bring their information back to each other and have a conversation about what they found. I figured that would lead to some natural synthesis of different sources. If all of the students had done their own research first and then shared with their groups, that would have led to new ideas.

In this transcript, Jolie uses parroting to highlight a significant word—synthesize—and then simply asks the teacher to elaborate. Notice that, through parroting, the coach is able to gain additional information about the teacher's vision and understanding without inserting any of her own thinking.

Paraphrasing. Unlike the parroting technique, in which a coach uses a teacher's exact words, paraphrasing allows a coach to repeat what a teacher has just said using new language. This allows a teacher to hear their own thinking in a new way. A paraphrase of the previous transcript might sound like this:

Jolie: So, by providing a topic that students were interested in, you thought they would engage in some independent work before sharing in teams and creating something new.

Although paraphrasing may not seem revolutionary (it is a technique for *simple* reflective listening statements, after all) paraphrasing is harder than it sounds because the natural tendency of adults is to interject their own opinions into conversations—to agree, disagree, and make connections. Because adults are naturally drawn to interjecting their own ideas and making meaning through connections, paraphrasing is a skill that will need to be developed and practiced. Just as it is more difficult than it sounds, it is also more powerful than it seems at first glance. The paraphrase, like the parrot, acts as a mirror, mirroring a teacher's words back to them. Everyone has said things before that they don't mean: "These kids will never learn to cooperate with each other!" The power of hearing this reflected from an external observer can cause a teacher to re-examine or clarify their own assumptions.

Summarizing. The final type of simple reflective listening is summarizing (Miller & Rollnick, 2013). Summarizing still repeats what the teacher has said, but unlike parroting and paraphrasing, it encompasses more than one idea. In fact, it may be a summary of the main points of the entire coaching conversation. While the summary helps the teacher see a new perspective, it also helps them see connections between things they have said that they may not previously have connected. For example, based on the transcripts given earlier, Jolie might summarize some of the key elements of the conversation to help Mr. Parsons begin making connections. A summary with a follow-up question might sound something like this: "So, we've talked about student interest, synthesis, collaboration, and group structure. What are the connections among these ideas?"

Simple reflective listening statements, including parroting, paraphrasing, and summarizing, can be paired with a probing question to stretch a teacher's thinking or followed by a pause to provide the teacher an opportunity to consider what they heard and to further elaborate. Coaches should keep in mind the value of "wait time." Just as students benefit from a teacher's wait time, so too can a teacher benefit from a coach's wait time. Providing time and space for a teacher to think can extend the depth of their thinking, provide opportunity for new insights, and provide them with a sense that they are respected by the coach. For tips on the ideal ratio between reflective listening statements and questions, see Box 4.10.

Box 4.10 Quick Tip: The Perfect Ratio

Reflective conversations are guided by reflective listening statements and powerful questions. A general rule of thumb is to use reflective listening statements at least twice as much as questioning to ensure the conversation isn't moving too fast (Miller & Rollnick, 2013). Reflective listening statements allow a teacher to explore their own thinking before the coach shifts the conversation with a question.

Of course, when actively listening, the coach should refrain from making suggestions. The goal of the coaching conversation is to build the teacher's own capacity for reflective thinking as well as their sense of autonomy and competence. Reflective listening statements are a way to ensure that teachers feel heard, to build trust, and to begin, perhaps, to provide a new perspective without the need for suggestions or external ideas.

Practice active listening with the exercise in Box 4.11 and learn more about how to interrupt when necessary in Box 4.12.

> **Box 4.11 On Your Own: Active Listening**
>
> Ask a friend to share a challenge they are currently navigating. This challenge does not have to be significant or heavy. Ask your friend to describe this challenge in detail. Instead of offering suggestions or even asking questions about this challenge, be an active listener by practicing simple reflective listening statements. Do not add anything original to the conversation; instead parrot, paraphrase, and summarize what you hear. What is the result? How does your friend respond? At the end of the conversation ask your friend how it felt to be listened to in this way.

> **Box 4.12 Coach's Dilemma: Interrupting**
>
> It is important to be an active listener, but it is also important for coaches to use their time wisely and to respect the time of the teachers they work with. So, what does a coach do when they suspect that a teacher has gotten off track, talking about a semi-related but very tangential topic with no end in sight? At times, a coach will need to interrupt a teacher to maintain focus on the goal at hand and to work within the time structures and constraints of schools. To set up for polite and purposeful interruptions, a coach can set the stage early in the coaching relationship. They can explain to the teacher that part of a coach's job is to help a teacher maintain focus on a particular goal and that at times she may need to refocus the conversation. After explaining the role, a coach can ask for the teacher's permission to interrupt as necessary.
>
> Follow these steps to ensure purposeful and empathetic interruptions:
>
> 1. Set the stage early. Help a teacher be prepared for interruptions by explaining your role and asking for permission to interrupt when necessary.
> 2. When you need to interrupt, again ask permission. Every time!
> 3. After interrupting, summarize what you have heard and ask if what you have heard is enough to continue moving forward.
> 4. Refocus the conversation with a powerful question.

Silence

Silence is an important and powerful tool for coaches. When coaches are unsure what to say or feel that what they are about to say may be suggestive or judgmental, they can simply pause for a pulse check. While brief pauses can be used to help coaches avoid suggestive or judgmental statements, more extended periods of silence (15–20 seconds) provide time for both coaches and teachers to engage in reflective thinking. More often than not, teachers will fill the space with additional reflective thinking, providing themselves and the coach with new insights.

The exercise in Box 4.13 aims to help you connect your practice with the approaches, models, and theories discussed here.

> **Box 4.13 On Your Own: Connecting with Research**
> - How do the foundations of coaching align with the approaches, models, and theories presented in chapter three?
> - How do specific strategies presented in this chapter align with the approaches, models, and theories?
> - What other strategies do you use in coaching that you would consider foundational for effective coaching?

Addressing Equity through Foundations of Coaching

Relationships and trust are the cornerstone of equity and the most effective tool for teacher growth and development (Adams, Ford, & Forsyth, 2015). Coaches model respect for a teacher's perspectives, thoughts, and experiences, and they model how to help someone lead their own learning. Modeling relationship-building and empowerment for teachers provides opportunities for teachers to see how to empower their own students, and empowered teachers are, in fact, more likely to empower their own students (Anderson & Blase, 1995). When used skillfully, the foundational techniques outlined in this chapter empower a teacher's voice and recognize the teacher's expertise and decision-making ability within the context of their classroom. Likewise, when the coach and teacher examine issues of equity, they do so in concert with one another through a reciprocal learning experience.

Conclusion

So, what should Jolie have done in the case of Mr. Parsons? To be an effective coach, Jolie first needed to empower Mr. Parsons to engage in reflective thinking on his own observations about his class. She needed to show him that his own evaluation of his work—not hers—was most important. To do this, Jolie needed to turn Mr. Parsons's question about how the lesson went back to Mr. Parsons. Additionally, Jolie needed time to consider the data and to plan for effective follow-up questions to support Mr. Parsons in reflective thinking about the data. To empower Mr. Parsons and to give herself time to plan for the follow-up conversation, Jolie's response should have looked like this:

Mr. Parsons: What did you think? How did it go?
Jolie: Mr. Parsons, I'm grateful for the opportunity to visit your classroom today. I'm also really interested in hearing from you. I know you have another class coming in, so let's set up a time for us to come back together to have a conversation. In the meantime, I'll leave the data I collected with you for you to think about. Would you prefer to meet after school today or during your planning period tomorrow morning?

Box 4.14 presents tips for foundational coaching based on the information in this chapter.

Box 4.14 Tips for Foundational Coaching
- Work to build, strengthen, and maintain relationships.
- Emphasize assets, autonomy, and empowerment of the teacher.
- Focus on the teacher's goals and leverage microcycles to ensure ongoing progress.
- Be intentional about how you use feedback.
- Remember the power of the probing question and reflective listening statements. Also remember the power of silence—when you want to make a suggestion, sit in silence.
- Manage your body language and arrange your face.
- If the teacher asks you to evaluate them (What did you think? How did it go?), turn it back on them (What do *you* think? How did it go?). This may feel strange at first but will become more natural with practice.

Part II
The CoachED Framework

5

An Introduction to the CoachED Framework

Opening Vignette: Jonathon and Ms. Varghese

Jonathon   Ms. Varghese

Ms. Varghese was a midcareer math teacher who at first resisted the idea of coaching. Whenever her coach Jonathon stopped by to chat with her, hoping to build a relationship that might lead to more formal coaching, Ms. Varghese often complained that her students were lazy, apathetic, and constantly on their cell phones; they didn't do their homework, they complained about class assignments, and their work was never up to her standards. She said that math was an important subject, that students needed it for lifelong achievement, and if only students would be more focused and motivated, they could all benefit from her teaching. After a while, she invited Jonathon to visit her classroom where students were sitting quietly in rows while she lectured about math content and completed practice problems on the board. Even though the students were quiet, only a few were taking notes and others had their heads on their desks or played on cell phones. When Ms. Varghese asked a question, she eventually answered it herself because her students did not volunteer, and when she called on them, they said, "I don't know," even if she had just reviewed the answer. In a debrief conversation about the visit, Ms. Varghese explained to Jonathon that students were unable to answer her questions because her course was very rigorous. Jonathon asked if Ms. Varghese would share some more of her lesson activities and assessments with him, and he noticed that they emphasized recall of content. Ms. Varghese believed that the information students were asked to remember in her course was really complicated, which made the course inherently rigorous no matter what activities she used or how the students were assessed.

Teachers are the experts of their own classrooms, their own teaching style and preferences, and their own opportunities for growth.

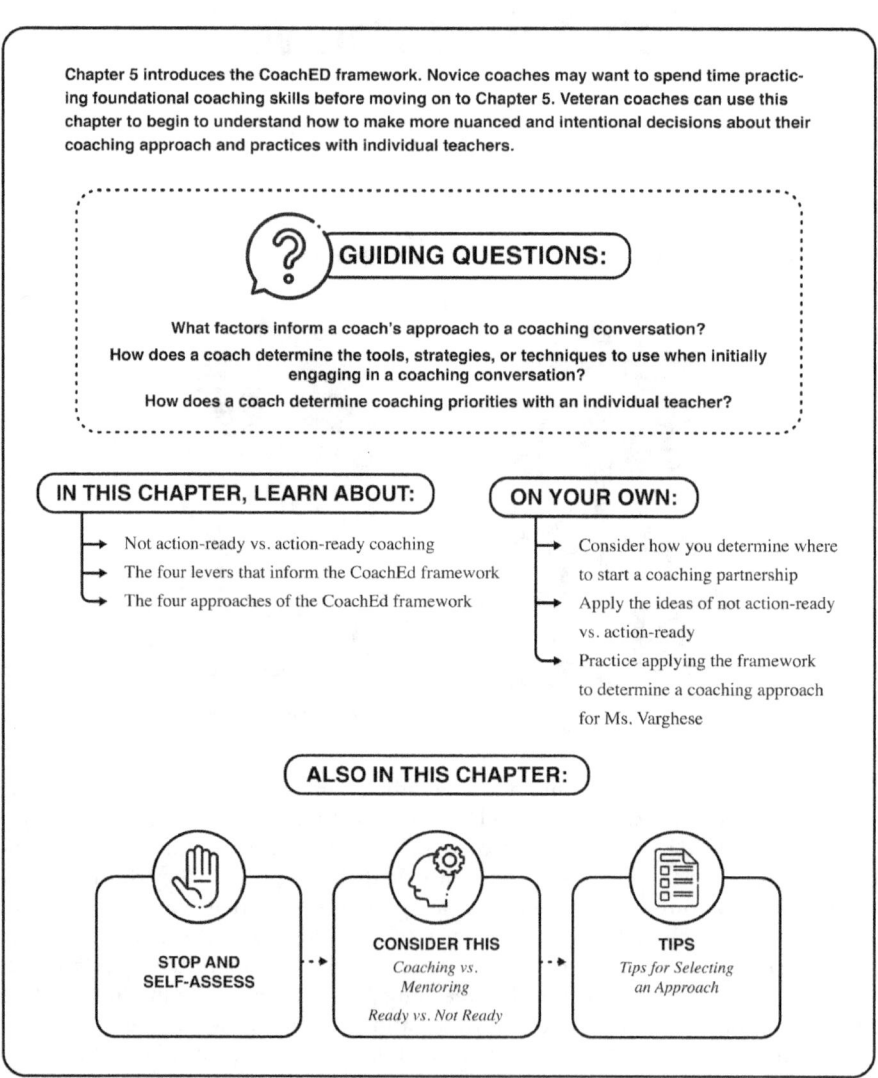

Figure 5.1 Chapter 5 Overview

Getting Started

Coaches must make decisions about how to move forward in each coaching situation given specific context and characteristics of an individual teacher. Just as teachers are most effective when their choices about students are intentional, informed, and differentiated, coaches, such as Jonathon in Box 5.1, are more effective when they make deliberate and informed decisions about their coaching approach based on the needs of individual teachers like Ms. Varghese.

Box 5.1 offers an exercise to help you reflect on your current practice.

> **Box 5.1 On Your Own: Determining Where to Start**
>
> Before you read on, take a few minutes to consider your own coaching approach and how you determine where you will start a coaching partnership.
>
> Where would you begin with Ms. Varghese? What might influence your decision?

Not Action-Ready vs. Action-Ready Coaching

The CoachED framework provides coaches with a way to think about how to approach coaching partnerships based on the unique context and characteristics of each individual teacher with whom they work. Broadly, the framework is divided into two categories based on a teacher's readiness for active coaching. These two categories are not action-ready and action-ready.

Not Action-Ready

Teachers who are not action-ready—that is, they are not ready to actively engage in the coaching process—sometimes are simply unaware of a need to change. If they are aware of a need for change, they may be unmotivated to engage in the change or lack confidence that they can make the change. For whatever reason, these teachers are not interested in actively engaging in coaching and may avoid coaching or seem resistant to coaching.

Jumping into coaching cycles with a teacher who is not ready to engage actively in the coaching process is unlikely to be effective. Instead, when a coach is working with a teacher who is not action-ready, the coach needs to focus on shifting the teacher's mindset so the teacher is actively motivated to engage with the coach, sees a need for change, and is confident in taking action toward change. The ultimate goal of shifting mindsets when coaching teachers who are not action ready is to get them action-ready so they are willing to engage in coaching cycles.

Foundational coaching strategies that support mindset shifts include building relationships, active listening, and asking powerful questions. All of these strategies provide opportunities for a coach to show a teacher that their own expertise is valued and that the coach is not trying to fix the teacher but to support them in reaching their goals. These strategies also provide opportunities for a teacher to examine their own practice and possibly identify an interest for growth and change that will help them become action-ready.

Action-Ready Coaching

Teachers who are action-ready understand a need for change and are motivated to engage in active coaching cycles in order to realize that change. When working with an action-ready teacher, a coach will likely find it easy to set macrocoaching goals with the teacher and engage in ongoing microcoaching cycles. Foundational techniques to use with teachers who are action-ready include intentional microcycles including planning, implementation, and reflective thinking, classroom visits for data collection, and analysis of data with effective feedback and questioning techniques.

Use the exercise in Box 5.2 to reflect on Ms. Varghese's state of readiness for coaching, and then perform the self-assessment in Box 5.3 before moving on.

Box 5.2 On Your Own: Not Action-Ready or Action-Ready?

Is Ms. Varghese not action-ready or action-ready? How did you make your determination?

Box 5.3 Stop and Self-Assess

Chapters 1 through 4 focused on foundations by defining coaching, addressing principals, theories, and models that support coaching, and describing foundational skills. In the second half of the book, we will turn to unpacking four distinct approaches to coaching and providing specific strategies and tools to implement each approach. Before reading further, stop for a self-assessment to determine your readiness level for moving forward. Based on your self-assessment, you may want to pause before reading further. If you'd like, spend some time practicing foundations of coaching and applying them to your current coaching partnerships before moving on to more complex ideas.

Use the following questions to guide your self-assessment:

- How confident are you that you can determine whether or not a teacher is ready for active coaching?
- Do you need to practice determining whether a teacher is action-ready or not before moving on to more specific approaches?
- How confident are you in your foundational coaching skills?
- Are there any foundational skills that you need to spend more time practicing before moving to more advanced skills?

If you need to practice more to get better at implementing these practices and identifying whether or not a teacher is ready for active coaching or not or simply to build your confidence, please do so before continuing in the book. When you are ready to learn more advanced coaching techniques for teachers who are ready for active coaching and those who are not, return and read on!

The Four CoachED Approaches

While determining whether a teacher is action-ready or not can certainly inform a coach's approach to coaching, understanding why and how a teacher is action-ready or not further defines what strategies will work best for each coaching partnership.

The coaching process and the concepts of not action-ready and action-ready can be further broken into four advanced approaches to coaching teachers. These four approaches—Coaching Values, Coaching Beliefs, Coaching Thinking, and Coaching Behaviors—compose our CoachED framework (Table 5.1).

Table 5.1 Foundations of the CoachED Model: Not Action-Ready vs. Action-Ready Coaching

Foundations of Coaching	
Not Action-Ready Coaching Coaches should focus on building relationships, active listening, and asking powerful and effective questions.	**Action-Ready Coaching** Coaches should focus on intentional microcycles including planning, implementation, and reflective thinking, classroom visits for data collection, and analysis of data with effective feedback and questioning techniques.

Coaching with Advanced Approaches			
Teachers who are not action-ready benefit from coaching related to their values or beliefs.		Teachers who are action ready are supported in active change through coaching related to their thinking or their behaviors.	
Coaching Values	**Coaching Beliefs**	**Coaching Thinking**	**Coaching Behaviors**
Coaching Values emphasize the alignment between what is important to a teacher and their practice. A teacher is most engaged in their work when their teaching and their values are aligned.	Coaching Beliefs emphasize exploring a teacher's beliefs about themselves, their students, their content, their community, and even education broadly in order to uncover assumptions that may be impacting their practice and to introduce new ideas and perspectives that help the teacher recognize a need for change.	Coaching Thinking emphasizes the alignment between intentional planning and outcomes. This involves understanding the importance of lesson plans, creating and implementing lesson plans, and reflective thinking on results to improve future plans.	Coaching Behaviors emphasize supporting a teacher by providing resources including strategies, tools, and techniques.
The goal of coaching teachers who are not action-ready is to prepare them to be action-ready.		The goal of coaching teachers who are action-ready is to engage them in a continuous process of macro- and microcoaching for ongoing improvement.	

Throughout the rest of this chapter, we will provide an overview of each approach. Advanced coaching techniques aligned to each approach follow in Chapters 6 through 9.

Defining the Levers

The CoachED framework relies on four levers, or specific indicators, that provide a coach with information about a teacher. The four levers—knowledge, application, engagement, and awareness—guide coaches as they determine the best approach to each coaching partnership. An overview of the levers is provided in Figure 5.2 and more detailed descriptions are provided afterward.

Knowledge (About Teaching and Learning)

Knowledge includes not only content knowledge—the knowledge of a particular subject—but also knowledge related to the students in the classroom, the teacher's own context within the school, and the context of the school as a whole. Teachers need to know about their students' strengths and struggles, both academically and personally. Teachers need to know about the communities where they teach and where their students grow up. Teachers need to know about diversity, including linguistic diversity, racial, ethnic, and cultural diversity, and diversity of learning types and learning needs. Teachers need to know about available resources they have to support diversity in their classrooms and to ensure that every student achieves their maximum potential. Additionally, teachers need to know multiple ways of teaching and multiple ways of learning. And, teachers must know how to navigate the educational system and advocate for equitable learning outcomes for their students. All of these concepts are essential for a deep understanding of teaching and learning.

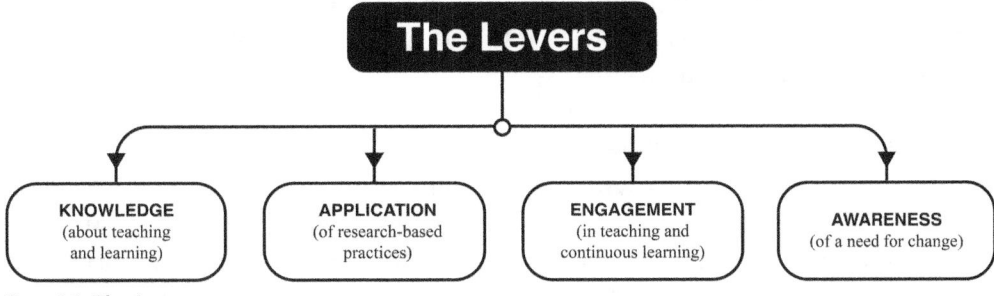

Figure 5.2 The Levers

Application (Of Research-Based Practices That Engage Students and Lead to Equitable and Rigorous Student Outcomes)

Although knowledge of content, students, context, pedagogy, and the educational system is essential for all teachers, we know from Bloom's Taxonomy that it is not enough just to be knowledgeable (Krathwohl, 2002). To effectively use an approach such as inquiry-based learning, culturally responsive pedagogy, social justice pedagogy, or issues-based science, a teacher must not only be able to describe that approach but also to implement it and do so successfully and intentionally. Further, successful implementation of a pedagogical approach should lead to engaged students and equitable outcomes. An effective teacher considers the students in their classroom both as individuals and as a group, applies context to their own understanding, evaluates their content, and chooses the best approach for each lesson. They create a plan and engage in reflective thinking about that plan, making revisions based on results from previous teaching. They engage in reflective thinking on their plan midstride and, if it is not working, change direction in the moment to ensure the success of their students. This application of knowledge requires not only a wealth of information about content, context, students, etc. and the flexibility to mine that wealth, but also the ability to use data analysis for intentional decision-making.

Engagement (In Teaching and Continuous Learning)

Every student deserves a teacher who can make the content exciting through a genuine interest in their work. For this reason, addressing teacher engagement through coaching is a top priority in the CoachED framework. Unfortunately, there are dispassionate teachers in schools who go through the motions of creating and teaching lesson plans but do not feel engaged in or energized by their work—not the content, the students, or the outcomes. At times, this lack of passion, excitement, or energy might be the result of stress on teacher well-being. Engagement in the CoachED framework is not only the extensive and frequent implementation of effective pedagogy but also the interest and curiosity needed to engage in reflective thinking on teaching and learning for ongoing growth and development, to make practice public to gain new perspectives, and to revise and refine teaching for continuously higher student achievement.

Awareness (Of a Need for Change)

Awareness is the extent to which a teacher understands and is aware of a need for change. Teachers who are not aware of a need for change may be in the precontemplation phase of change or in the unconscious incompetence stage of learning. Conversely, teachers who are aware of a need for change are at minimum in the contemplation phase of change or the conscious incompetence phase of learning. They know there is something specific they can improve, and they are interested in beginning the process of change. This awareness is often key for action-ready teachers to work in partnership with a coach. When a teacher is aware of a need for change, they are typically ready for active coaching.

Using these indicators, a coach builds a CoachED profile about each teacher with whom they work. This profile helps them make intentional coaching decisions throughout the coaching process.

The Approaches in Detail

The CoachED framework relies on an analysis of the four levers described earlier to determine a priority approach for coaching individual teachers. The priority approach identified to begin working with a teacher helps a coach emphasize particular coaching techniques based on the teacher's individual profile.

Figure 5.3 indicates how a specific combination of levers can be used to inform a coach's priority approach.

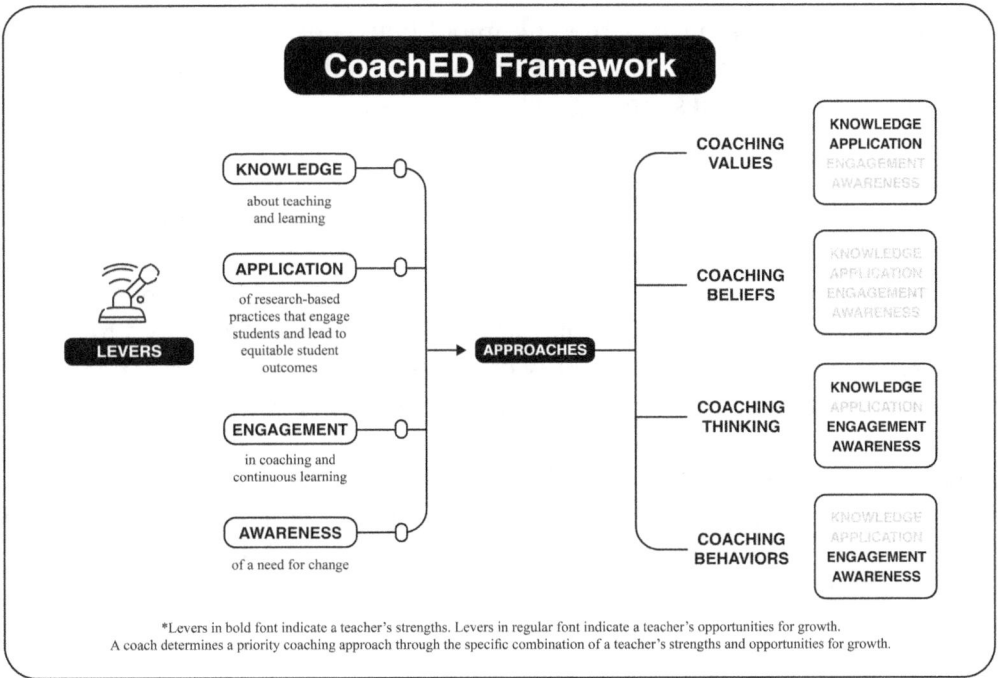

Figure 5.3 The CoachED Framework

To determine a priority approach for coaching, coaches might ask themselves the following questions:

- Does the teacher have the resources to implement a change in the classroom?
- Does the teacher have the skill to implement new ideas effectively and take risks?
- Does the teacher seem ready to take a risk by trying something new in the classroom?
- Does the teacher seem aware of a need for change and eager to make a change?
- Does the teacher seem highly engaged in change and continuous learning, or does the teacher seem burned out?
- Does the teacher seem overwhelmed or dispassionate?

An analysis of Ms. Varghese from our opening vignette, for example, would likely show an opportunity for growth when it comes to knowledge since she seems to misunderstand the meaning of "rigor" as it applies to her content; she does not have a high level of knowledge related to rigorous instruction. A detailed description of each approach will follow.

Coaching Values

Coaching Values emphasizes the alignment between what is important to a teacher and their practice. A teacher is most engaged in their work when their teaching and their values are aligned.

The Example

Ms. Barnes is a veteran teacher. She has been teaching for 23 years and has taught students in all elementary grades, including students with special needs and students in accelerated programs. She attends professional learning on a regular basis and is a mentor and department chair. She has a Master's degree in curricula and writes highly effective and engaging curricula for her district. Her students excel on all accountability measures. Recently, however, Ms. Barnes has lost interest in her work. She has started recycling lesson plans so that she does not have to stay after school or come in early to prepare. She is not sure why she feels this way. She has always loved teaching, but she is just not feeling excited anymore and she doesn't have the energy to engage in active coaching cycles. Ms. Barnes could benefit from values-based coaching.

The Levers

Coaches prioritize Coaching Values when a teacher's knowledge and application are strengths but engagement and awareness are opportunities for

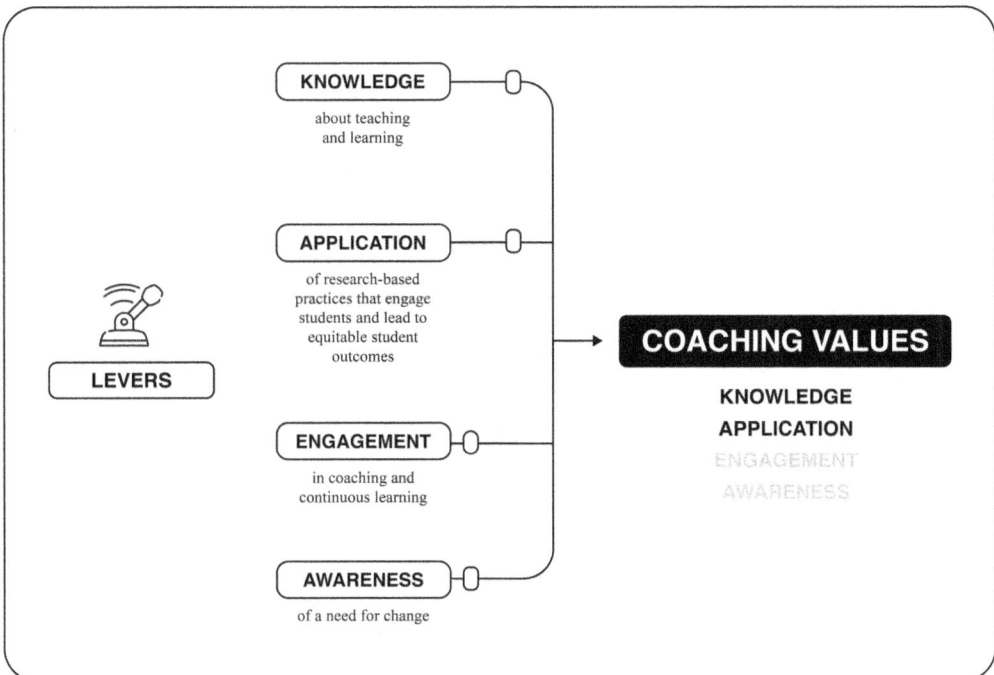

Figure 5.4 The Coaching Values Levers

growth (Figure 5.4). The teacher does not need support with knowing content, context, students, or pedagogy and understands how to apply research-based practices to teaching and learning; however, engagement with coaching and change and awareness of a need for change are low. Although this teacher has the ability to apply research-based practices in theory, they may not currently be exhibiting these best practices on a consistent basis because of a lack of interest and energy in the classroom.

The Approach
Coaching Values emphasizes an exploration of a teacher's values and the alignment between those values and the teacher's instruction. Coaches work with a teacher to consider and make explicit the teacher's values for intentional alignment between values and teaching practices.

The Reason
Alignment between values and classroom practice will help teachers remain engaged in the classroom. For teachers who are disengaged, emotionally exhausted, or burned out, realigning their work to their values, decreasing isolation through a partnership approach, and increasing feelings of self-efficacy can re-energize their practice.

The Goal
The ultimate goal for Coaching Values is to support teachers in aligning their practice in the classroom more closely with their values about students, teaching, and learning to maintain or improve interest in and energy for teaching through partnership, intellectual stimulation, and emotional engagement. Increasing energy and engagement will, in turn, lead to an increased likelihood that a teacher will become ready for active coaching.

Coaching Beliefs
Coaching Beliefs emphasizes exploring a teacher's beliefs about themselves, their students and their community, their content and their practice, and even education broadly in order to uncover assumptions that may impact their practice and to introduce new ideas and perspectives that help them recognize a need for change.

The Example
Mr. Stone is a high school biology teacher, and he loves what he does. Biology is fascinating to him, and he spends hours reading biology journals and keeping up to date on the most recent advances in science. Mr. Stone has been teaching for seven years, and he just cannot understand why his students are not doing well in his classes or why they never seem excited about learning. He cannot imagine why they do not see the importance of biology. When asked about his teaching, Mr. Stone describes the lectures and PowerPoints he has carefully crafted over the years. He says that his vision for teaching is to be just like one of his biology teachers in college whose lectures he found fascinating. Mr. Stone does not connect his teacher-centered approach to the lack of engagement displayed by his students. Beliefs-based coaching could help him explore what he believes about how and why students engage in learning.

The Levers
Coaches prioritize Coaching Beliefs when all levers—that is, knowledge, application, engagement, and awareness—are opportunities for growth (Figure 5.5). This combination of indicators will often occur under two circumstances:

1. When a teacher's beliefs do not align with effective and equitable learning practices supported through research—for example, a teacher who does not believe students learn in collaboration with one another
2. When a teacher's instructional practices do not align with existing effective beliefs—for example, a teacher who believes collaboration between students is an effective way of learning but relies on lecture and independent study to teach their students

An Introduction to the CoachED Framework ◆ 79

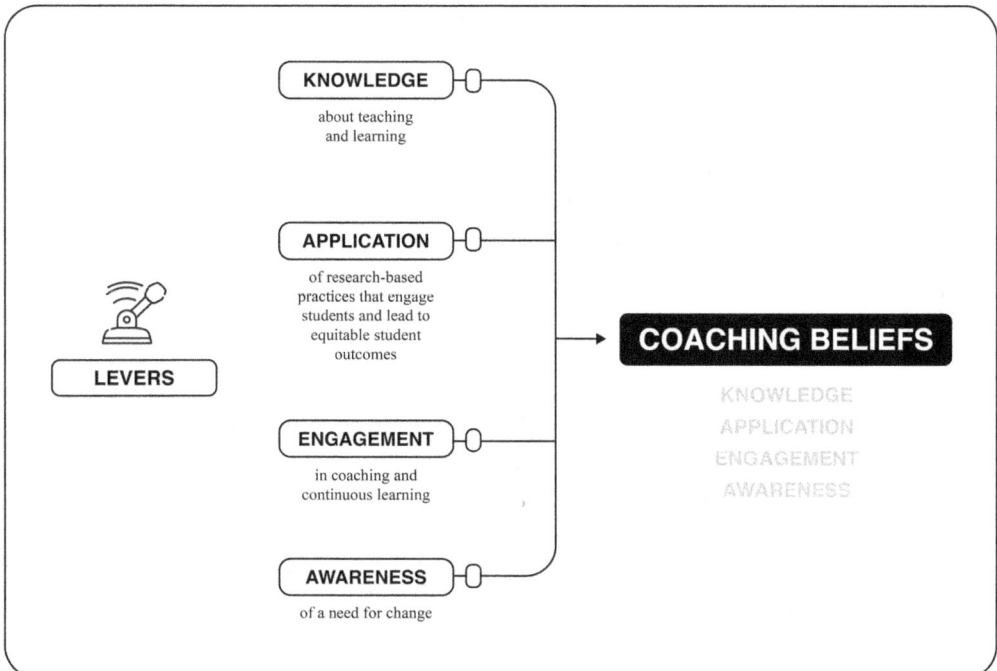

Figure 5.5 The Coaching Beliefs Levers

A teacher's beliefs might include, for example, what students should learn and how they should learn, attitudes about specific individuals or groups of students, and beliefs about a teacher's role in the classroom. A teacher's beliefs that are not in line with effective and equitable teaching practices may stem from personal experience or a "blame-the-victim" approach resulting from cynicism and emotional exhaustion.

Sometimes, a teacher who would benefit from beliefs coaching may, in fact, believe in effective and equitable learning practices and even have the best interest of their students at heart; however, because of a lack of awareness in their classroom, their teaching practices may not align to these beliefs. This might occur, for example, when a teacher believes all students can learn but because of a fear of embarrassing their special programs students or English language learners, the teacher only gives them the easiest of prompts to answer during class discussions. The teacher may not even be aware of what they are doing or the impact of their practice on these students.

When a teacher's beliefs do not align with effective and equitable learning practices, their knowledge of research-based instruction is likely low. When a teacher's instructional practices do not align with effective beliefs, their knowledge of themselves, their students, or their classroom practice may be low. Either way, application of good instruction, awareness of a need for change, and engagement with coaching are impacted.

The Approach
Coaching Beliefs focuses on either changing a teacher's beliefs about teaching and learning or realigning their practice to their beliefs. A coach supports this work through facilitation of conversations and experiences that provide new perspectives and open a path toward more effective and equitable teaching practices.

The Reason
Because a coach's work is to help teachers change *to improve the achievement of students*, coaching is defined by student outcomes, and coaches must support teachers in ensuring equitable opportunity and achievement for all students. This means supporting teachers in using evidence-based practices in their classrooms; however, to use high-leverage practices, teachers must first believe in those practices and then implement them with fidelity and equity.

The Goal
The goal of Coaching Beliefs is to help teachers orient or reorient their practice to a more effective and equitable approach either by realigning their practices with existing beliefs or by supporting a change in their beliefs. Realizing that their practices do not match their beliefs or that their beliefs do not align with what is best for students will help a teacher identify a need for change. Understanding a need for change is a big step in becoming ready for active coaching.

Coaching Thinking
Coaching Thinking emphasizes the alignment between intentional planning and outcomes. This involves understanding the importance of lesson plans, creating and implementing lesson plans, and reflective thinking on results to improve future plans.

The Example
Ms. English is a young and enthusiastic teacher. She has achieved great success so far with her students' academic outcomes, and she has recently become aware of a new approach she would like to try—competency-based education. Although she has been to a training and watched a few videos online, she seeks out a coach to help her implement this work in her classroom. She knows that it is going to take quite a bit of time and planning to implement this approach to assessment well, and she wants all the support

she can get. Ms. English is ready for some coaching related to her thinking to help her intentionally and effectively reach her goal.

The Levers

A coach will prioritize this approach when knowledge, engagement, and awareness are strengths but application is an opportunity for growth (Figure 5.6). Coaching for thinking occurs when a teacher has deep content knowledge and knows their students, their context, and their pedagogy but struggles with applying their knowledge. This struggle may manifest in a lack of intentional implementation or in misconceptions about the impact of teaching choices. Perhaps the teacher is selecting learning targets and activities not based on data but rather on interest or personal preference. The teacher must have the knowledge, energy, passion, and commitment to engage with a coach and the awareness that they need to make a change for this approach to be successful. Teachers who will benefit from a Coaching Thinking approach may be new teachers who have a plethora of theoretical knowledge but limited classroom experience or veteran teachers trying a new approach for the first time after a professional learning workshop. Teachers who exhibit this combination of levers are often the most excited about coaching.

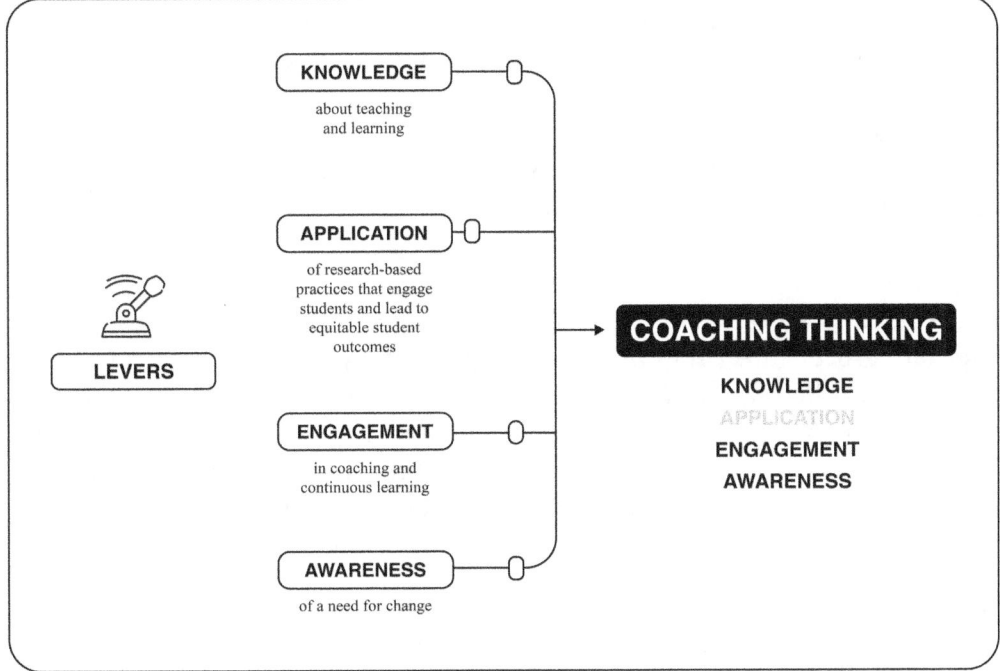

Figure 5.6 The Coaching Thinking Levers

The Approach
Coaching Thinking focuses on intentional application of instructional practices, data analysis to align intention with outcomes, and data-based reflective thinking and revision. Coaching Thinking includes support with intentional planning and implementation and reflective thinking to ensure a continuous process of improvement over the course of new learning.

The Reason
Supporting teachers in making connections between intentional design and student outcomes increases effectiveness and equity in the classroom. Additionally, as teachers more effectively align intentional decisions with data-based student needs, student achievement increases. As student achievement increases, teachers' self-efficacy does too. Teachers begin to see a direct impact between their choices and student achievement.

The Goal
Coaching Thinking starts with engaging teachers in meaningful and purposeful reflective conversations. Reflective conversations, when done meaningfully and purposefully, allow teachers to become more intentional about application of their practice. Through facilitated reflective thinking, teachers more explicitly consider their practice and the results of that practice on equitable outcomes for all students. The goal, then, is to support teachers in becoming more intentional about relationships among classroom data, knowledge of students, content, context, and pedagogy.

Coaching Behaviors
Coaching Behaviors emphasizes supporting a teacher through resources including strategies, tools, and techniques.

The Example
Mr. Adams is a brand-new teacher who was recently certified through an alternative licensure program. He was previously an engineer and is now teaching middle school math. He enjoyed his licensure program and feels it prepared him for much of what he encounters in his classroom, but he knows he has a lot to learn and feels like his teaching tools (resources, strategies, techniques, etc.) are limited. He would like new ideas to help him add variety to his classroom as well as ongoing support in using these new ideas well.

The Levers
A coach uses the Coaching Behaviors approach when knowledge, and thereby application, are opportunities for growth but engagement and awareness of

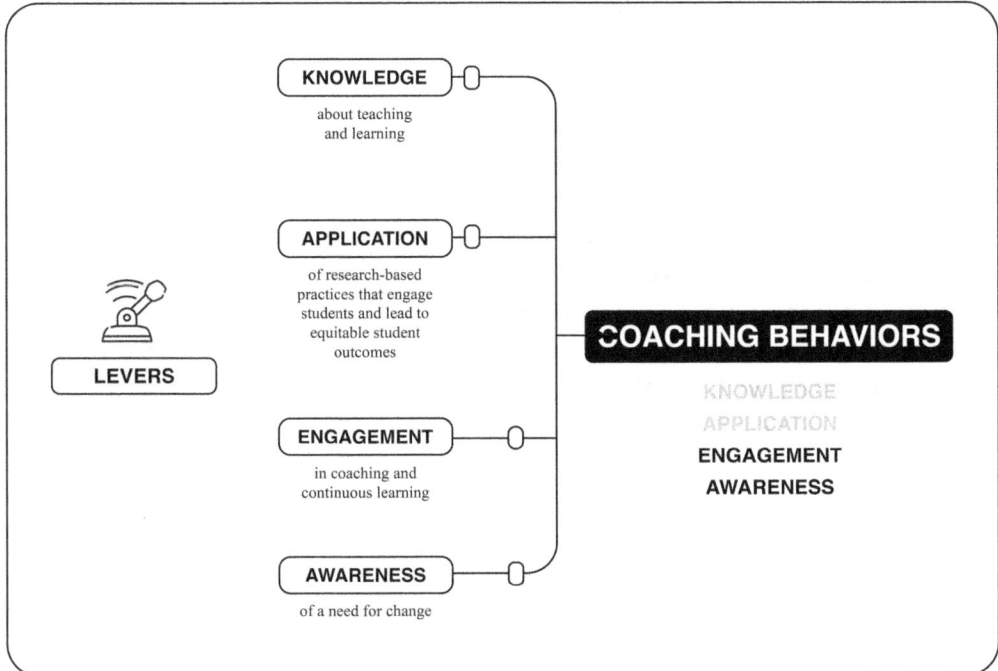

Figure 5.7 The Coaching Behaviors Levers

a need for change are strengths (Figure 5.7). While the goal of all coaching is to empower a teacher to use their own expertise to make their own choices in their classroom, there are times when a teacher simply does not have enough expertise to make an informed choice. Unlike the Coaching Thinking approach, which occurs when a teacher knows about and can explain a particular practice, method, or tool but is not implementing it effectively, Coaching Behaviors occurs when a teacher does not have the knowledge to identify a practice, method, or tool they would like to use. Often, these teachers are lateral-entry or early-career teachers; however, this is not always the case because even veteran teachers can lack knowledge about new teaching methods and resources for which they have received no formal training.

The Approach

Coaching Behaviors is a technique that allows for more explicit guidance and support of a teacher. During this approach, a coach will assume a mentoring position with a teacher. Because this is a slippery slope, potentially leading the coach to enable the teacher, make choices for them, and provide suggestions even when the teacher does have the capacity to make their own choices, this approach always *considers the teacher's voice first*. This means providing multiple choices rather than one suggestion, asking first what the teacher does know before providing additional information, and asking the teacher to determine their own priorities.

The Reason

Teachers new to the profession or teachers trying a new approach sometimes lack information and resources or lack the time to seek out information and resources on their own. Although the role of a coach is most often to elicit ideas from teachers with whom they work to support capacity building, if a teacher simply does not have any information to draw from, this practice becomes frustrating. Coaching Behaviors allows a coach to temporarily act more like a mentor whose role is often to provide resources to teachers learning a new practice.

The Goal

There are two goals of Coaching Behaviors: one for teachers and one for coaches. The goal for teachers is to ensure that they have the resources and the support they need to use those resources in the appropriate ways and at the appropriate times. In addition to this teacher-centric goal, the goal of a Coaching Behaviors approach includes getting out of the Coaching Behaviors approach as quickly as possible! Coaches should move to a different coaching approach as soon as a teacher with whom they are working feels they have the resources needed to move forward.

Coaches take on a mentoring stance during the Coaching Behaviors approach—providing teachers with resources, suggestions, and ideas—that, when overused, may lead to disempowerment of the teacher. To mitigate this risk, a coach should stay in this role only as long as it takes to provide a teacher enough ideas to move forward. Additionally, the approach should only be used when a teacher is truly out of resources, and it should be used in a manner that supports an immediate shift into an alternative approach as the teacher becomes aware of new tricks, strategies, and techniques. Tools and strategies for making the shift out of Coaching Behaviors and for using the approach in the most empowering way are provided in Chapter 9.

Bringing the Pieces Together

We have described four distinct approaches for coaching and will focus on each with more depth in the next four chapters. It is important to understand that coaching is fluid and even within one coaching conversation, a coach may use tools from multiple approaches, often borrowing from one approach to enhance another; however, thinking about the approaches distinctly will increase a coach's awareness of different ways to approach coaching. Understanding a variety of approaches and how and when to apply them based on a teacher's needs can increase the intentionality of coaching. We will address ways to integrate the approaches more in Chapter 10.

Conclusion

Coaching from a one-size-fits-all perspective disempowers and devalues the professionalism of teachers; therefore, the CoachED framework recognizes that each teacher is an individual with different needs and different experiences and is designed to support instructional coaches in thinking explicitly about how to coach individual teachers to allow them the most autonomy possible within the coaching partnership. This autonomy is essential because we seek to treat teachers as the professionals they are. Teachers are the experts of their own classrooms, their own teaching style and preferences, and their own opportunities for growth. Providing them the opportunity to make their own decisions about their students, their classrooms, and their professional learning increases their agency and empowerment and positions them as leaders. The outcome we seek to achieve as coaches is maintenance and improvement of teacher well-being in order to create a system of engaged teachers who have the intrinsic motivation, curiosity, and passion to continuously improve their practice and outcomes for students. In turn, these engaged and passionate teachers will empower their students to have a sense of agency over their own academic and social and emotional outcomes and their own futures.

Box 5.4 provides extra practice for applying the framework, and Box 5.5 offers some summary tips for selecting the best approach.

Box 5.4 On Your Own: Apply the Framework

Return to the opening vignette at the beginning of this chapter. Given the CoachED framework, which approach would you choose to get started with Ms. Varghese and why? What details of the vignette support your decision?

For our answer, see Box A.5 in Appendix A.

Box 5.5 Tips for Selecting an Approach

- When a teacher is not engaged, energetic, passionate, and curious in the classroom, the coach will prioritize a Coaching Values approach.
- When a teacher's beliefs about students, teaching, and learning do not lead to equitable outcomes, the coach will prioritize a Coaching Beliefs approach.
- When a teacher's practice does not align with beliefs that lead to equitable outcomes for all students, the coach will prioritize a Coaching Beliefs approach.
- When a teacher is using effective pedagogy but is not intentional in planning or in analyzing results to inform their direction in the classroom, the coach will prioritize a Coaching Thinking approach.
- When a teacher does not have the foundational knowledge to reach their goal, the coach will prioritize a Coaching Behaviors approach to provide those resources.

6

Coaching Values

Opening Vignette: Jolie and Mr. Martinez

Jolie   Mr. Martinez

Mr. Martinez has been teaching English at the elementary school level for 20 years. In his career, he has held a number of leadership positions: department chair, School Improvement Team co-chair, Student Support Team co-chair, and mentor, among others. In addition, he was a Nationally Board Certified Teacher (NBCT) and volunteered his time to work with and support other aspiring NBCT candidates. His colleagues looked up to him, spoke about his teaching with the utmost respect, and commented that Mr. Martinez's test scores had met expectations of growth for years, but when Jolie stopped by his classroom, he was uninterested in coaching. Instead, Mr. Martinez said things like, "My test scores are fine. Your time is better spent with teachers who need you." Although Jolie understood that Mr. Martinez was meeting expectations for growth on academic outcomes, she had also noticed that he didn't always engage with his students. She had seen him sit at his desk between classes and ignore his students when they entered the room. When she walked by his classroom, she most often saw his students sitting in rows while he lectured from the front of the room. She had even seen him ignore students who knocked on the door during lunch or before school, locking his door and pretending he hadn't heard them. What Jolie saw in Mr. Martinez didn't fit with what his colleagues said about him or what Jolie knew about his past practice.

Visioning allows a teacher to imagine their classroom as it would be if it were aligned to their values without any constraints.

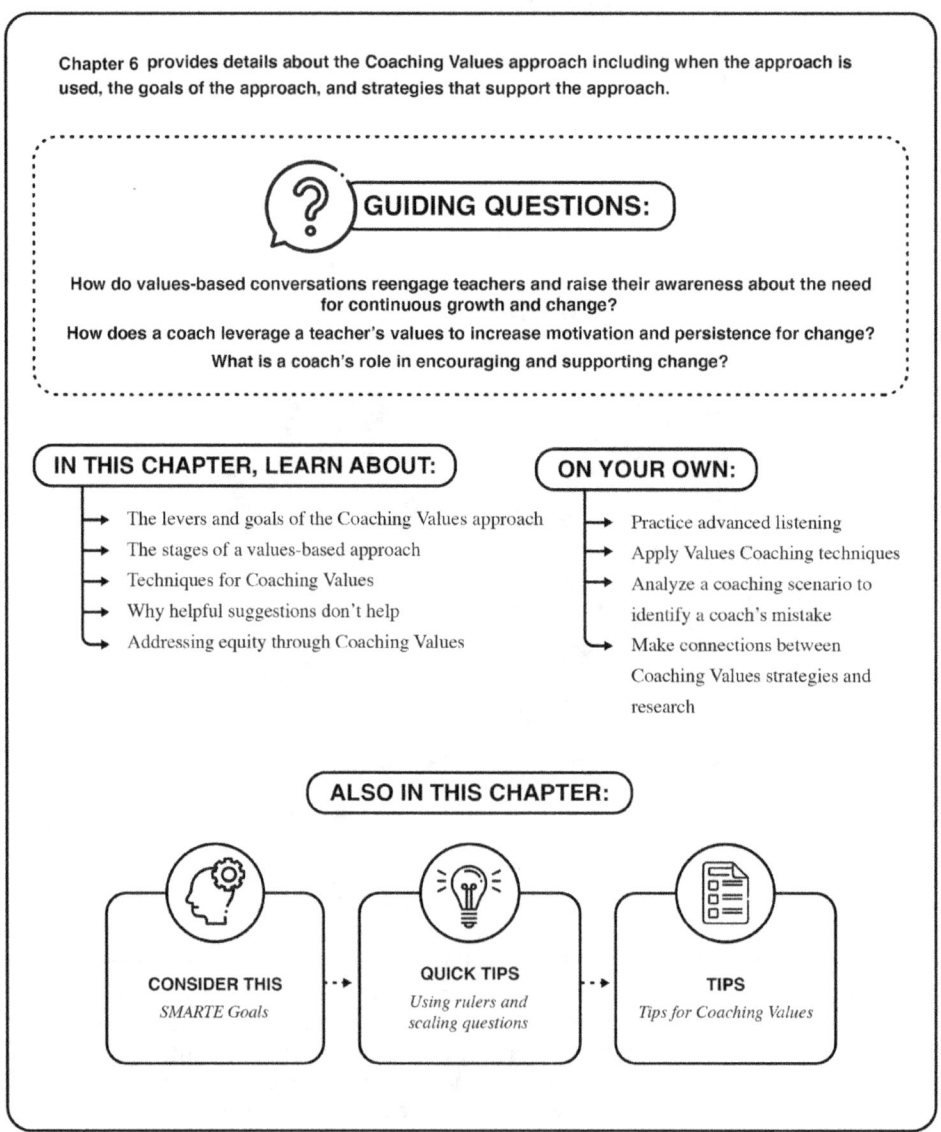

Figure 6.1 Chapter 6 Overview

The Levers

As we have described, principals and teachers often assume that coaching is for teachers who struggle with pedagogy and have low test scores; however, coaching can *and should* be about more than just implementation of powerful teaching techniques and student achievement. In fact, coaching can be used to bring energy to a classroom. In the case of Mr. Martinez (in the Opening Vignette), we know that his knowledge of teaching is high—he has been teaching for 20 years—and his application of effective pedagogy is high—his test scores consistently show growth and he has achieved National Board certification. In the past few years, his pedagogy may have slipped since he has become less inclined to try new things, but this is not because he doesn't know how to teach. In this scenario, the key levers for determining a priority approach are Mr. Martinez's lack of energy and engagement and his lack of awareness that something needs to change to reignite his interest in his students and his teaching practice, both of which impact not only his own enjoyment with his work but also student experiences in his classroom (see Figure 6.2 for the Coaching Values Levers). This is a case for values-based coaching!

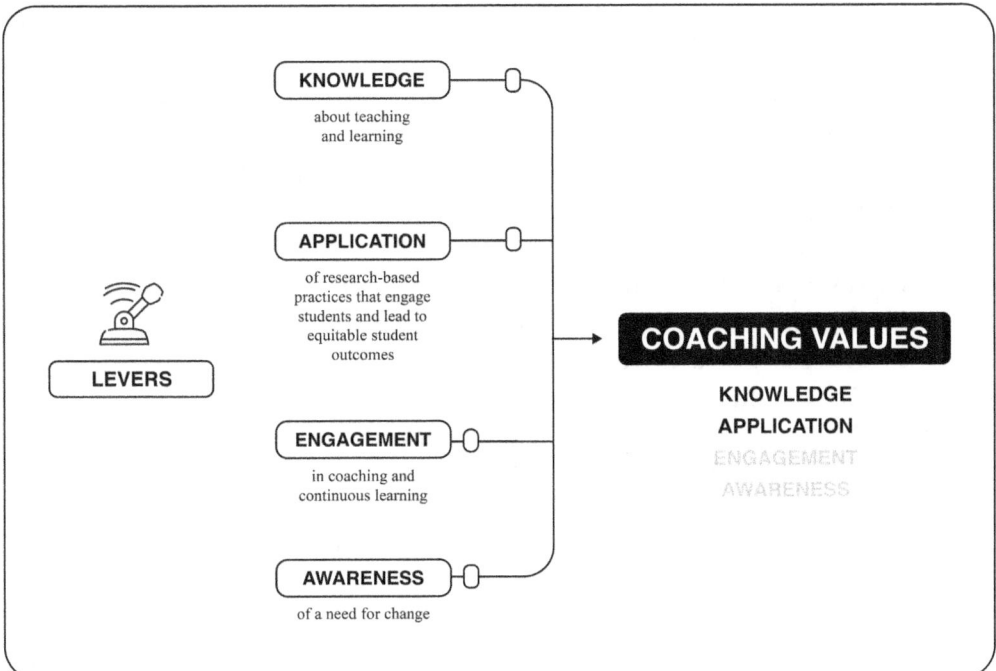

Figure 6.2 The Coaching Values Levers

Goals of the Approach

The goal for Coaching Values is to support a teacher in more closely aligning his practice in the classroom with his values about students, teaching, and learning in order to increase a teacher's social and emotional well-being, alleviate burnout, and increase energy in the classroom.

Stages of a Values-Based Approach

Like all approaches to instructional coaching, Coaching Values has a specific cadence, or cycle, that a coach can follow to create a path for the coaching relationship. This cycle is based on a health coaching approach and focuses on supporting the teacher to find alignment between their practice and their values. Coaches will notice that this cycle includes components similar to those of the macrocoaching phase (visioning, goal setting, and planning) and microcoaching cycles (planning, implementation, and reflective thinking) presented in Chapter 4.

The process for Coaching Values is different from other coaching cycles only in the amount of time spent deeply exploring a teacher's values before actively discussing classroom change in order to prepare the teacher to become ready for active coaching. Although it may be difficult to set aside time for these discussions and although a coach may feel like they need to move a teacher to action quickly, Coaching Values takes time. If time is not taken to explore values when a teacher is not action-ready, not only does the coach miss an opportunity to support the teacher in reconnecting their practice to their values, but it is also less likely that any movement toward change will be sustainable. If the change decided upon is not fully aligned to a teacher's values—what is most important to them—they will be less intrinsically motivated to pursue the change and persevere through any challenges that may arise.

Let's take a look at a process for coaching values adapted from the Health Coaching Process Model developed by Pacific Institute for Research and Evaluation (PIRE) for the Veteran's Health Administration Whole Health Coach Training (Whole Health Coaching Participant Manual, 2018). The Veteran's Health Administration model includes four stages: Develop Personal Mission, Assess and Choose, Plan for Action, and Execute the Action. Figure 6.3 shows the steps we have adapted for use with teachers in Coaching Values.

Stage 1: Exploring Values

The first step in this process is to find out what is most important to a teacher like Mr. Martinez by exploring their values.

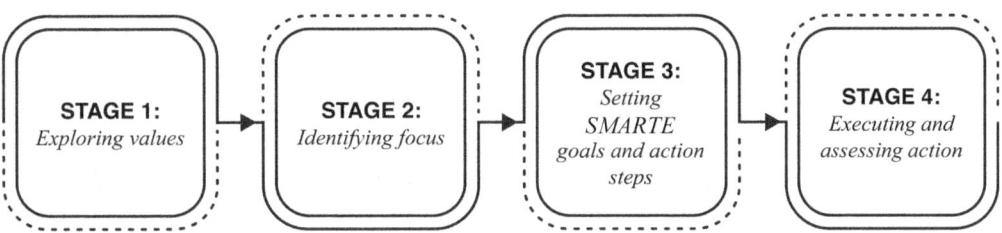

Figure 6.3 Stages of a Values-Based Approach

Let's imagine that Mr. Martinez became a teacher 20 years ago because he wanted to make a difference in students' lives; this motivation represents his values. It was important to Mr. Martinez, when he began teaching, to focus not only on academics but also on the social and emotional needs of his students. He purposefully decided to work in a high-needs school where he could make a difference for students who didn't always get the love, connection, and support they needed at home due to challenging circumstances. He began his career by incorporating social and emotional lessons into his academic content. He didn't always get through his curriculum, but he felt good about what he was doing. Then came an increased focus on testing.

At first, Mr. Martinez was able to resist the pressure of the testing movement. He continued incorporating social and emotional lessons into his content, but then he started getting chastised by his administrator for not keeping up with the pacing guide. Mr. Martinez's values began to conflict with his environment and context, and avoiding reprimands from his principal became a priority over the social and emotional learning of his students. He addressed social and emotional issues less and less and kept up with the pacing guide instead. He no longer had time to truly get to know his students, their struggles, or their personal contexts. He was able to rationalize this shift for a while—his students were doing well on their tests and he was praised every year because his students were meeting or exceeding growth. But, as the years have gone by, he has had less and less interest in school and in his students. He feels terrible when he turns off the light and closes the door during lunch, but he just doesn't have the capacity to be emotionally present for his students anymore during the one moment of the school day that he has some time to himself.

In this scenario, the conflict between Mr. Martinez's values and his teaching context has caused chronic stress and impacted his engagement with teaching. Coaching Mr. Martinez must begin with emphasizing his values so that the coaching process can support realignment between his values and his practice in the classroom.

Questions a coach might ask during this stage of the conversation include the following:

- What brought you to the teaching profession?
- What is most important to you about your teaching approach?
- What do you value most about your classroom? Your students? Your role?
- What do you enjoy most about your work and why?
- What matters to you most in your classroom?
- What was most important to you when you began teaching?
- What brings you joy and happiness in teaching?

Importantly, this values conversation may take up the entire first coaching session (or even multiple sessions) with a teacher, and coaches should prompt teachers to explore their values by following a teacher's responses to opening questions with questions or statements that ask for deeper thinking, including, "What else?" "Say more," and "Tell me more about that." Moving forward without first understanding Mr. Martinez's values and without helping him to reconnect with his values will lead to ineffective coaching and ultimately waste more time than it will save.

For a full coaching transcript of a values conversation with Mr. Martinez, see Appendix B.

Stage 2: Identifying Focus

After providing the time and space for a teacher to name and explore their values, the next step is to identify a focus area for change that will help them find a better alignment between their values and what happens in their classroom. Additionally, as always, the coach empowers the teacher throughout the journey by increasing feelings of autonomy and self-efficacy and by helping them identify and act on aspects of their context that are under their control or influence. When teachers are able to connect their actions directly to results, they feel more autonomous and empowered.

Techniques for Identifying Focus

In choosing a focus, teachers and coaches will need to intentionally consider their options for change. This consideration should include what changes are within the teacher's control as well as the potential impact of those changes and the energy the teacher feels related to making the change. Tools that can be used to support these conversations include spheres of control and decision-making matrices.

Spheres of control. Elena Aguilar (2014) wrote about spheres of control, which can be used anytime someone seeks opportunities for change. The spheres of control model differentiates between those factors that are entirely within a person's control, those factors that are not in someone's control but within their ability to influence, and those factors that are entirely outside their control. Of course, making changes to aspects of a situation that a person can entirely control will be more energy efficient and are more likely to be successful than changes that are not entirely within a person's control.

When using this tool to explore values, a teacher first identifies all variables that have an influence on the conflict between their values and current context. After identifying these variables, the teacher categorizes them into those variables they can directly control, those that they have at least some influence on, and those that are completely out of their control and influence. Mr. Martinez, for example, has complete control over how he organizes his lessons, can influence how his principal understands his work with students, but cannot control his required curriculum. Focusing on how he organizes his lessons to address SEL needs of his students is likely to be the easiest and most successful change Mr. Martinez can make. Mr. Martinez might also be successful in helping his principal understand the importance of SEL to his classroom. Mr. Martinez will not, however, be able to change the requirements of his curriculum, and spending time focusing on this frustration will not be time well spent.

Categorizing variables in this way allows a coach and a teacher to focus on those things within the teacher's control and influence and let go of those things that cannot be changed. Accepting that there are things outside of a teacher's control can, in fact, lead the teacher to a greater sense of efficacy as they shift focus to those things within their control and begin to make progress.

Decision-making matrices. There are a number of matrices that can help a teacher sort, categorize, and evaluate goals to make effective decisions about focus. These include an action priority matrix (Mind Tools Content Team, n.d.)—also called an impact/effort matrix—and an urgent/important matrix (Covey, 2004)—also called a time management matrix (Figure 6.4). Plotting factors within a teacher's control on these matrices can help them further define their coaching goal. For example, a goal with high impact and minimum effort might be something the teacher chooses to implement immediately on their own without a coach's support. On the other hand, a high-impact/high-effort strategy will be a goal likely to warrant support from a coach while a low-impact/high-effort strategy may be one the teacher avoids altogether.

Likewise, the time management matrix can not only help a teacher establish time-sensitive priorities and make better choices about how they use their time, but the matrix can also be used by a coach to gauge motivation and

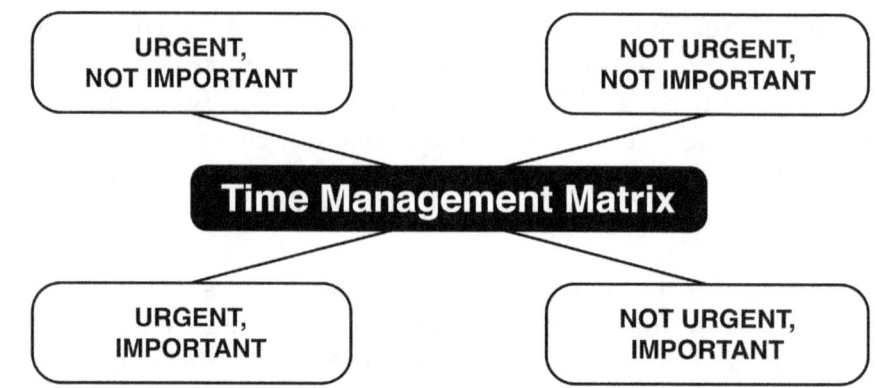

Figure 6.4 Time Management Matrix

support intentional coaching decisions. If a goal is urgent but not important to the teacher, the coach will need to use strategies like the ones presented later in this chapter to increase the teacher's motivation for the change. On the other hand, if a goal is important to a teacher, they are more likely to follow through on action steps, and the coach can quickly move into more active coaching.

Questions for a discussion about identifying focus might include the following:

- What are all the different variables that impact your ability to align your practice with your values?
- Which of these variables are within your control? Which can you influence? Which are entirely out of your control?
- Thinking about those variables that are within your control, what possible change excites you the most?
- Of these variables, what possible change is most important to you? Most urgent?
- Which possible change feels as if it would be most impactful for you and your students?
- Which possible change would most closely align your work with your vision and values?
- Which change are you most motivated to make?
- Which change are you most confident you can successfully achieve?

Stage 3: Setting SMARTE Goals and Action Steps

After identifying a focus area in stage 2, the teacher begins to plan for the change in stage 3. This planning stage begins with intentional goal setting aligned to a teacher's core values and should include a SMARTE goal (Box 6.1) to the extent possible. Ending this stage with at least one concrete action step the teacher can complete during the following week sets the teacher and coach up for the final stage.

In determining goals as well as action steps, the coach should maintain focus on spheres of control. If the overall goal is within the teacher's control but they choose a first step that is not, they may easily become frustrated with the change.

Box 6.1 Consider This: SMARTE Goals

The SMART acronym, originally developed by George Doran (1981), is

Specific
Measurable
Action-oriented
Realistic
Timebound

Over time, the original SMART goal acronym has been adjusted to include an E and the E has stood for many things: "evaluate," "extend," "environment," "equitable." We have chosen to include the **E for equitable**. When teachers consider the implications their goal might have on an equitable learning environment, they take into consideration their impact on all students. Equitable goals bring a specific focus toward actively disrupting patterns that may contribute to a lack of student success (Green & Hauser, 2020).

A SMARTE goal might be framed in the following way: By [insert date], I will [insert specific and action-oriented goal] as measured by [insert data-collection method]. [Insert subgroup] will [insert equity outcome].

For example, a teacher's goal might be, "By December 4, 2020, I will increase the number of students who participate during whole class discussions as measured by classroom data collected by my coach. I will provide English Language Learners with tools that support their active participation in order to ensure they participate in class discussions at least as much as other students."

Questions for setting SMARTE goals and corresponding action steps include the following:

- Based on your focus area for change, what is a realistic goal for you?
- How can you make your goal more specific?

- How confident are you that you can meet that goal? What might make it more realistic for you?
- How will you know when you have met your goal?
- What is your timeline for meeting your goal?
- What are some of the things you need to do to reach your goal?
- What's your plan for getting started?
- What is one thing you could do tomorrow that would set you up for success?
- When do you plan to take that action step?
- How confident are you that you will be able to take that step [by desired date]?
- What do you need to be successful with the first step?
- How do you know the goal and first step are within your control?

Challenges and Barriers

Although the ultimate goal of stage three is to create a SMARTE goal and an action plan with at least one specific step for the immediate future, it is also important to recognize that during this stage a coach might want to guide a teacher to anticipate challenges and barriers that may arise. The purpose of addressing challenges and barriers at this stage of the work is to proactively plan for ways to mitigate and overcome them. Questions for addressing challenges and barriers with a proactive stance include the following:

- What might prevent you from taking that action step?
- What might derail your good intentions?
- What can you do in advance to minimize the possibility that something will come up to prevent you from being successful?
- Are there any barriers or challenges you can identify now that might impede your progress?
- What might you be able to do to ensure that barrier or challenge doesn't occur?
- If you do encounter that challenge, what resources or supports do you have to manage it?
- If you get stuck, who might help you out?

Stage 4: Executing and Reflecting

In stage 4, a teacher implements an action step which is followed by a reflective conversation to assess the action. At this stage, coaching is as much about the process as it is about the final outcome. Whether or not the action step was completed is not the focus of the reflective conversation. Rather, the conversation focuses on what the teacher learned about themselves, their values, their teaching, and/or their students during the process. The conversation emphasizes the way this new understanding can be applied to further change. In this way, this stage is similar to microcycles introduced in Chapter 4, and stage 4, like microcycles, repeats as a teacher engages in cycles of implementation and reflection in pursuit of the big-picture SMARTE goal.

Figure 6.5 shows three possible outcomes that create starting points for the reflective conversation (Whole Health Coaching Participant Manual, 2018).

The coaching conversation that takes place after an action step will be different depending on the outcome of the action step. Following this are some potential questions for each possibility.

Outcome #1: Success!

Success can be broadly defined. For example, if a teacher planned one step but took another with successful implementation and outcome, that is success. The coach may want to facilitate a discussion about why one step felt better or easier than another, but the teacher was successful in moving toward their goal despite the change in action.

- What have you learned through this process and your success?
- What supported your success?
- How do you feel about your goal after your success?
- What can you learn from this success that will help you as you continue toward your goal?

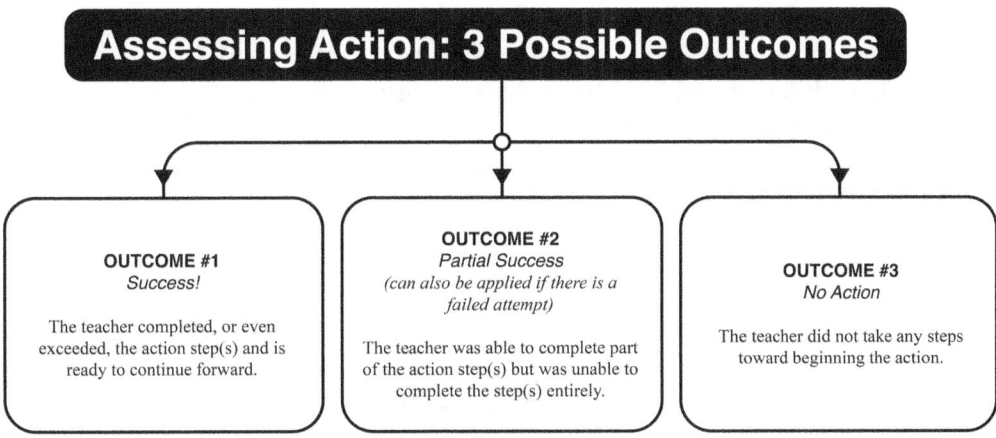

Figure 6.5 Assessing Action: Three Possible Outcomes

- Were there any challenges or obstacles along the way? What helped you to overcome them?
- What's the next step?
- What will you change, if anything, about your approach moving forward?

Outcome #2: Partial Success

Partial success includes partially completing a step successfully, completing a step that was only partially successful, or even a failed attempt.

- What have you learned about yourself or your teaching through this experience?
- What were your successes with this step? (Even if a step fails, there is success in attempting.)
- How do those successes make you feel?
- What got in the way of completing the step?
- How can you apply what you learned to complete this step?
- Given the importance of this goal to you, how will you move forward?
- What do you need to complete the step in the next few days?

Outcome #3: No Action Taken

If no action is taken, it is important for the coach to ensure that the goal was aligned with the teacher's values, seen as important and achievable by the teacher, and within the teacher's control. If any of these are not true, the teacher will be unlikely to take a first step.

- What have you learned about yourself or your teaching through this experience?
- Does this still feel like the right goal for you?
- On a scale of 1 to 10, how important is this goal to you (1 equals not important at all while 10 equals extremely important)?[1]
- Does this still feel like the right first step?
- How confident are you that you can complete this step?
- How can you use what you learned to be more successful this week?
- What can you commit to in the next week to get you started?
- What do you need to be successful this time?

Techniques for Coaching Values

While the stages of the conversation can provide a big-picture map for moving through a Coaching Values approach, additional techniques can be used

Figure 6.6 Techniques for Coaching Values

throughout to support coaching conversations. These include visioning, advanced listening techniques, and the Importance Ruler (Rollnick et al., 2008; Miller & Rollnick, 2013) (Figure 6.6).

Visioning

Although there are more complicated techniques for Coaching Values—and we will get to those—emphasizing the visioning process is a simple way to help a teacher get in touch with their own values about teaching and learning. *Visioning allows a teacher to imagine their classroom as it would be if it were aligned to their values without any constraints.* Visioning alone might cause a transformational learning experience as a teacher recognizes the differences between their ideal classroom and their current classroom; however, this process may need to be helped along through additional coaching conversations and strategies.

Visioning conversations often, though not always, come at the beginning of a coaching relationship and are revisited throughout the coaching process. Visioning helps a teacher set goals for action and improvement and strengthens motivation for change as a teacher explores the possibility of a future desired state.

Visioning begins with a conversation about that future desired state; moves to a consideration and examination of the present state, often with an emphasis on classroom data; and ends with goal-setting and action steps. A series of questions for this type of coaching conversation might include the following:

Step 1: Future State

- If your teaching and students' learning were exactly the way you wanted them to be with no constraints, what would happen in your classroom that isn't happening now?

- Of those things that would happen but aren't now, which is most important to you? Which would make the biggest difference for your students?
- How might your desired state align with your values about your students, your practice, and your role?

Step 2: Current State

- What does your current classroom look like?
- What evidence do you have to support your description of your classroom?
- How does your current state compare to your desired state?

Step 3: Goal-Setting and Action Steps (Notice How These Questions Begin to Address Spheres of Control, Impact, and Importance)

- What, within your control, can you do to begin to close the gap between your current state and your desired state?
- What are some of the steps that will help you reach your desired state?
- Of those steps, which are you most excited about? Which are you most likely to take first? Which will be most challenging? Which will be most impactful to students?
- Which will be your first step?
- What challenges or obstacles might you encounter as you take this step? How will you mitigate challenges and obstacles?
- How would you like to be held accountable for this first step? How can I support you as a coach?
- How will you know when you have been successful with this step? How will you know when you have reached your overall goal?

Advanced Listening Techniques

DARN-CAT

The acronym DARN-CAT is intended to help coaches remember to listen for and focus reflective listening statements on change language (Rollnick et al., 2008; Miller & Rollnick, 2013), that is, anything a teacher says about the possibility of change. When a teacher is in the contemplation phase of change, they are considering a change but have not yet committed. It can be difficult for a teacher to commit to a change that will take energy and engagement to implement, especially when they are not at their optimal well-being. Focusing on change language is a way a coach can highlight the possibility of and positive impact of change and thereby increase the teacher's motivation and confidence for change. For this reason, it is important that a coach pay close attention to change language for teachers like Mr. Martinez who are burned out and for any teachers who are not yet committed to change.

DARN-CAT can help a coach remember the various types of change language that can become powerful levers for accelerated action. Each of the letters in the DARN-CAT acronym stands for one type of language that represents the possibility for change.

D—Desire for change
A—Ability to change
R—Reason for change
N—Need to change
C—Commitment to change
A—Activation of change
T—Taking steps toward change

Let's consider an example with Mr. Martinez:

Jolie: During our last visit, we discussed the difference between your ideal vision of your classroom and your classroom as it exists now. Have you thought more about this?
Mr. Martinez: I have, and I really want to work on making some changes, but I know it's going to take a lot time to figure out how to balance my academic content with social and emotional learning and ensure that I keep my principal happy. I'm just not sure that I have the energy to figure out how to balance everything.
Jolie: You are still interested in making some changes.

During a conversation with a teacher *contemplating change*, it is important to open and expand possibilities for change rather than closing and narrowing possibilities for change. Listening for and focusing reflective listening statements on change language is one powerful way coaches can impact and open possibilities for change. Notice that, in this short transcript, Jolie made a very intentional choice regarding her reflective listening statement. Instead of focusing her reflective listening statement on Mr. Martinez's language about how much time and energy the change was going to take, Jolie listened for and intentionally reflected language that portrayed a desire for change. What's the difference in the reflective listening in the following transcript?

Jolie: During our last visit, we discussed the difference between your ideal vision of your classroom and your classroom as it exists now. Have you thought more about this?

Mr. Martinez: I have, and I really want to work on making some changes, but I know it's going to take a lot of time to figure out how to balance my academic content with social and emotional learning and ensure that I keep my principal happy.

Jolie: It's going to take a lot of time for you to make a change and it's going to be hard work.

In this transcript, Jolie has likely diminished Mr. Martinez's desire to make the change by focusing on the difficulty of the change. The rest of the conversation may go something like this: Jolie will attempt to find ways to help persuade Mr. Martinez that he is ready for the change while Mr. Martinez, now focused on the time and effort it will take, will resist. On the other hand, when Jolie reflects a desire for change by saying, "You want to make a change," she emphasizes the opportunity for change.

Here we present other DARN-CAT statements Mr. Martinez might have made. Importantly, reflective listening statements are not posed as questions. The coach is not questioning the teacher's possibility of change but rather emphasizing it.

Ability to Change

Mr. Martinez: I know that I can create lesson plans that include social and emotional learning. It's what I love and I'm really good at it. It's just so time consuming, and I'm not sure I want to commit to that.

Jolie: You feel confident that you can do this.

Reason for Change

Mr. Martinez: Honestly, I'm not sure I can focus on social and emotional learning given all the emphasis on testing and accountability, but if I can incorporate social and emotional learning into my lessons on a more regular basis, I know that I would be doing so much more for my students. They would really benefit from understanding more about social and emotional learning and having the opportunity to practice those skills during class.

Jolie: You want to do more for your students than just provide academic content, and you think this is a way to really make an impact on them.

Need to Change

Mr. Martinez: If I can't figure out a way to make a change, I am just going to continue to burn out, and I'm going to have to quit this job. The kids really need me, but I don't have it in me anymore.

Jolie: You see a real need to make this change, both for your own benefit and the benefit of your students.

Commitment to Change
Mr. Martinez: I know it is going to be hard, but it is something important to me, so I'm going to make it happen.
Jolie: It's important enough to you that you are committed to seeing it through.

Activation of Change
Mr. Martinez: I am going to start next week when we start our STEM unit. We are going to be reading *Charlie and the Chocolate* Factory, which is great for STEM. I think is also has some good opportunities to talk about SEL skills like fairness and selfishness. I know that I can incorporate discussion and presentation standards into a lesson being fair.
Jolie: Sounds like a great time to start, and you already have a first step!

Taking Steps Toward Change
Mr. Martinez: Yesterday I finished my lesson plan on being fair. It included text analysis, student discussion, and presentation skills. Students are already making connections with Charlie and his family and thinking about how to keep different perspectives in mind when we build things using STEM. I hit multiple standards in this lesson and was still able to address social and emotional issues.
Jolie: You took a successful step toward your desire to balance content with social and emotional learning!

Practice advanced listening with the exercise in Box 6.2.

Box 6.2 On Your Own: Advanced Listening

A coach should practice listening for and reflecting change language, that is, any language that represents a possibility for change. Have a conversation with a friend who is considering a change. As you engage with your friend, listen for and reflect anything they say about the possibility of change. What is the impact of your reflective listening statements?

Double-Sided Reflective Listening Statement
Another way to incorporate reflective listening statements related to change language while still hearing, acknowledging, and affirming a teacher's feelings

and perhaps frustrations is to use double-sided reflective listening statements (Miller & Rollnick, 2013). In this reflective technique, a coach listens for language that represents a values conflict or other struggle and reflects both the struggle and the change language in a structured way to ensure a positive impact on the change. Let's look at another example between Mr. Martinez and his coach:

Jolie: During our last visit, we discussed the difference between your ideal vision of your classroom and your classroom as it exists now. Have you thought more about this?
Mr. Martinez: I have, and I really want to work on making some changes, but I know it's going to take a lot of time to figure out how to balance my academic content with social and emotional learning and ensure that I keep my principal happy.
Jolie: On one hand, you know that this is going to be a lot of work, and on the other hand, it is important to you to start making some changes.

Like a simple reflective listening statement, the double-sided reflective listening statement gives a teacher the feeling of being heard. Additionally, when structured in a specific way, the double-sided reflective listening statement can also emphasize change. The reflective listening statement in this example, "On one hand, you know that this is going to be a lot of work, and on the other hand, it is important to you to start making some changes," ends with an emphasis on the change and is likely to lead to further discussion of the change. Ordering the reflective listening statement to end with the change impacts the trajectory of the conversation. If Jolie had said, "On one hand, you want to start making some changes and on the other hand you know it is going to be a lot of work," the structure of the reflective listening statement emphasizes the difficulty ahead and may lead to more discussion of this difficulty than of the desire for change.

The language of a coach matters and, although reflecting is always an important coaching skill, if a coach can be selective and intentional about what they choose to reflect and how they reflect, they can increase the possibility of change.

Complex Reflective Listening
In Chapter 4 we introduced simple reflective listening statements (parroting, paraphrasing, and summarizing). Complex reflective listening statements involve adding meaning to what a teacher has said (Miller & Rollnick, 2013). The meaning a coach adds is their interpretation of information, such as values, underlying what the teacher says. In other words, the coach guesses at a deeper, underlying meaning based on the teacher's language. Although it

is important not to be wildly wrong—otherwise a teacher might think his coach hasn't been listening at all—it is okay to be not quite right. If a coach's guess at an underlying meaning is incorrect, the teacher will fill in additional information as necessary. One way of guessing at underlying meaning includes identifying potential values that may be informing the teacher's thinking.

We know that tying a change to a teacher's values increases the teacher's internal motivation and likelihood of success. If a teacher knows that a change is important to them, they are more likely to persevere through any challenges or obstacles that may arise. Sometimes, though, a teacher needs help identifying their values and connecting their actions to those values. Listening for and offering reflective listening statements about the underlying values portrayed through a teacher's language can help them to tie change to greater meaning and purpose by connecting to their values. Here is an example:

Mr. Martinez: I get so frustrated with all of this testing. It takes so much time, and I don't have time to get through my content, let alone anything like 21st-century skills. I need to teach my students how to be problem solvers and critical thinkers, and instead I'm teaching them to fill in bubbles on answer keys. We have benchmarks every six weeks, and they are really impacting my ability to do any real teaching.
Coach: You value deep thinking and problem-solving skills. Can you tell me more about that?

Again, what the coach chooses to reflect in this example is important. Listening for underlying values allows the coach to bring those values to the surface and begin discussions about how a teacher's practice aligns or doesn't align with those values. Through these discussions, a coach can impact a teacher's awareness of a need for change.

The Importance Ruler

Another tool used in Motivational Interviewing is the Importance Ruler (Rollnick et al., 2008; Miller & Rollnick, 2013). Rulers can be used in a number of ways to measure values, motivation, confidence, readiness, and progress (Rollnick et al., 2008; Miller & Rollnick, 2013). The Importance Ruler specifically measures how important a change is to a teacher and, therefore, addresses values.

Rulers are created with scaling questions (Berg & de Shazer, 1993), that is, questions that ask the teacher to determine for themselves where they are on any given scale. Scaling questions provide a coach insight into a teacher's perspective. A coach might choose a scale of 1–10, 1–5, or even 1–100. When using scaling questions to explore values and motivation for change, a coach might ask, "On a scale of 1 to 10, how important is this change to you (with a 1 being not important at all and a 10 being very important)?"

Like the double-sided reflective listening statement, in which the structure of the paraphrase is a part of the tool, the structure of a set of scaling questions used in a ruler is essential to its effectiveness. First, a scaling question should always be followed by a request for more information—what does that number look like to you or what does that number mean to you? This allows a teacher to further explore their own thinking and identify objective reasons for the selected number on the scale. The following dialogue shows how to use a ruler in a coaching conversation:

Jolie: On a scale of 1–10, with 10 being very important, how important is this change for you?
Mr. Martinez: I'd say about a 6.
Jolie: What does that 6 mean to you?
Mr. Martinez: Well, it means that it is important to me, but there are other things I am evaluated on that have to be important, too. I have to keep my job, so even though I wish it were a 10, it can't be. On a day-to-day basis, it comes after all the things my principal tells me I have to do.

Now, let's look at how scaling questions can help a teacher explore their thinking about a change by increasing their internal motivation for change based on values.

The next question, "Why not a lower number?" is perhaps the most important question in the series of scaling questions when they are used to create a ruler. Notice that this question does not ask the teacher why they did not place themselves at a higher number. This is because the purpose of the question is to guide the teacher to begin to identify all the reasons *why the change is important to them*. When a coach asks a teacher why they placed themselves at a 5 instead of a 3 or 4, for example, the teacher immediately focuses on all the reasons why the change is important. This discussion may even lead the teacher to determine that they are higher on the scale than they initially placed themselves, further boosting their internal motivation and the likelihood that they will engage in the change. Notice the importance of reflective listening statements in this process as well:

Coach: Can you tell me why you didn't say a 5 or even a 4?
Mr. Martinez: Of course! These kids aren't getting these skills at home. This is what is going to make them successful in life, not dates and famous people.

Coach: You said a 6 because these are the skills that will make kids successful.
Mr. Martinez: Well, when you put it that way, I guess it's maybe more like an 8 to me personally! I was thinking about what other people thought—like all those test makers.

Finally, the third question, which asks the teacher how to scale to a higher number, begins to move the teacher toward action:

Coach: This is an important change to you personally. Now what would make it a 9 or even a 10?
Mr. Martinez: It could be a 10, even an 11, if I could get my Professional Learning Community to buy in so that we were all doing it together and could work as a team to figure out how to align these skills to our pacing guide.
Coach: Getting some help from your Professional Learning Community is important.
Mr. Martinez: Yes, I think that could be a first step.

Used with the Importance Ruler, scaling questions not only help a coach make intentional decisions about what to emphasize and how to guide a teacher through change based on a better understanding of a teacher's context and internal motivation, but they can also help a coach build a teacher's motivation for change and begin to move them toward action. Box 6.3 provides further tips on using rulers and scaling questions.

Box 6.3 Quick Tip: Using Rulers and Scaling Questions

Remember that rulers with scaling questions have a specific form and a specific order (Rollnick et al., 2008; Miller & Rollnick, 2013). The three scaling questions should be presented as follows:

1. On a scale of 1 to 10, how important is this change to you (with a 1 being not important and a 10 being very important)?
2. Describe what that 6 means to you.
3. Tell me how you decided a 6 and not a 5 or even a 4.
4. What would it take for you to decide a 9 or even a 10?

The actual numbers you use will depend on the teacher's initial response. This example assumes the teacher responded with a 6. No matter the number the teacher chooses for the initial response, question 3 will always ask why not a lower number while question 4 will ask how to get to a higher number.

We will return to rulers using scaling questions to see how they can be used to help build a teacher's confidence by emphasizing asset-based thinking in the next chapter.

Apply the techniques in this chapter using the exercise in Box 6.4.

Box 6.4 On Your Own: Applying Values Coaching Techniques

Read Transcript 1: Exploring Values in Appendix B.

- What techniques can you identify that support the Coaching Values conversation?
- How do these techniques impact the coaching conversation?

Why Helpful Suggestions Don't Help

Now that we've reviewed the stages of values-based coaching as well as a few tools for supporting values-based coaching, let's look again at Mr. Martinez. Let's assume that Jolie learned early on in their relationship that the misalignment between Mr. Martinez's values and his practice was impacting his joy in teaching.

Now, let's say Jolie reacted to this discovery by suggesting that Mr. Martinez incorporate a 20-minute social and emotional learning lesson every Friday to teach more to his values and get that spark back. Let's also imagine that Mr. Martinez seems to think this is a good idea—after all, this is important to him! He says that he will start next week.

After the following Friday, Jolie returns to check in with Mr. Martinez. When Jolie asks how the first 20-minute social and emotional learning lesson went, she is surprised to hear that Mr. Martinez didn't follow through. Jolie encourages him to try again next week, reminding him of the importance of aligning his values and his practice and reminding him of his own realization that not addressing social and emotional learning in his classroom was causing him to lose interest in teaching. Mr. Martinez again promises to incorporate an SEL lesson the following week, but Jolie returns after the next week to check in and is frustrated to learn that, for the second week in a row, Mr. Martinez has failed to implement the social and emotional learning lesson that Jolie had suggested and he had agreed to implement.

Explore this scenario further with the exercise in Box 6.5.

>
> **Box 6.5 On Your Own: What Went Wrong?**
> Reflect on the previous scenario. What do you think is the problem with this coaching scenario?

Based on the transtheoretical change model, we know that Mr. Martinez may not yet be ready for change. Although he has recognized a need for change, he may still be in the contemplation phase of change, weighing the effort of the change against its impact and urgency. If Mr. Martinez is still contemplating the change, Jolie needs to take the time to continue emphasizing his values, reflecting change language, identifying locus of control, and sorting priorities until Mr. Martinez decides for himself that it is time to act on the change.

A suggestion to a teacher who either is not currently committed to a change (contemplation phase) or is not even aware of a need for change (precontemplation phase), will, at best, be ignored. At worst, a coach who makes a suggestion before a teacher is ready to change risks impacting the trusting relationship she has with the teacher. Making suggestions before someone is ready to hear them and seriously consider them is a waste of time and can be damaging to the coaching relationship.

Reflect on connections between the Coaching Values and approaches, models, and theories using the questions in Box 6.6.

>
> **Box 6.6 On Your Own: Making Connections**
> - How does the Coaching Values approach align with the approaches, models, and theories presented in Chapter 3?
> - How do specific strategies presented in this chapter align with the approaches, models, and theories?
> - What other strategies do you use in coaching that might support a focus on Coaching Values?

Addressing Equity through Coaching Values

Every student deserves not only a technically competent teacher but also a wholly engaged teacher. A Coaching Values approach is designed to improve or maintain a teacher's energy in the classroom. Revisiting a teacher's values and engaging them in change processes helps them avoid stagnation and reinvest in their teaching practice. When a teacher has the opportunity to engage in reflective thinking about why they became a teacher and what is important to them about their role, they may be more likely to actively devote their time, effort, and energy into student success (Gay, 2010). As a result, they are more likely to engage in practices such as creating culturally relevant classrooms, communicating precise instructions for success, acknowledging when students meet expectations, holding all students to high expectations, fostering and modeling growth mindset, and building authentic relationships with students, their families, and their community (Frank, 2018). Coaching Values includes helping a teacher become aware of how they show up in the classroom and how their presence impacts the health and well-being of their students.

Conclusion

The best approach to coaching Mr. Martinez, given the scenario at the start of the chapter, is to spend time talking with him about what is most important to him as a teacher, reflecting change language to help him prepare and become motivated for change, and implementing strategies that might provide a transformative experience to jump-start the change process.

Box 6.7 provides additional tips for Coaching Values.

Box 6.7 Tips for Coaching Values

- Use a values approach when a teacher seems burned out or has low energy.
- Emphasize what is most important to the teacher so that coaching work can focus on alignment between values and practice.
- Remember that action-oriented questions do not work when a teacher is still in the contemplation phase of change.
- When deciding what part of a teacher's comments to reflect, reflect change language as often as possible.
- When using a double-sided reflective listening statement, always end with the side of the desired change.
- When using a ruler with scaling questions, always follow up by asking the teacher to define the number they have chosen. After discussing the meaning of the number chosen, ask a follow-up question eliciting the reason why the number was not *lower* than the number chosen.

Note

1 This is an example of using the Importance Ruler (Rollnick, Miller, & Butler, 2008), which is described in this chapter on page 105.

7

Coaching Beliefs

Opening Vignette: Jonathon and Ms. Harris

Jonathon   Ms. Harris

Ms. Harris was a 13-year veteran and chairperson of the science department. Her students consistently performed well on the end-of-course test, and she welcomed her coach Jonathon into her classroom to see the procedures she had in place to help her students do well. Perhaps by learning from her, she said, Jonathon could help the other science teachers in the school.

During a coaching conversation early in their partnership, Jonathon asked Ms. Harris to tell him how she structured the last months of school in preparation for testing. Ms. Harris told Jonathon that she targeted her review on those students who were "on the bubble." These students would benefit most from end-of-year review and would come out proficient on the exam if they focused and engaged. She said that she was not worried about her highfliers at the end of the year because she knew they would do well on the end-of-course test no matter what she did.

With confidence, Ms. Harris also shared that there were four students in the class whom she felt would not do well on the tests and so she didn't worry about them either because nothing she could do would result in a proficient score anyway. She described the four students. Damien, a Black male student who was a star athlete but who was "just not getting it"; Josh, a White male student athlete who was simply lazy; Matias, a Hispanic male and English Language Learner (ELL), who turned in his class work, but according to Ms. Harris must be copying from friends because he always did poorly on quizzes and exams; and Abigail, a White female who didn't appear to have friends in the course to help her with her work and had been failing all year. As they talked, Jonathon asked Ms. Harris if she would be willing to place these four students in a group during the lab on his next visit so that he could collect some data on how (or if!) they were working during class.

Ms. Harris agreed, saying that it would be nice to get confirmation that state benchmark and prior-year predictions were correct about these students—that they wouldn't be proficient at the end of the year—and justified the way she differentiated in class, focusing specifically on students "on the bubble" and ignoring those who wouldn't pass anyway. She wanted to know if these four were attempting to do the work or just copying it from others as she suspected. She wanted to know if they were talking to one another, and if so, what they were talking about; she was sure it wasn't class content. Jonathon and Ms. Harris co-constructed a data tool that would capture what she was looking for, and Jonathon observed during the next class period.

The Levers

A Coaching Beliefs approach should be taken when all levers present opportunities for growth (Figure 7.2); this makes coaching for beliefs one of the most difficult coaching scenarios. Coaching Beliefs takes a lot of time and patience but can be extremely rewarding because it can lead to powerful changes for students. In the Opening Vignette, for example, Ms. Harris is using effective teaching practices for *some* of her students. She is providing adequate instruction for many of them; however, her ineffective application of best practices for *all* of her students is creating inequity in her classroom.

Although Ms. Harris does know how to teach *some* of her students, her knowledge of other students and her application of effective instructional practices for them is low as is her engagement. Ms. Harris has given up on a number of students in her classroom and doesn't seem to have the energy or investment in these students to teach differently. Finally, Ms. Harris's awareness of how she was disenfranchising these students is low, and she is not aware that she needs to make a change to more equitably serve her students.

Beliefs, like values, are often deeply rooted in experience. They form when repeated experiences lead someone to begin to make assumptions about what is true. Unlike values, however, which are very difficult to change, beliefs are malleable and can change for the better or worse (for more on the difference between values and beliefs, see Box 7.1). Take Ms. Harris for example.

Beliefs, like values, are often deeply rooted in experience. They form when repeated experiences lead someone to begin to make assumptions about what is true. Unlike values, however, which are very difficult to change, beliefs are malleable and can change over time.

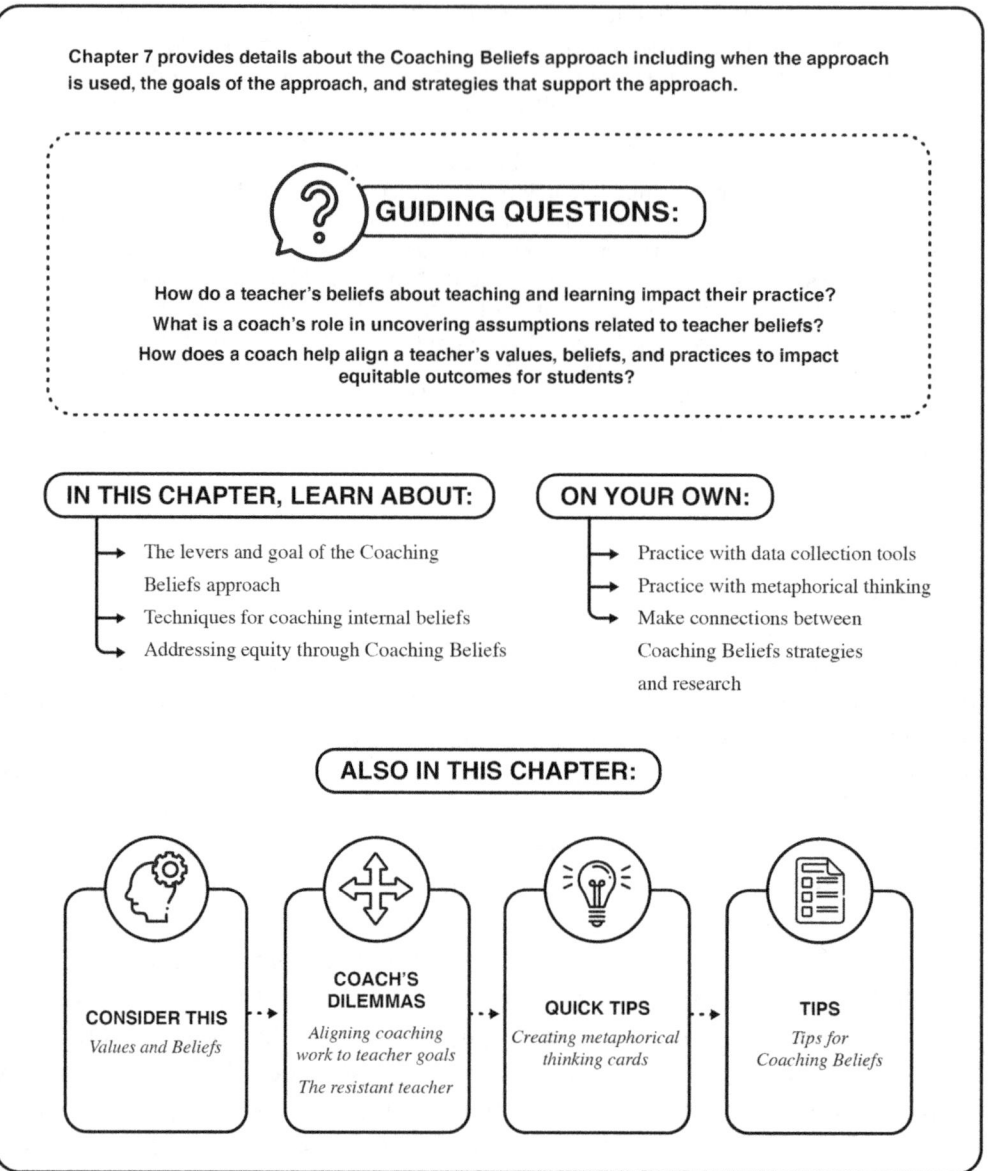

Figure 7.1 Chapter 7 Overview

Maybe at one point in her career Ms. Harris believed that *all* of her students could learn and pass end-of-course tests; however, after years of teaching, she has begun to make more assumptions about her students based on her prior experiences. This is a natural way of responding to an environment

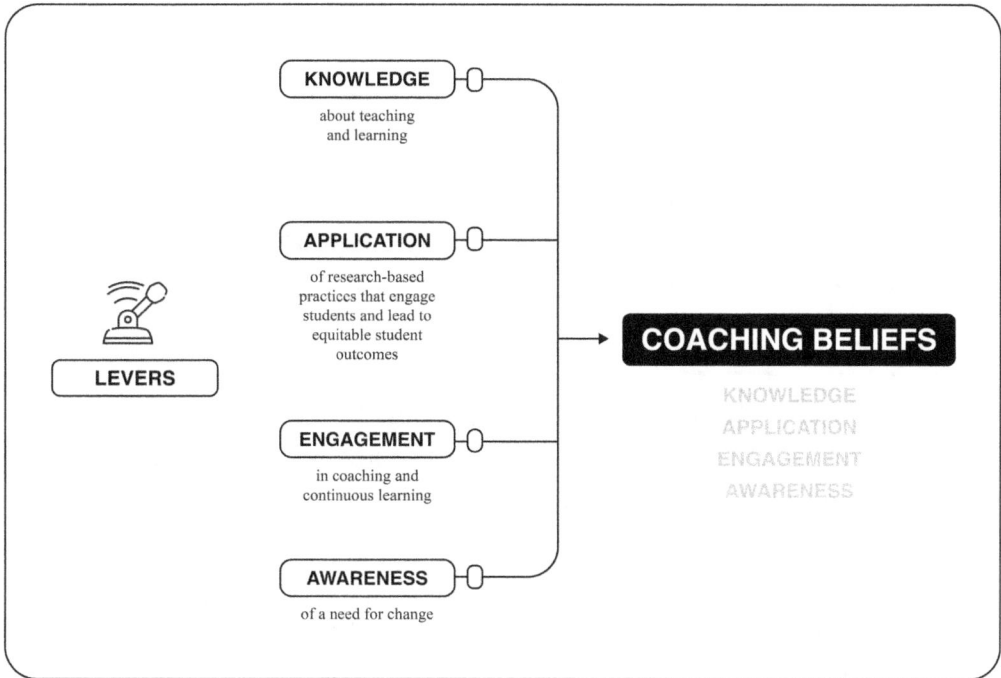

Figure 7.2 The Coaching Beliefs Levers

with as many inputs as a classroom has. Teachers, like everyone else, filter information and select only portions of information to inform their thinking. As a result of many kinds of data including predictive test scores, opinions from other teachers, and stereotypes that are perpetuated in schools, teachers' beliefs often change over time. This is one explanation for how Ms. Harris came to underestimate a particular group of students.

Teacher beliefs come in many forms and can be external as well as internal.

External beliefs are beliefs about people and ideas outside oneself including beliefs about:

- children and young people—what they know and can do, how they are similar to and/or different from children of the teacher's generation, what they prioritize, etc.;
- the role of the teacher—the teacher's responsibility for teaching and learning, the most effective approach for student achievement, how and when to engage with parents and the community, etc.; and
- education and learning—the purpose of school, the best model for schools, the best pedagogical approach, etc.

Internal beliefs are beliefs about oneself including beliefs about:

- one's own ability and self-efficacy in the classroom, and
- how one may be seen by students, parents, colleagues, etc.

When teacher beliefs, external or internal, seem to be getting in the way of the teacher's ability to be their best self in the classroom, it is time to use a Coaching Beliefs approach.

Box 7.1 Consider This: Values and Beliefs

Values and beliefs are different. Values represent fundamental ideas about what is most important to an individual. Values are often tied to our upbringings, are highly constant, and are very difficult to change. Beliefs are assumptions that we make based on our experiences, and they are malleable. From our experiences we make assumptions of what we believe to be true about the world around us. Beliefs can be changed when we experience new events or engage in new situations that may not fit with our existing assumptions. To better understand how this occurs, review Transformative Learning Theory in Chapter 3.

Goal of the Approach

The goal of Coaching Beliefs is to help a teacher orient or reorient their practice to a more effective and equitable approach, either by realigning their practices with their beliefs or by realigning their beliefs with their values.

Realigning a Teacher's Practices with Their Beliefs

At times, a teacher's practices in the classroom do not align with their beliefs. This may occur, for example, when a teacher *says* they believe that all students are capable of high-level thinking and learning but then they do not hold a certain set of students—English Language Learners, students with special needs, or athletes, for example—to the same rigorous standards as other students.

Perhaps, instead of giving these students the same rigorous work with additional scaffolding to ensure success, the teacher simply gives them easier work. Maybe they don't expect these students to learn certain material and let them off the hook when it comes to classwork. Perhaps they only call on those students to answer the easy questions out of fear that they will be embarrassed if they don't have the correct answer. Or maybe, like Ms. Harris, the teacher simply ignores those students in the classroom. This disconnect between a teacher's beliefs and actions may occur because of past experiences with English Language Learners, students with special needs, or athletes who did not perform well. Often, a teacher whose practices do not align with their beliefs isn't even aware of the disconnect and needs help to recognize that their beliefs and their practices are out of alignment. The teacher may also need coaching to begin to identify practices that help them teach in alignment with their beliefs. Their coaching goal will be to better align their practices with their beliefs about students.

Realigning a Teacher's Beliefs with Their Values

Another instance in which a coach may focus on Coaching Beliefs occurs when a teacher's beliefs do not align with their values. For example, a teacher may value equity for all students but say things like, "That kid will never learn," or a teacher may value 21st-century skills like engaging with technology but say, "These kids just can't be trusted to work on computers." Remember, these statements are not internal flaws of the teacher; rather, the assumptions the teacher makes may be a result of repeated experiences and not a result of their beliefs at all. Experiences that impact a teacher's beliefs can be their own experiences as a parent—they may be challenged with their own children balancing the use of technology for homework and gaming—or from repeated experiences over time in their own classroom. Perhaps the teacher has not set up clear expectations for assignments students complete using the computer or the assignments were not rigorous and interesting to students. Over time, because technology assignments didn't work for the teacher, they came to assume that technology assignments never worked at all. In any case, the coaching work focuses on realigning the teacher's beliefs with their values first, reminding them of their values through coaching conversations using powerful questioning techniques and other values-based tools (see Chapter 6), uncovering their assumptions, and working to align their practices with their beliefs.

Techniques for Coaching External Beliefs

Techniques that support external beliefs—beliefs about children, the role of the teacher, and education and learning, for example—include classroom data collection; focusing on specifics; and modeling, co-teaching, and co-planning (Figure 7.3).

Figure 7.3 Techniques for Coaching External Beliefs

Classroom Data Collection

Classroom data provide one type of objective feedback a coach might rely on when using a Coaching Beliefs approach. As we discussed in Chapter 4, when using classroom data, it is important to determine what data the teacher would like and how they would like that data to be collected. These decisions should be tied to the overall coaching goal. Here's an example of what this looked like for Ms. Harris.

Coaching Goal

The baseline data Jonathon collected during his first data collection visit to Mrs. Harris's classroom (described in the earlier vignette) revealed that the four students Ms. Harris was concerned about were, in fact, discussing the topic but struggling with the work. Ms. Harris realized she had been wrong about the assumptions she was making about them and with Jonathon she decided that she needed to vary her instructional strategies and differentiate for her four struggling students—Josh, Damien, Abigail, and Matias—by providing more scaffolding to increase their opportunities for success.

What Data Were Collected?

During her next coaching conversation with Jonathon, Ms. Harris decided to implement a differentiated review activity that provided additional scaffolding for Josh, Damien, Abigail, and Matias. While most students in the class would be engaged in predicting genetic crosses, these four would also predict genetic crosses but would have additional supports including a vocabulary bank and a graphic organizer to guide them through the analysis.

How Were the Data Collected?

Together, Jonathon and Ms. Harris decided to collect data on how students throughout the class (not just Matias, Damien, Abigail, and Josh) were discussing the topic. Ms. Harris wanted to compare and contrast the way Matias,

Damien, Abigail, and Josh talked about the topic to the way the rest of the class talked about the topic. This comparison would give her insight into how better to scaffold learning for Matias, Damien, Abigail, and Josh. Through reflective thinking about the data, she hoped to identify new strategies that she might incorporate to more effectively support these students.

Jonathon and Ms. Harris decided to use a scripting approach to data collection. In order to fully analyze how the small group talked about the topic similarly to or differently than the rest of the class, Ms. Harris wanted to see exactly what they said as they worked, so Jonathon visited each group during the activity and rotated from group to group every two minutes. While he was at each group, he scripted their conversations and clearly identified group number and student name. He rotated to each group three times. At the end of the classroom visit, he handed the data to Ms. Harris.

How Were the Data Used?

During Ms. Harris's planning period the next day, she and Jonathon engaged in a follow-up reflective conversation during which Ms. Harris reviewed the data and reflected on what the data could tell her about her students and her own practice. Based on the data, which showed that the vocabulary bank supported student understanding, Ms. Harris decided her next step would be to provide a vocabulary bank on the students' next quiz to see if their outcomes improved.

Explore data collection further with the exercise in Box 7.2.

Box 7.2 On Your Own: Data Collection

Consider the scenario with Ms. Harris. Imagine that she was interested in understanding whether or not Matias, Damien, Abigail, and Josh were using the additional scaffolds she provided and if the scaffolds were supporting their learning.

How might you go about collecting data for Ms. Harris? Create a data tool for collecting this information and consider how you would use it.

See Appendix A for sample data collection tools to support your thinking.

Data Conversations

Once classroom data are collected, they are a powerful tool for reflective conversations. Reflective conversations using data typically follow the steps outlined in Figure 7.4.

Figure 7.4 Steps for Facilitating a Reflective Conversation

Step 1: Teacher Perception

Data conversations often begin with a teacher's perception of the data. The coach might ask questions such as the following:

- What did you think the data would show?
- What was your perception of how the lesson went before you looked at the data?

Step 2: Data-Based Reflective Thinking

Next, the coach engages the teacher in reflective thinking about the classroom by specifically referencing the data collected. Questions during this time might include the following:

- What stands out to you when you look at the data?
- Do the data align to your beliefs about your students? Your lesson? Your practice?
- Does anything surprise you? If so, what? Why or why not?
- In your ideal classroom, what would these data look like?

During this step, the coach might also ask specific questions about data points that stand out to them.

Step 3: Data-Based Next Steps

After an exploration of the data, final questions like the following help the teacher identify next steps to align the data with their vision of their classroom:

- What would it take to make the data align more closely with your beliefs about your students?
- What are you willing to try to make the data look different?
- What one change *within your control* do you think would make the biggest impact on these data?

While these questions can be asked regarding coach-collected classroom data, they can also be used for additional types of data. Student work, for example, is another type of data that can be used for data conversations. Ms. Harris may have collected the graphic organizers Matias, Damien, Abigail, and Josh used to support their conversations to see what additional insight she could glean from these artifacts. Other student work that can be collected and discussed includes formative and summative assessments, student work, self-reflections, peer reviews, and journals.

Focusing on Specifics

Data collection is certainly a highly effective way of focusing on specifics and using details to help a teacher change their beliefs; however, sometimes a simple conversation can help a teacher focus on specifics.

Beliefs are often generalizations. When teachers say things like, "These kids just don't care," or, "That group is never going to pass the end-of-course test," they are making a generalization about students and using their experiences with specific students to make assumptions about all students. To begin to shift a teacher's beliefs in these cases, a coach can simply ask them to consider a specific example. Considering a specific example can help them question their beliefs and assumptions. Here's an example of a conversation focusing on specifics that might have taken place with Ms. Harris:

Ms. Harris: You know, there are always a few in every class who just aren't going to do the work or pass the test, no matter what a teacher does. I can't reach everybody, so I just do the best I can with those students who will be successful.

Jonathon: Do you have students like that in this class?

Ms. Harris: Of course! Every class!

Jonathon: Okay, who are they in this class?

Ms. Harris: Josh, Damien, Abigail, and Matias. Damien's an athlete and cares more about the next game than his classes, and Matias is ELL. ELL kids just don't do well on tests.

Jonathon: Would you mind if we spent a few minutes getting specific about Matias?

Ms. Harris: Sure, he's a nice kid, but he is ELL. He really struggles with the vocabulary in this class. He just can't pass the end-of-course test with that language barrier. He turns in all of his homework and it's always correct, but he fails all of the tests and quizzes, so he must be copying from other students. I also see him on his phone all the time. I think it's just going to take him a while to get up to speed with the English language, and then he'll have to retake the class in a year or two.

Jonathon: Language can be a barrier for him, and there is a lot of vocabulary in your class.

Ms. Harris: Exactly. That's why ELL kids don't pass biology end-of-course tests.

Jonathon: Let's keep talking about Matias. We know that he struggles with the vocabulary. What have you noticed about his learning during labs and class discussion?

Ms. Harris: He does great in labs. He actually comes up with some really innovative ideas during labs.

Jonathon: How does Matias understand the vocabulary used in labs?

Ms. Harris: Well, he has access to his classmates to help him with the vocabulary, and I also let him use his phone to look up words.

Jonathon: He has additional scaffolds during labs to help him with his vocabulary and so he does well on those assignments.

Ms. Harris: Well, now that you say that, maybe he's not copying his homework. Maybe he's using his phone to help him with the vocabulary when he's at home. He could be using his phone for vocabulary support during class, too.

Jonathon: How do you think we can test the theory that he might not be copying his homework?

Ms. Harris: I guess I need to know if he does well on tests and quizzes if I scaffold the vocabulary for him. Maybe I can give him a vocabulary cheat sheet on the next quiz and see how he does.

Jonathon: That sounds like a plan! I look forward to the results.

Notice how getting specific about one ELL student helped Ms. Harris identify assumptions she was making about Matias and begin to consider Matias as an individual student with strengths and weaknesses instead of a member of a particular group with deficits.

Box 7.3 provides more information about how to align coaching work with teacher goals.

> **Box 7.3 Coach's Dilemma: Aligning Coaching Work to Teacher Goals**
>
> Back in Chapter 4, we said that sometimes a teacher will choose a goal different than the goal a coach might have chosen for them. Although the coach should prioritize the teacher's goals, that doesn't mean they should ignore other opportunities to improve the teacher's practice.
>
> For example, Ms. Garcia has asked Jonathon to help her as she improves her classroom discussion structures. She is hoping that through consistent

and explicit planning for classroom discussion she can improve her students' abilities to disagree respectfully with one another. Ms. Garcia is interested in trying specific activities to support this work, and she has identified scaffolding strategies like sentence stems that she plans to incorporate into discussions. Ms. Garcia has asked Jonathon to help her co-plan some specific lessons and activities and then to collect data in her classroom to track how students respond to and disagree with one another.

During data collection requested by Ms. Garcia, Jonathon notices inequitable classroom management and accountability. A group of girls in the front of the classroom whisper with one another constantly and are ignored, while two male students in the back—one is Black—are reprimanded any time they speak to one another even though Jonathon notices that one of the young men is actually asking for help from the other. Furthermore, Ms. Garcia sends the Black male student out of class after asking him to stop talking to his neighbor for the third time. Jonathon knows that this disparity needs to be addressed, but Ms. Garcia has not invited a conversation related to her beliefs about students or her classroom management strategies. So, what does Jonathon do?

Because teachers are often unaware that their beliefs don't match their values or that their actions don't match their beliefs, they are most likely to invite a coach in for a Coaching Thinking or Coaching Behaviors approach (more on these approaches in Chapters 9 and 10). A coach has to find their own opportunities to address beliefs. This is true for values as well. Teachers will often allow coaches to provide support in strategies and implementation, but they will rarely ask for values or beliefs coaching, often due to a simple lack of awareness. Values and beliefs are typically subconscious and require a coach's support to uncover, analyze, and respond. This means that coaches should be aware of underlying values and beliefs while applying Coaching Thinking and Behaviors approaches and will often have to incorporate values and beliefs coaching into these approaches.

In the scenario of Ms. Garcia, Jonathon might find an opening to address beliefs while discussing the data collected on classroom discussion. After discussing Ms. Garcia's observations and progress related to her goal, the coach might point out the two seats where the young men sit and simply ask Ms. Garcia to tell him more about these two specific students. As Ms. Garcia shares information, Jonathon will listen for her underlying beliefs and use strategies like those presented in this chapter to help her better align her values, her beliefs, and her practice. If Jonathon is able to have this conversation *within* the teacher's own goals for improvement, he is more likely to be successful. If, on the other hand, Jonathon says to Ms. Garcia something like, "I know you want to work on classroom discussion, but I noticed you have some classroom management issues we need to discuss," he is more likely to encounter resistance and negatively impact the coaching partnership.

Modeling, Co-Teaching, and Co-Planning

Modeling, co-teaching, and co-planning can also support Coaching Beliefs by providing opportunities for transformative and experiential learning.

Modeling

Modeling allows the teacher to have a transformative experience as they watch their students engage with a different teacher in their classroom. For example, if the teacher believes that students don't care enough about the subject to engage in conversation but then sees their coach structure an activity that supports more discussion than usual, the teacher will need to confront their beliefs about their students as well as their own responsibility in planning for successful discussions. To provide an even more impactful experience for the teacher and data to discuss during the post-visit conversation, the coach can ask the teacher to collect data on student learning as the coach teaches.

Co-Teaching and Co-Planning

If the teacher prefers not to give control of the classroom to the coach—or if, after the coach models, the teacher believes students engaged in the conversation because someone new was standing at the front of the room—the coach can co-teach or co-plan with the teacher to support intentional planning of a lesson that will scaffold and structure a more effective conversation. In both co-teaching and co-planning, the teacher should drive final decisions about their own classroom and students.

Whether modeling, co-teaching, or co-planning, the goal is to provide the teacher with a single experience or series of experiences that challenges their current perspective. This challenge might lead to a disorienting dilemma that the teacher must seek to understand through a new way of thinking. Modeling, co-teaching, and co-planning experiences can include or be followed by data collection and reflective conversations that subsequently help a teacher confront their own assumptions and make sense of a new way of thinking.

Techniques for Coaching Internal Beliefs

It is often easier for a coach to remember to focus on a teacher's ideas about their students and their practice than to remember to address a teacher's thinking about themselves. After all, the coach's focus is ultimately on student learning. A teacher's beliefs about themselves, however, are extremely important in the change process. The more competent a teacher feels and the more confidence a teacher has in their ability to change, the more successful they are likely to be. On the other hand, when a teacher lacks confidence,

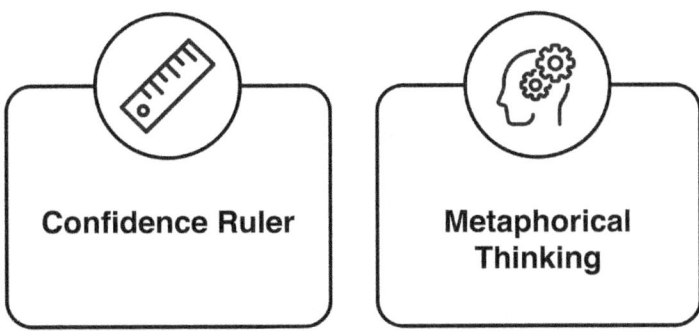

Figure 7.5 Techniques for Coaching Internal Beliefs

the likelihood of failure increases. There are specific tools a coach can use to discuss and even improve teacher confidence, including rulers (Rollnick et al., 2008; Miller & Rollnick, 2013) and metaphorical thinking (adapted from Ting & Scisco, 2006) (Figure 7.5).

The Confidence Ruler

The Importance Ruler, a tool drawn from Motivational Interviewing, was introduced in Chapter 6, where scaling questions were used to explore and increase motivation for change by focusing on the importance of the change and alignment to values. Scaling questions can also be used to discuss and build confidence through a Confidence Ruler (Rollnick et al., 2008; Miller & Rollnick, 2013). The following steps, which mirror the steps of the Importance Ruler, show how to use scaling questions to explore confidence and to begin to build a teacher's self-efficacy:

1. The coach asks the teacher a scaling question about confidence: On a scale of 1–10, how confident are you that you can make this change or implement this strategy?
2. The coach asks the teacher to explain what their number means to them. Ask probing follow-up questions as necessary to explore meaning.
3. The coach asks the teacher why they didn't rate themselves lower than they did.
4. The coach asks the teacher what it would take for them to increase their rating to a higher number.

Like the Importance Ruler, which is designed to increase motivation, the Confidence Ruler is designed to increase confidence. Asking the teacher why they didn't respond with a lower number is an asset-based approach; the teacher's response has to focus on what they do well that keeps them from rating themselves lower on the scale. In this way, the coach begins to build confidence simply by providing the teacher an opportunity to identify their own assets. Ending with the final question moves the teacher toward action by identifying a next step that might increase their feelings of self-efficacy.

For a transcript example of how to use the Confidence Ruler and scaling questions for motivating change, see Appendix B.

Metaphorical Thinking

Metaphorical thinking, adapted from Ting and Scisco, Eds, 2006, is another way to begin to identify and change a teacher's beliefs about themselves in the classroom, their approach to teaching, and even their students. Metaphors have the power to reveal deep truths and, because they provide concrete images with shared understandings, they can provide safety as teachers express powerful emotions and internal beliefs in a very concrete way. For example, consider the following statement:

> I Am a Sinking Ship!!

It may be much easier for a teacher to share this statement with their coach than it would be to say, "I am overwhelmed and feel as if I am going to fail. I am afraid of the damage I will do to my students if I am unable to carry my load. I don't believe that I am capable of doing all that I need to do in the next few weeks to ensure my students' success and well-being." The sinking ship metaphor provides the teacher with a safe place to start, ensures that their coach quickly understands their feelings, and provides a concrete anchor (pun intended) for continued discussion.

One way coaches can use metaphorical thinking is with a deck of cards that shows a variety of images wholly unrelated to education. Perhaps the deck includes an image of a highway with speeding cars, an image of that sinking ship, an image of wholesome vegetables at a farmer's market, a serene field, and a farm animal—perhaps a chicken. The steps in Figure 7.6 show how to use the deck to explore a teacher's feelings and then begin to impact their beliefs and action.

Step 1: Identify Current State

The coach asks the teacher to scan through the deck and choose the image that most represents their beliefs or feelings about a specific topic. For example:

- Which image best represents your understanding of yourself as a teacher?
- Which image best represents your understanding of your students?
- Which image best represents your feelings about this coaching experience?
- Which image best represents how you feel about today's class?

Figure 7.6 Steps for Using Metaphorical Images

Step 2: Explore Current State

The coach uses powerful questions to help the teacher explore the image. Questions might include the following:

- What characteristics of this image stand out to you?
- What does this image mean to you?
- How do these characteristics relate to what you believe (about yourself, your students, coaching, today's class)?

Step 3: Identify Desired Future State

After exploration of the current state, the coach uses the same deck of images to identify a desired future state.

The coach asks the teacher to scan through the deck and choose the image that most represents what they would like to believe or feel about the topic. For example:

- Which image best represents how you would like to see yourself in the classroom?
- Which image best represents your vision for your students?
- Which image best represents how you would like to feel about this new strategy?

Step 4: Explore Desired Future State

Again, the coach uses powerful questions to help the teacher explore the chosen image. Possible questions are the same as in Step 1 and include the following:

- What specific characteristics made you choose this image?
- What is the relationship between this image and your vision?

Step 5: Shift to Action

Finally, the coach asks the teacher to begin to identify steps to close the gap between the current state and the desired future state.

- What is one thing you can do tomorrow to begin to move from image 1 to image 2?
- What resources do you need to begin to move from image 1 to image 2?

Boxes 7.4 through 7.7 offer an opportunity to explore metaphorical thinking further and to reflect on the Coaching Beliefs approach.

Box 7.4 Quick Tip: Creating Metaphorical Thinking Cards

This is a tip we've been sharing for years though we're not sure who the original tipster is. To create your deck of images, visit a discount store in mid-January and buy a variety of last year's calendars. Or, search the Internet for open-source stock photos. Print and laminate.

Box 7.5 On Your Own: Metaphorical Thinking

Practice using metaphors with family members, friends, or colleagues to describe your feelings at the end of a day, the end of a meeting, or the end of a work session.

Spread out a set of images and ask family members, friends, or colleagues to choose one that represents their current feelings. Ask them to explain why they chose their image. If anyone's current state is less than ideal, use your coaching skills to help them figure out how to improve their state through action!

Box 7.6 Coach's Dilemma: The Resistant Teacher

Ms. Daniels is a second-year teacher. She teaches third grade. Her coach Jonathon is aware that she is struggling with classroom management and, in fact, her principal asked Jonathon to provide support to Ms. Daniels at the beginning of the year.

Jonathon spent most of the first semester building a relationship with Ms. Daniels so that she would be willing to be coached. Ms. Daniels finally let Jonathon visit her classroom right before the winter break. During this visit, Jonathon saw students talking to their neighbors while Ms. Daniels was teaching, getting out of their chairs to wander around the room, and throwing things at each other when Ms. Daniels's back was turned. Although there were rules posted in Ms. Daniels's room, there was no follow-through for students when they broke the rules. When Ms. Daniels tried to teach, she asked the students to settle down with constant verbal reminders like, "Shhhhh," "Settle down," "Come on guys," and, "I need your attention," but she did not provide consequences when she was ignored.

It was now February and Jonathon was hoping that the semester shift would allow Ms. Daniels to reset and start fresh with a solid classroom management plan, but that didn't happen. Ms. Daniels is aware that her students are loud and disruptive, and when Jonathon works with her, she often breaks into tears because she is so frustrated with the behavior of her students and completely exhausted by the end of the day. She desperately wants to improve her classroom management, and she knows some strategies she might use. She even identified a strategy that might work for her and her students and promised to implement it before Jonathon's next visit. The next time Jonathon saw Ms. Daniels, he asked how the strategy was going, and Ms. Daniels said that she hadn't tried it yet and doesn't think she will be able to do it this year. She shared that coaching felt like just another thing she doesn't have time for, so while she appreciates Jonathon's time and efforts, she thinks he would be more effective working with other teachers.

****

Jonathon might be tempted at first to chalk Ms. Daniels's resistance up to a gap in her readiness for change. Or maybe Jonathon thinks that Ms. Daniels's resistance might be a misalignment between the change goal and her values. However, in this instance, neither is the case. Ms. Daniels has clearly indicated that a change in her classroom management is important to her and that she wants to make this change. So, what's the problem?

Sometimes teacher resistance disguises a lack of confidence. What if, this time, the resistance disguised Ms. Daniels's belief that she was not capable of changing student behavior? After repeated failures, her sense of self-efficacy might be extremely low and, just as some students choose not to do classroom assignments in order to avoid failure, she may be choosing not to attempt a new strategy because it is easier than failing yet again. Scaling questions and metaphorical thinking can be used with a "resistant" teacher when the coach suspects that their resistance may be a lack of confidence.

Resistance can also be related to other beliefs a teacher might have, including beliefs about the purpose and process of coaching. As we have mentioned, many teachers—and administrators—believe coaching is intended to "fix" poor teachers. Emphasizing the teacher's autonomy and empowering the teacher to make decisions about their own classroom will begin to break down these beliefs, but it may take time.

Engaging resistant teachers takes patience, good listening skills, empathy, and a lot of humility and resilience. Resistant teachers may avoid coaches; complain incessantly about coaching, students, and school leadership; or actively lash out against coaches. We have had doors closed in our faces on more than one occasion when resistant teachers have seen us coming. Coaches should always remember that resistance is not an inherent or unlikeable characteristic of a teacher; rather, it may be tied in some way to a teacher's beliefs about coaching, themselves, or education in general. A coach should remain curious about a teacher's resistance and ask questions that may uncover opportunities for Coaching Beliefs and Coaching Values.

>
> **Box 7.7 On Your Own: Making Connections**
> - How does the Coaching Beliefs approach align with the approaches, models, and theories presented in Chapter 3?
> - How do specific strategies presented in this chapter align with the approaches, models, and theories?
> - What other strategies do you use in coaching that might support a focus on Coaching Beliefs?

Addressing Equity through Coaching Beliefs

All humans are prone to cognitive bias. Cognitive bias is a habit of thinking that occurs as individuals take shortcuts when processing and interpreting information from the world around them (Box 7.8). There are times when these habits of thinking or mental shortcuts lead to unintended consequences because they impact our decisions and practices; therefore, it is important to be aware of them. Racial bias, gender bias, and ability bias are common biases, but there are many more types of biases that exist and impact students in schools. Understanding both the prevalence of cognitive bias and how to combat cognitive bias is critical to reaching educational equity.

Data collected in the classroom can uncover assumptions a teacher is making about who has the ability to answer their most complex questions. For example, if a teacher notices in their data that they ask girls more follow-up questions than boys—whether they answered correctly initially or not—the teacher may begin to realize that they are holding different expectations for different students as a result of the students' genders. It is a coach's role not only to collect the data but also to use other techniques for Coaching Beliefs to engage in coaching conversations that critically examine data and what it reveals about issues of equity.

>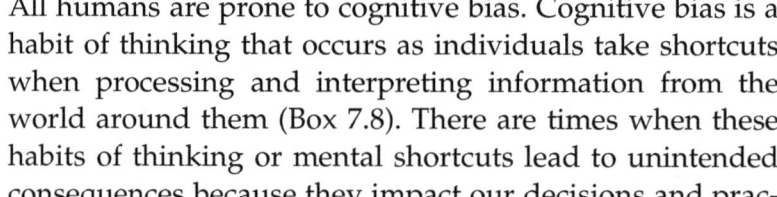
> **Box 7.8 Consider This: Cognitive Bias**
> Cognitive bias is a type of error in thinking that occurs when we process and interpret information from stimuli in the environment. Cognitive biases are the result of mental shortcuts that humans take in order to survive in the world. With over 40 million bits of informa-

tion coming to us at any one minute, shortcuts are necessary. Tversky and Kahneman (1973) observed that because information processing, time, and ability are limited, humans must use shortcuts to breakdown information in systematic ways, which naturally leads to biases. For example, we saw in the case of Ms. Harris that she jumped to conclusions about her struggling students. This was not because Ms. Harris was a bad or uncaring teacher; rather Ms. Harris, who taught 120 students in the course of a single day, began taking mental shortcuts and simplifying information she saw and heard to help her save time and energy.

To learn more about cognitive bias, read *Blindspot: The Hidden Biases of Good People* by Banaji and Greenwald (2016).

Conclusion

After Ms. Harris realized through a transformative experience that she was making assumptions about her students, she set the following immediate next steps for herself:

1. Greet each student individually to build stronger relationships;
2. Hold student conferences with Matias, Damien, Abigail, and Josh, as well as with other students to help them self-assess and set learning goals for their review;
3. Differentiate her lessons more; and
4. Change her expectations about what students could and could not do based on who they were and how they may have performed earlier in the semester.

Ms. Harris completed the first two steps of her plan on her own and asked Jonathon to help her think through her options for changing her lesson plans and routines. Together, Ms. Harris and Jonathon spent the next two months engaged in microcoaching cycles that helped Ms. Harris purposely consider her instructional practice; realize that the practices she had used year after year didn't always work for every student; and uncover the assumptions she was making about Matias, Damien, Abigail, and Josh as well as other students like them. In the end, Ms. Harris told Jonathon that new data helped her to see the bigger picture and become more conscious of those students who she believed would not pass the end-of-course test.

Box 7.9 provides further tips for Coaching Beliefs.

Box 7.9 Tips for Coaching Beliefs

- Begin with an experience that will help the teacher begin to question their assumptions and open up to new learning.
- Focus on specifics! Discuss specific data points and specific students. Ground discussions in evidence and objective feedback.
- Remember to address not only the teacher's beliefs about their students, their practice, and teaching in general, but also the teacher's beliefs about themselves.
- Changing beliefs is hard. Be patient, empathetic, and supportive throughout the transition.
- Expect extreme reactions from resistant teachers, and remember that resistance can mask fear, uncertainty, and a lack of confidence.
- As you work to uncover a teacher's assumptions, be aware of your own assumptions and remember to question them and avoid projecting them onto the teacher.

8

Coaching Thinking

Opening Vignette: Jolie and Mr. Dudley

Jolie   Mr. Dudley

Mr. Dudley was a high school art teacher who was passionate about his content. He loved supporting students as they learned to create things, but something was missing. He wanted to teach students to create their own art, but he also wanted to teach them to talk about art—and not just what they liked or didn't like about art. He wanted them to discuss the theory of art, the form of art, the meaning and symbolism of art. For Mr. Dudley, these were all important aspects of being an artist.

When Jolie and Mr. Dudley began working together, Mr. Dudley said that the one thing he wanted to change in his classroom was his students' ability to have real conversations about art, but, he said, they just weren't interested in talking about art. He had tried on multiple occasions to implement Socratic seminars, debates, and art critique discussions, but they never turned out well.

When Jolie asked what discussions about art looked like in his classroom, he stated that he provided students with a question about a piece of art, and the ensuing discussion lasted about two minutes. The same students participated every time, and after two or three students shared what they liked or didn't like about the art, no one else volunteered to share anything. He said that he tried follow-up questions but that either the same few students would answer, or the class would sit in silence. He hadn't gotten any traction, and so mostly he just avoided planning classroom discussions completely because he expected students to disengage, and he was tired of feeling frustrated. He had seen effective classroom discussions facilitated by other teachers, so he knew it could happen. He just wasn't sure how to make it happen in his classroom.

The art of teaching comes when teachers know how, when, and why to use the particular tools in their toolbox. Part of the joy of teaching, one could argue, is borrowing, adapting and tweaking a practice so that it fits just right within the context of an ever-changing environment!

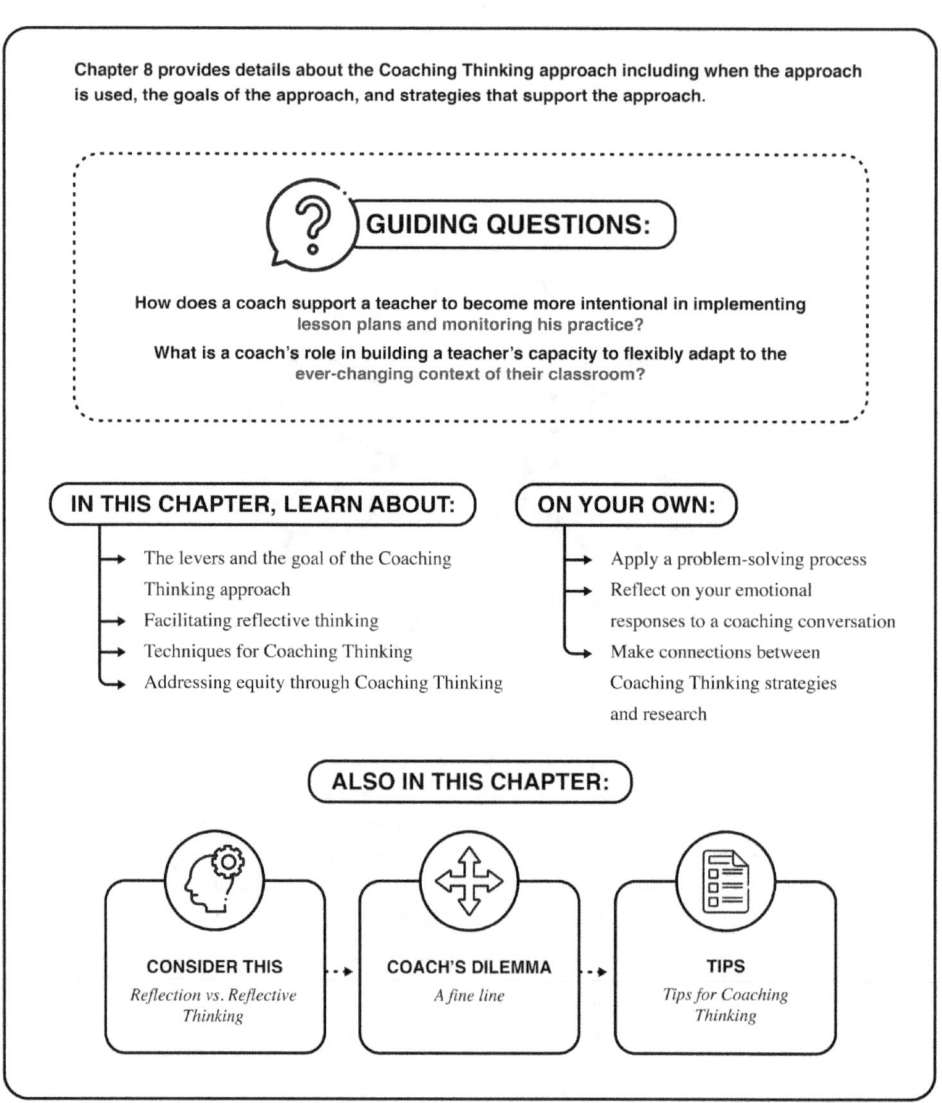

Figure 8.1 Chapter 8 Overview

The Levers

Coaching Thinking occurs when a teacher's knowledge is a strength—they are aware of a strategy and can explain how to implement it from a technical standpoint; however, their intentional implementation—application—of the strategy is an opportunity for growth. They may use the strategy, for example, without understanding why the strategy might (or might not) work for a particular set of students or content standards. They may implement the strategy without intentionally considering the details of the implementation, or they may implement the strategy and miss or ignore results that show the strategy isn't working to reach their intended outcomes. A teacher might have a hard time explaining why they planned their lessons a certain way. Typically, a teacher who is ready for a Coaching Thinking approach is aware that there is an area for growth within their practice and is engaged with the coaching process (Figure 8.2).

Mr. Dudley (in the Opening Vignette), for example, has a high level of knowledge about discussion strategies. He can name and describe strategies he has tried to implement in the past; however, when Jolie asks about his implementation of the strategies—how he prepared students for the discussion, how he scaffolded their conversation, and what students needed to be

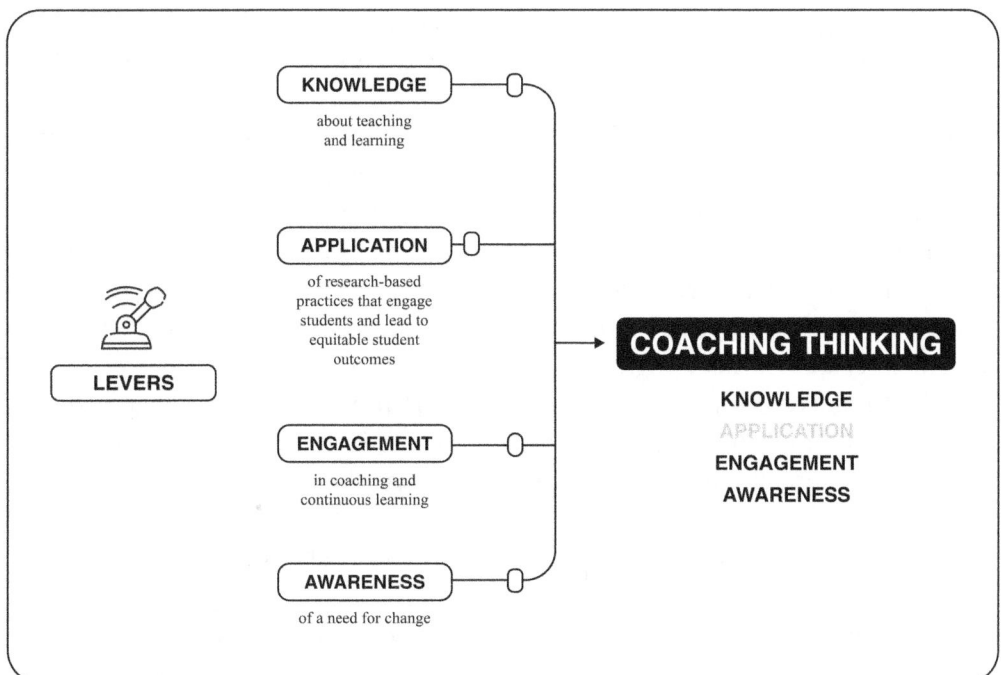

Figure 8.2 The Coaching Thinking Levers

successful—he is unable to provide a direct and concrete response. Mr. Dudley knows that his implementation of the discussion practices he has used has been ineffective, so he stopped holding classroom discussion entirely. Mr. Dudley's engagement with the coaching process is high, though, and he is excited about the changes that he might make to classroom discussions with coaching support.

Goals of the Approach

Coaching Thinking starts with engaging teachers in meaningful and purposeful inquiry with an emphasis on reflective thinking. Reflective thinking guides teachers to become more intentional about the planning, implementation, and results of their practice on equitable outcomes for all students. The goal for Coaching Thinking, then, is to support teachers in becoming more intentional about relationships among their knowledge of students, content, context, pedagogy, and classroom data.

Anyone who has spent any time in a classroom knows that what works with one set of students does not necessarily work with another. A lesson plan that went swimmingly one year may be tossed out the next because it does not fit with the needs of the current students. The same goes for a class or lesson taught at the beginning of the day compared to that same lesson with similar pacing taught in the afternoon to a different set of students. Practices, strategies, and tools that are used in teaching are not one-size-fits-all. Different tools are used for different reasons and different tools are needed for different groups of students. *The art of teaching occurs when teachers know which pedagogical practices, tools, strategies, and techniques to use to positively impact student learning and can explain how and why they have made the decisions they've made regarding their practice. Part of the joy in the art of teaching, one could argue, is borrowing, adapting, and tweaking a practice so that it fits just right within the context of an ever-changing classroom environment!*

Coaching Thinking is designed to support the ability to flexibly respond to the teaching environment and adapt instructional practices to a specific context. Coaching Thinking supports teachers as they

- intentionally match strategies to students' learning needs and the classroom context;
- implement practices and notice in-the-moment results;
- use in-the-moment results immediately to change course and respond appropriately to student needs; and

- reflect on outcomes after a lesson to further refine understanding of relationships among students, content, context, pedagogy, and classroom data.

In addition to supporting intentional planning and a flexible response to changing contexts, Coaching Thinking emphasizes research-informed and evidence-based teaching practices. Evidence-based teaching, in turn, supports teachers in understanding what effective instruction looks like and can contribute to an equitable classroom environment.

Coaching Thinking often begins with powerful questions that engage teachers in reflective thinking and are intended to build a teacher's instructional capacity. When coaches employ a Coaching Thinking approach, teachers use reflective thinking as a source to identify their own areas of strength and growth and explore specific questions related to the relationships that exist between student learning and their practice. Additionally, when engaged in reflective thinking teachers intentionally work toward identifying and using the appropriate tools in their toolbox for student success. Essentially, these teachers become students of their own teaching practice.

Coaching Thinking involves setting time aside for a teacher to engage in metacognition—that is, monitoring and directing their own cognitive (thinking) processes (Young & Fry, 2008). Researchers who study adult learning and metacognition argue that effective teachers are "more metacognitive" and are personally able to adapt to changes in their environment and respond more effectively to the variability that exists in classrooms (Duffy, Miller, Parsons, & Meloth, 2009; Manasia, 2015). Effective teachers thus evaluate, monitor, and regulate their own cognition or mental functioning (Flavell, 1979). These activities go beyond mere "reflection," which often centers on thinking *about* an experience but not one's own *learning* related to that experience (Box 8.1).

Box 8.1 Consider This: Reflection vs. Reflective Thinking

Reflection and reflective thinking (metacognition) are different. Reflection often involves surface-level thinking while reflective thinking involves more analysis and evaluation. Notice the differences in these two examples:

Reflection: Students were unable to answer the questions posed during discussion.

Reflective thinking: I think I began asking students to use all of the elements of critique in describing this painting too soon. I need to consider how I am scaffolding students' learning to engage in art critique because they were unable to answer the questions posed during the discussion.

Facilitating Reflective Thinking

Many teachers jot brief notes on lesson plans or assignments to remind themselves of what went well during a lesson or what they want to change for the next year, while other teachers engage in passing conversations with colleagues in the hall or over lunch to talk about how a lesson went. These types of quick chats or written notes don't always lead to long-term, sustainable change in practice because the thinking is not *metacognitive* and has not been fully explored, analyzed, and tied to actionable next steps. Teachers may find it hard to engage deeply in meaningful reflective thinking because of time constraints or lack of energy. Other teachers may get caught in overanalysis of a situation and become stuck in "analysis paralysis" missing the learning and growth opportunities presented through classroom challenges.

It is a coach's role in Coaching Thinking to support deep, intentional, and sustained analysis of thinking by facilitating reflective conversations and helping teachers move beyond surface-level thinking or analysis paralysis. Coaches help teachers engage in reflective thinking that *does* lead to long-term change in teacher practice through ongoing coaching cycles that focus on a single line of inquiry and emphasize active experimentation with data collection and progress monitoring. In facilitating reflective thinking on an experience, a coach focuses on three elements of a teacher's practice: knowledge, skill, and experience (Jiang, Ma, & Gao, 2016) (Figure 8.3).

Reflective Thinking: Focusing on Knowledge

A teacher's knowledge includes knowledge of self, including strengths and opportunities for growth and preferred teaching style as well as knowledge about pedagogical strategies to use in specific contexts. Mr. Dudley, for example, may have a wealth of knowledge about art and art critique. He may also know a variety of discussion strategies. What he may not know is that his students need scaffolds—included scaffolded questions—to fully engage in art critique.

Figure 8.3 Elements of a Teacher's Practice for Reflective Thinking

Questions that engage teachers in reflective thinking about their knowledge may include:

- How might your interest (or lack of interest) in this topic impact how you teach it?
- What do you know about yourself that impacts how you engage with students?
- How do you know when and if you have chosen the right pedagogical strategy for a specific activity?
- How did you determine how students will work in this lesson (independently, in pairs, in small groups, or as a whole class)?
- How does student grouping during this lesson impact the activities in which they will engage?

Reflective Thinking: Focusing on Skills

A teacher's skills include the ability to intentionally plan and implement a lesson that aligns and leads to expected outcomes. Implementation includes not only the ability to carry out the lesson plan as intended but also to respond in the moment to student learning and to self-monitoring of one's own teaching practice.

- **Planning for Student Learning (before instruction):** identifying and setting instructional goals, selecting appropriate instructional strategies for a lesson, and making predictions about how students will respond to a lesson when implemented;
- **Responding to Student Learning (during instruction):** maintaining awareness of how students are processing the information and engaging in the activities during instruction; awareness of students' short-term and long-term growth and achievement; and
- **Responding to One's Own Teacher Practice (during instruction):** engaging in self-monitoring and adjusting teaching practice in response to lesson outcomes and student formal and informal feedback during instruction.

For example, Mr. Dudley had tried a variety of whole-class discussion strategies, including Socratic seminar, debates, and art critique discussions, but his implementation of these strategies was not leading to the right outcomes. Mr. Dudley needed to build competence in how he planned for and responded to student learning and reflected on his own practice:

- **Planning for student learning:** Mr. Dudley may have chosen a discussion activity that did not align with his goals for the lesson, or he

may have planned questions for a discussion without providing the structures and scaffolds students needed to enter in to the discussion.
- **Responding to student learning:** Mr. Dudley may not have realized prior to the discussion that students did not understand the art at the focus of the conversation or the instructions for the discussion. He may have missed the impact of students' misunderstanding on their ability to critique the art. Perhaps in the moment, he made ineffective course corrections, further frustrating and shutting down his students.
- **Responding to one's own teaching practice:** As students disengaged, Mr. Dudley may have misinterpreted his students' disengagement in the lesson and missed the impact of his own frustration on his students.

Mr. Dudley recognized that discussions weren't working in his class, but he was not effectively planning for discussions and he did not have the skill in the moment to pivot and respond to resulting classroom conditions.

Questions that engage teachers in reflective thinking about their skill can focus on planning, responding to student learning, and/or responding to one's own teaching practice and may include the following:

- How do you ensure that your class activities align to your lesson's intended outcomes?
- What is hardest for you in planning for a lesson?
- What about the lesson planning process is automatic for you?
- When students do not initially engage in a class activity, how do you respond?
- How does your facilitation of an instructional strategy impact student response?
- How do you adjust when you realize that your teaching is not aligned to intended outcomes of the lesson?

Reflective Thinking: Focusing on Experience

When using the Coaching Thinking approach, coaches actively listen to teachers as they explore, analyze, and evaluate specific experiences in their classrooms. Through the use of clarifying and probing questions, coaches provide teachers with opportunities to consider experiences from both a cognitive (thinking) perspective and an emotional perspective. Although a coach typically focuses a teacher's reflective thinking on one specific lesson, including elements that came before and after the lesson helps a teacher to make explicit connections among various classroom events. Further, a teacher's understanding of a lesson is often influenced by a culmination of experiences and related emotions. Therefore, reflective conversations about experiences may include discussion about:

- feelings, judgments, and past experiences and how each may impact thinking about the current experience; and
- what happened before, during, or after an experience.

For example, while Mr. Dudley and Jolie are engaged in a reflective conversation about a specific lesson during which Mr. Dudley tried a new discussion strategy, Mr. Dudley may comment, "I am feeling worn out. I feel as if I am doing all the work. The kids looked absolutely bored today. Can I even teach art critique to these kids?" This comment may be based on the results of the specific lesson being discussed, but it may also be based on heightened emotions that occur after an ineffective lesson or due to the culmination of experiences that led him to feeling frustrated in the first place.

To support Mr. Dudley during reflective conversations, Jolie should use specific data to help Mr. Dudley focus on the lesson at hand; however, she should also use questioning paths that explore Mr. Dudley's emotions and how his actions and perceptions led to these emotions. Additionally, Jolie must ensure that Mr. Dudley keeps a focus on his goals and is able to make sense of how his reflective thinking about this experience can help him make in-the-moment decisions during future lessons to respond to students' learning needs.

Questions that engage teachers in reflective thinking about their experiences may include the following:

- What makes this experience stand out to you?
- Have you had an experience before that was similar/different?
- What happened before class started? What was the transition into the lesson like?
- How do you think students felt during the lesson? What evidence do you have?
- What emotions came up for you during the lesson?
- How do you think the way you are feeling and thinking about this lesson will impact how you engage with and teach students tomorrow?
- Does an experience like this lesson never happen, rarely happen, typically happen, or happen all the time? Tell me more.
- If you could recreate this experience with the same students next week, what would you need your students to do differently? What do you need to do to support this change?

Techniques for Coaching Thinking

While specific questions are useful in facilitating a teacher's reflective thinking about their knowledge, skills, and experiences, there are also specific techniques aligned to the goals of a Coaching Thinking approach that support teachers in deep inquiry about their practices. These include the three-stage problem-solving technique, identifying a single layer of inquiry, progress monitoring, advance questioning techniques, and exploring emotions (Figure 8.4).

Three-Stage Problem-Solving Technique

When teachers are ready for active coaching, coaches help them become clear about what they are curious about. Typically, teachers who are ready for a Coaching Thinking approach have in mind what they would like to investigate about their practice but need support identifying a goal and concrete action steps. There are many different problem-solving techniques that can be used to help teachers identify their macrocoaching goal. The problem-solving technique we describe in Figure 8.5 draws on and modifies James Henderson's (1992) problem-solving process.

Step 1: Explore the problem. The coach and teacher will begin by exploring the problem that needs to be solved.

Questions Jolie might ask Mr. Dudley during stage 1 include the following:

- What problem are we trying to solve with engaging students in art critique?
- What makes this problem worth exploring?

Figure 8.4 Techniques for Coaching Thinking

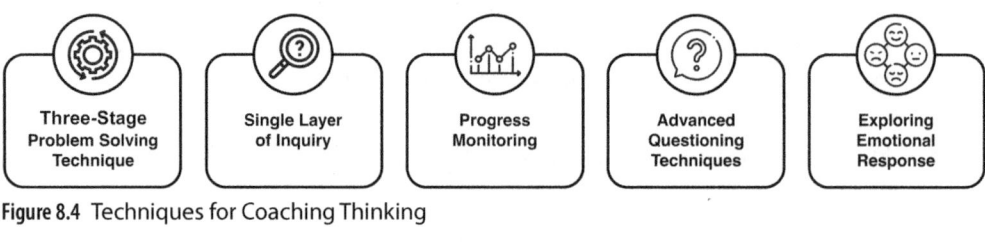

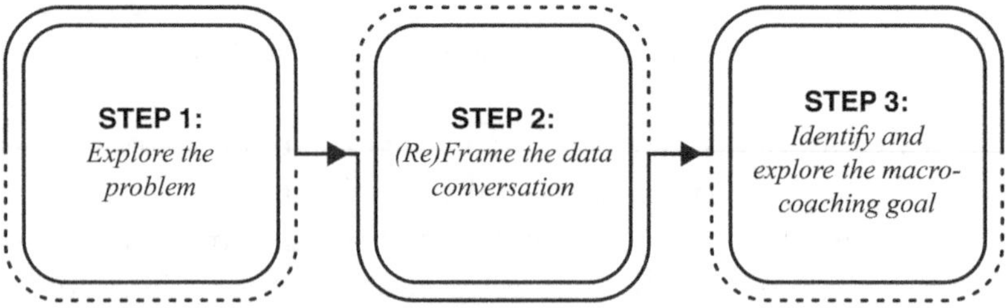

Figure 8.5 Three-Stage Problem-Solving Technique

- What evidence do we have that sheds light on this problem of practice?
- What class is this happening in?
- Who are the students in this class?
- When is the problem most noticeable?
- What other data do we have to understand the problem of practice?
- Have you explored similar problems in prior years?
- What question can we use to frame this problem of practice?

Step 2: (Re)Frame the data conversation. After a teacher explores and articulates the problem of practice they intend to solve, the coach supports further exploration of the existing data that currently informs the problem **and** will inform analysis of progress regarding the change the teacher intends to make. It is important during this stage of problem-solving that teachers begin to think about what data they use and how data is influencing their decision-making processes.

Questions Jolie might ask Mr. Dudley during stage 2 include the following:

- What adjustments have you already made to help students engage in art critique?
- What evidence do you have that students are not able to critique art?
- Does the evidence apply to all students?
- What specific work would students produce if they were proficient in art critique? Have they already produced any of this work?

During Coaching Thinking, the goal of data conversations is to help teachers begin to think about what type of data, both formal and informal, can be collected related to their problem of practice. Decisions should be based on specific outcomes relative to the problem. At this point, the teacher has not set goals or identified what success looks like. The intention behind the process is that often conversations about data help to refine the problem so that when the teacher moves toward identifying actionable next steps, those steps are purposeful, intentional, and measurable.

Step 3: Identify and explore the macrocoaching goal. During stage 3 of the problem-solving process, a teacher identifies a macrocoaching goal, explores what success looks like, and begins to identify actions toward solving their problem of practice and meeting their goal. Mr. Dudley's goal, for example, might be stated as, "By the end of the unit, 100% of my students will participate in whole-class discussion related to art critique."

Once a macrogoal is identified, the coach will guide the teacher in a discussion of what success looks like. The teacher and coach may also identify key stakeholders who can support the change process, clarify teacher expectations, and explore readiness for change.

Questions Jolie might ask Mr. Dudley during stage 3 might include the following:

- What does success look, sound, and feel like when students in this class are critiquing art during whole-class discussion?
- How will students know that they are successful in critiquing art?
- What do you think are viable solutions to engaging more students in whole-class discussion?
- I understand that students' ability to critique art is important to you. As we continue to implement strategies that help students get better at this skill, what happens if it takes longer than you expect?
- What should our process be to monitor progress?

Now that a macrogoal has been identified and both the teacher and coach understand the macrogoal and the value it has for the teacher and for students, the coach supports the teacher in focusing on a single layer inquiry question to guide each microcoaching cycle.

Practice problem-solving with the exercise in Box 8.2.

Box 8.2 On Your Own: Applying the Problem-Solving Process
With a peer coach, work through the problem-solving process with an inquiry into your own practice as a coach.

- What problem are you trying to solve?
- What evidence helps you understand this problem?
- What question(s) helps to frame the problem to be solved?
- How have strategies or techniques used in the past, if any, attempted to solve the problem?
- What additional evidence emerged from those attempts help to clarify the problem?
- What new data can you collect to track your progress as you make adjustments to address this problem?
- What will success look like and how will you know when you get there?

Identifying a Single Layer Inquiry Question

There are many layers of learning that will support Mr. Dudley in meeting his macrogoal: "By the end of the unit, 100% of my students will participate in whole-class discussion related to art critique." The layers of his inquiry might include the following:

- how to plan effective questions to scaffold the discussion,
- how to implement the scaffolded questions and adjust based on student engagement, and
- how to reflect on the outcomes of his questions and make improvements for the next discussion.

To successfully carry out a microcycle, a teacher must narrow their focus for learning to one layer of inquiry. This allows the teacher an opportunity to investigate a single aspect of their teaching related to their macrogoal. The aim is to develop a single layer inquiry question that will guide a single microcoaching cycle with a teacher.

To develop a single layer inquiry question, the coach might use a series of prompts such as:

- If you had no constraints, what would you investigate about this experience?
- What about your students would you like to know more?
- What about student learning would you like to know?
- What about your planning process would you like to know?
- What about your implementation of the lesson would you like to know?
- What about the classroom environment would you like to know more?
- Based on the ideas you would like to investigate, choose the top three that you think knowing more about would have resulted in a different experience.
- Choose one of these three ideas for us to investigate during a coaching cycle and let's develop a single layer inquiry question to guide our work together.

A single layer inquiry question is designed within the context of the macrogoal and is focused on one change, is open-ended, and is designed to make an impact on teacher practice.

For Mr. Dudley, the inquiry might be focused on the following question: "How can I better plan for and support all students to engage in whole-class discussions about art critique?" Once Mr. Dudley has a single layer inquiry question, Jolie will navigate Mr. Dudley through a microcycle including planning for a better discussion, implementing the plan, and engaging in reflective thinking about the outcomes.

Focusing a microcycle on a single layer of inquiry helps to build teacher capacity, improves teacher self-efficacy, and prevents teachers from being overwhelmed and stressed out as they engage in the process of change.

Progress Monitoring

Within a microcycle, opportunities for monitoring progress build a teacher's capacity to engage in inquiry by analyzing a problem, using data, and organizing next steps. Additionally, monitoring progress provides opportunities to identify and celebrate incremental successes along the way to meeting the overall macrogoal.

Examples of ways to help teachers monitor their progress during microcoaching cycles include the following:

Conduct Classroom Visits

Baseline data. To support monitoring, the coach can help a teacher identify baseline data. This baseline data could be data collected as part of a coach's classroom visit or through student work samples. It is not necessary for a teacher to make a change before inviting the teacher into the classroom for data collection. Rather, visiting the classroom to collect baseline data and to begin to understand the context of the class can help both the teacher and the coach as they work toward implementing a change to meet the teacher's macrogoal or respond to their single layer inquiry question. Subsequent classroom visits will allow a comparison to help track the teacher's growth as well as the impact of that growth on their students. To ensure that changes to instruction are impacting student learning in equitable ways, it's essential to monitor samples of student work that are produced as a result of the changes. This monitoring occurs through ongoing coaching cycles.

Ongoing data. Ongoing classroom visits support data collection in a variety of forms and can lead to powerful reflective conversations that debrief the data and identify a specific, evidence-based next course of action. Classroom visits should be aligned with the teacher's overall goal, based on a single layer inquiry question, and occur when teachers are in active experimentation.

Assess Student Work

Analyzing student work samples is at the heart of teaching. The National School Reform Faculty and School Reform Initiative have data analysis protocols that work well in analyzing student work. Additionally, partnering with teachers to examine student work from different tasks, different student subgroups, and students of varying proficiency levels engages teachers in reflective thinking that impacts equity in their classrooms.

Celebrate success. Recognizing and celebrating successes builds a teacher's recognition of their own competence. Oftentimes we want a teacher to reach benchmarks that demonstrate their progress, and once they do, we look for the next benchmark without first pausing to recognize accomplishments. Coaches should take time to ask a teacher what hey have noticed about their own progress and that of their students after key benchmarks.

Write it down/journaling. Teachers can record questions and ideas related to their single layer inquiry question by chronicling their investigations, recording thoughts, actions, and ideas generated during reflective thinking. Over time, these written notes can demonstrate the relationship between a teacher's knowledge and skills, implementation experiences, and student outcomes, thereby building their capacity to solve similar problems in the future.

Engage in action research. Action research projects are excellent opportunities for teachers (along with their colleagues, if they'd like) to work on a sustained dilemma over time. Action research includes a series of steps a teacher can engage in to improve their teaching or to evaluate the impact of their teaching (Harmer, 2001). During action research, teachers engage in theorizing about their practice and researching their practice to test their theories. The coach's role is to support the teacher throughout the process of theorizing, identifying questions for investigation, providing partnership support for active experimentation, and engaging teachers in reflective thinking to turn their knowledge into practice and improve student learning outcomes.

Advanced Questioning Techniques

In their coaching toolkit for social and emotional learning, Yoder and Gurke (2017) call out question categories that can be applied to a reflective conversation. Their questioning categories include objective, reflective, interpretive, and decisional (Figure 8.6). These types of questions can be used to help a coach plan the structure of a reflective conversation, beginning with objective questions and ending with decisional questions. We will describe and identify the purpose of each of these types of questions and then use the vignette from the beginning of the chapter to illustrate.

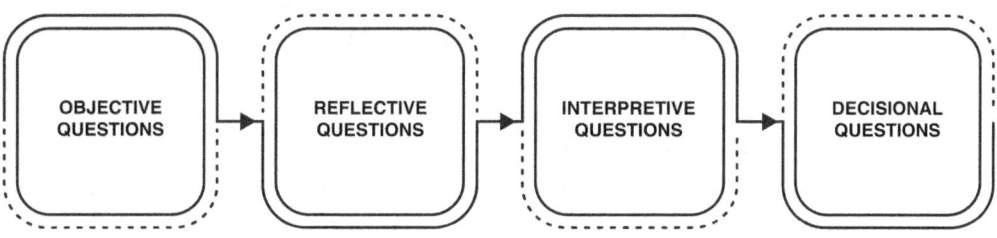

Figure 8.6 Yoder and Gurke's Question Categories

Objective. Objective questions focus on the data of a classroom experience—often data formally collected by a coach during a classroom visit—and help a teacher avoid jumping to conclusions or making inferences based on previous experiences or assumptions about students. When using objective questions, the coach should ensure that the teacher provides only objective responses and that those responses are specific and detailed and reflect what actually happened in the classroom. For example, let's imagine that when Jolie follows up with Mr. Dudley, he is unhappy with the results of the day because the students did not engage in discussion the way he wanted. Perhaps, after he tries a new approach, Mr. Dudley says, "These kids just can't engage in discussion with each other. They're not interested!"

However, what if the data actually showed that more than half of the class engaged in the discussion? Maybe Mr. Dudley is focusing only on the students who do not engage and is missing information about those who do. His response is a generalization and signals that he may have filtered out evidence that contradicted his assumptions about how students would respond to the classroom discussion. Filtering in this way is both a normal and a natural process because humans are designed to take shortcuts in their thinking in order to handle the amount of information available to them each day. In fact, Danielson (1996) estimates that a teacher makes more than 3,000 nontrivial decisions every day. There is an extraordinary subtlety involved in making discretionary decisions about which student to call on, how to frame an impromptu question, or how to respond to an interruption. With this many decisions to make in a day, it is no wonder that teachers are not always able to adequately or even correctly identify and analyze key evidence in their classrooms. Coaches use objective questions to help teachers identify gaps in their own thinking and assumptions in their analysis.

Examples of objective questions Jolie might ask Mr. Dudley to help him see things he missed include the following:

- What did you see students doing while you were posing questions for discussion?
- What did you hear students saying about the art?
- What evidence do you have that students were disengaged from the conversation?
- What evidence do you have that students were thinking, or not thinking, about the critique?
- What do the data show you about who participated and who didn't participate?
- What's the relationship between the number of students who participated and the number who didn't?

Questions like these help a teacher to slow down in their thinking, reconsider what they saw and heard, and come to a more informed decision about what was happening in their classroom. In the case of Mr. Dudley, perhaps through the data collected, he may come to realize that over half of his class participated and some were even using language of art critique. With this information, he can now more purposefully consider those who didn't participate and those who did not use the language of art critique. He can begin planning an experimental approach with a more focused understanding of what is happening in his classroom.

Reflective. Reflective questions provide opportunities for a teacher to consider their reaction to the classroom experience and should be used in comparison to the objective data.

Examples of reflective questions Jolie might ask Mr. Dudley include the following:

- How do you feel about the data that we just discussed?
- Did anything about the data surprise you?
- Does this data align with what you experienced during the class?

Interpretive. Interpretive questions begin to help the teacher make connections between their teaching actions and the students' responses. For example, Jolie might ask Mr. Dudley the following questions:

- How did your planning impact student discussion?
- What is the connection between your planning for discussion and its impact on students?
- What were students most successful at during the whole-class discussion? What were they least successful at?

Decisional. Finally, after objective data have been analyzed, reflected on, and interpreted, coaching conversations should move into a decisional phase. This is the phase in which a teacher determines next steps for their own growth and improvement. Coaching conversations must include next steps so that growth and improvement are ongoing between coaching cycles. Additionally, the teacher must determine next steps to build their sense of autonomy and efficacy as well as their capacity for independent growth and development.

- What will you do differently the next time you plan for discussion?
- What's another way to engage students in discussion that might support students who didn't speak today?
- How will you change this lesson before you implement it again?

Planning with Yoder and Gurke's question types allows a coach to prepare a conversation that will move a teacher in a logical manner from what they noticed during a lesson to implications of what they noticed on decisions for their classroom. Using these question types can provide support and structure for a coach in planning a single coaching conversation. Additionally, these question types are not limited to inquiries about social and emotional learning or to instructional practice. They can also be used to explore student work, to understand a problem of practice, or to develop a single layer inquiry question.

Exploring Emotional Responses

A key component of any experience is the emotional response the experience may evoke, and emotions often surface during reflective conversations. A coach should use this opportunity to help a teacher explore emotions that surface including a teacher's feelings of self-efficacy—or lack thereof. For tips on engaging with a teacher's emotions, see Box 8.3.

> **Box 8.3 Coach's Dilemma: A Fine Line**
>
> Coaching is not therapy and yet, because effective coaches build strong and trusting relationships with teachers, coaches are sometimes faced with coaching conversations that seem to border on therapy sessions. Frustrated and overwhelmed teachers who have to leave their personal lives at the classroom door may open up to their coaches about challenging personal situations, and the coaching conversation may end abruptly as the coach searches for tissues, a bottle of water, and the right words to say. When this happens, coaches should be empathetic, draw on the teacher's assets, and use relationship-building skills to remind the teacher that they are in conversation with a partner who values who they are as a person, the work that is being done together, and the drive toward student success.

For example, as Mr. Dudley prepares to attempt a discussion strategy again, Jolie should be aware that he may experience trepidation as he wonders if the new strategy that he has chosen will fail and become yet another example of his inability to effectively structure a whole-class discussion for his students. Acknowledging and discussing these fears and other emotions is an important aspect of Coaching Thinking.

Goleman (2001) places emotional intelligence into four main domains: self-awareness, self-management, social awareness, and relationship management. By asking specific questions about emotions related to these domains, coaches can help teachers identify feelings that impacted an experience. Exploration of these feelings can help teachers further analyze the experience and identify their own actions and reactions that may have impacted the outcomes. For example, a coach may ask Mr. Dudley the following questions:

- How were you feeling at the moment when only a few of your students responded during the whole-class discussion?
- How are you feeling now as you reflect on the experience of implementing whole-class discussion for the third time?
- I heard you say that you were disappointed; is there another emotion you can think of?
- What would make you feel your best?
- How does making additional attempts toward engaging students in art critique make you feel?
- What can you do to change your emotional response to ineffective classroom discussions? How would a different response impact results?

As always, a coaching conversation that includes reflective thinking about emotions should also include actionable next steps. Coaches should not spend an entire coaching session asking teachers to engage in reflective thinking and exploration of emotions without identifying steps that can move teachers forward.

Box 8.4 explores reflection on your own emotional responses, and Box 8.5 connects Coaching Thinking to approaches, models, and theories presented in Chapter 3.

Box 8.4 On Your Own: Explore Your Emotional Responses

Consider your last coaching conversation. Reflect on the following questions:

- How did you feel throughout the conversation?
- What triggered your specific feelings?
- How did you feel heading into the conversation, at different transition points, and immediately after the conversation?
- Did your feelings change throughout the conversation?
- Overall, was the coaching conversation a delightful experience for you? Was it frustrating? Did you feel successful?
- What can you learn about your coaching approach based on these feelings?

> **Box 8.5 On Your Own: Making Connections**
> - How does the Coaching Thinking approach align with the approaches, models, and theories presented in Chapter 3?
> - How do specific strategies presented in this chapter align with the approaches, models, and theories?
> - What other strategies do you use in coaching that might support a focus on Coaching Thinking?

Addressing Equity through Coaching Thinking

As teachers engage in reflective thinking, it is important that they consider the impact of their decisions on equitable learning outcomes. For example, is a literacy strategy involving student groups meeting the needs of all learners or only a few? Are the tasks that teachers assign to students allowing students to work with grade-level content and engaging students in high cognitive demand? Additionally, as coaches engage teachers in reflective thinking conversations, they should help teachers focus on specifics. In the Coaching Thinking approach, coaches should focus on building teacher instructional capacity to improve the learning experiences of all students. Addressing issues of equity facilitates this process.

Conclusion

Coaching Thinking begins with a problem-solving process to identify a macrogoal related to knowledge, experiences, or skills. The three-step problem-solving process prompts a teacher to explore a problem of practice, which leads to identification of a macrogoal and subsequently related single layers of inquiry. Engaging in an investigation related to something they are curious about ignites a teacher's willingness to engage in a change effort. As a result, the coach is positioned to support the teacher through cognitive scaffolding, where they partner with the teacher to engage in microcycles that allow the teacher to investigate their own problem of practice.

Coaching Thinking focuses on supporting the teacher who is knowledgeable, engaged in the coaching process, and aware of the needs of their students. Teachers draw upon evidence-based strategies during their lesson-planning process and should understand the best practices for teaching their grade level, students, and content areas. When focusing on Coaching Thinking, the intent of the coach is not to persuade or influence how the teacher is making decisions about the tools that they are using but to build the teacher's capacity to plan for, implement, measure, and take action as a result of using the tool to address student learning needs.

Box 8.6 offers tips and strategies for Coaching Thinking.

Box 8.6 Tips for Coaching Thinking

- Be an active listener and determine if the teacher is reflecting on their knowledge of self or pedagogy, experience, or skills.
- Help build the teacher's capacity for instruction by identifying a single layer inquiry question related to their reflective thinking and the outcomes they would like to see with student learning.
- Let teachers know the impact that change can have on their practice and their feelings.
- Use progress-monitoring strategies to help teachers celebrate success and to inform the need for or revisions to change efforts.

9

Coaching Behaviors

Opening Vignette: Jonathon and Ms. Shah

Jonathon   Ms. Shah

Jonathon had been working with Ms. Shah for about eight months. She was an early-career teacher and Jonathon's coaching had focused on using a variety of instructional strategies in her classroom. As an early-career teacher, she needed some tools in her toolbelt. Then, Ms. Shah went to a conference where she heard about PBL. This wasn't a new tool—this was a whole new toolbox! She returned from the conference energized and ready to implement PBL in her classroom. The only problem was that she had heard about PBL in one short 90-minute session of an entire conference, and one short session is only enough to open the lid of the toolbox, not enough to learn about those tools, when to use them, or how to use them. The toolbox was open, and she was looking at shiny new tools that she didn't know how to use.

When Ms. Shah told Jonathon about her interest in PBL, Jonathon was excited. He had spent the last two years supporting a schoolwide PBL initiative at a nearby school. He understood the characteristics of high-quality PBL; he knew how to plan for a PBL unit; he had lots of ideas for unit launches, final products, and culminating events; and he was aware of potential pitfalls and ways to avoid or mitigate those pitfalls. While Ms. Shah had seen the toolbox, Jonathon understood the tools and knew how and when and why to use them.

The commonality among teachers who need coaching with a mentoring approach is that they have limited internal resources to rely on themselves to answer their own questions or arrive at their own solutions.

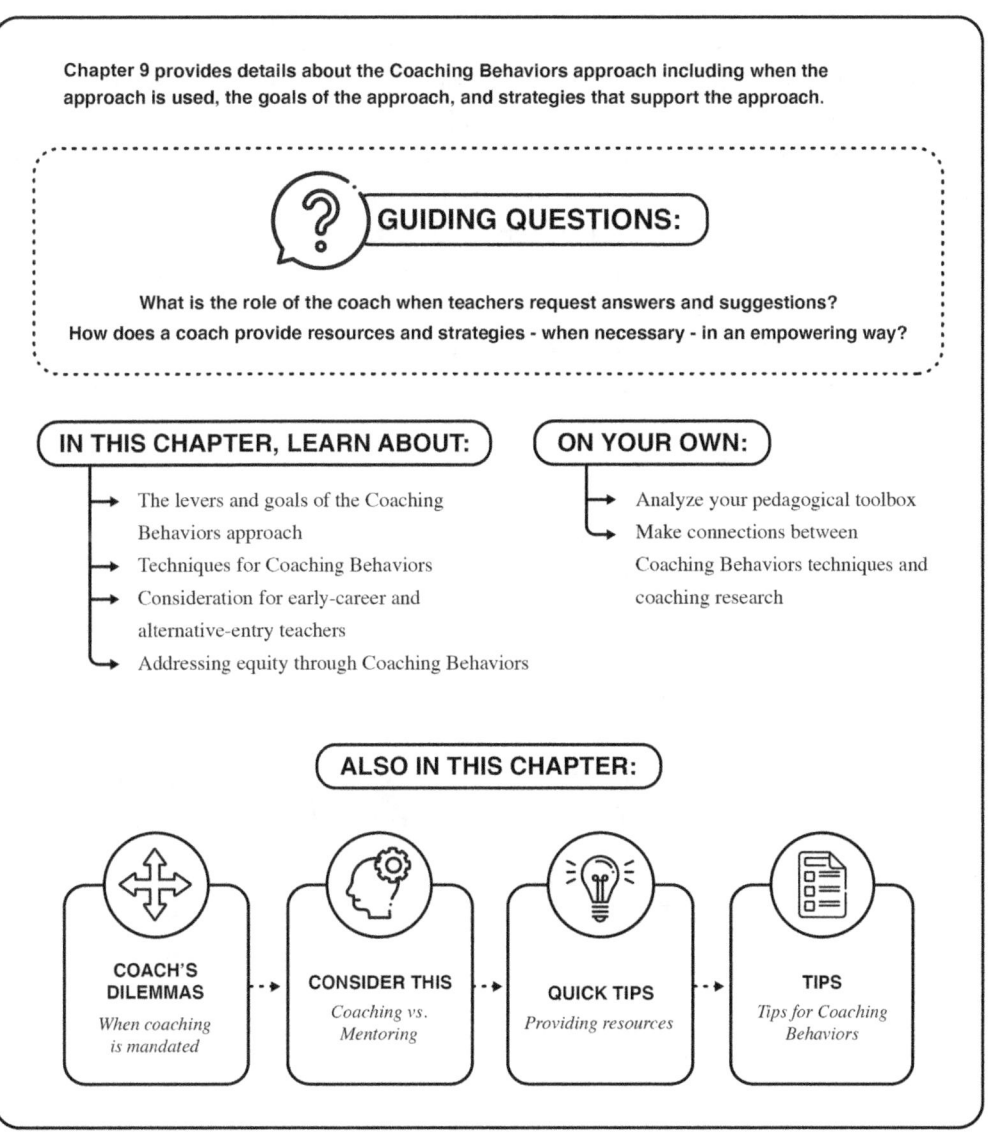

Figure 9.1 Chapter 9 Overview

The Levers

The defining levers for Coaching Behaviors are a gap in knowledge regarding an approach or practice and, therefore, a low level of application. A teacher who does not know any discussion strategies, for example, will have limited implementation of those strategies. To effectively engage in Coaching Behaviors, both awareness and engagement must be high. A teacher must be aware enough of their needs to ask for help, and they must also want the coach's support and be engaged in the coaching process (Figure 9.2).

Coaching Behaviors, which draws on a mentoring stance, may seem at first glance to be the easiest and most comfortable approach for many coaches, especially those who have had any experience in schools as mentors. Coaching Behaviors involves supporting teachers who have limited experience with teaching in general or limited knowledge of a particular pedagogical or instructional approach they are interested in implementing. Teachers in this category may be early-career teachers with little experience or they may be veteran teachers who want to try something new with which they have no previous experience. *The commonality among teachers who need coaching with a mentoring approach is that they have limited internal resources to rely on themselves to answer their own questions or arrive at their own solutions.* For these

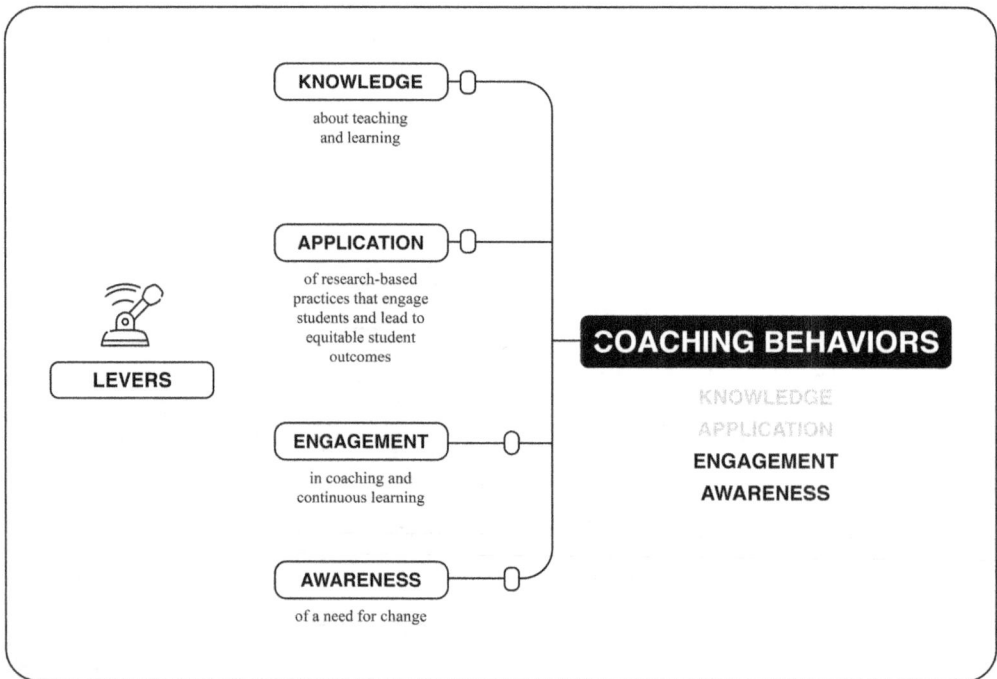

Figure 9.2 The Coaching Behaviors Levers

teachers, the coach is positioned in more of an expert role than in any of the other approaches. Often, these teachers request support for implementation of innovative approaches just as Ms. Shah did in the Opening Vignette. This request makes the entry into initial coaching very easy because the teacher is eager for coaching support. While the approach may seem easy, coaches must be wary not to provide *too much* support with this approach, thereby disempowering the teacher. Box 9.1 provides guidance for situations in which coaching has been mandated.

> **Box 9.1 Coach's Dilemma: When Coaching Is Mandated**
>
> Sometimes a coach will find themselves working with a teacher who has asked for their support—hence, the teacher is aware of a need for change—but who is not engaged in the coaching process. Perhaps an administrator has told the teacher that they *must* improve their use of collaborative strategies, or perhaps the teacher may have been *required* by their school or district to implement an initiative that the teacher either does not value or does not believe in. Although a coach may at first believe that Coaching Behaviors is the priority approach—after all, the teacher has asked for specific pedagogical support—it will quickly become clear that the teacher is not invested in the strategy or the process of coaching. In this case, the coach will need to provide support and strategies as the teacher requested, but they will also need to incorporate Coaching Values and/or Beliefs to help better engage and motivate the teacher through alignment to what is most important to the teacher.

Goals of the Approach

There are two goals of Coaching Behaviors—one for teachers and one for coaches. The goal for teachers is to ensure that they have the resources and the support they need to use those resources in the appropriate ways and at the appropriate times. In addition to this teacher-focused goal, it should be the goal of the coach using a Coaching Behaviors approach to get out of the Coaching Behaviors approach as quickly as possible! A coach should move to a different coaching approach as soon as the teacher with whom the coach is working feels they have the resources needed to move forward.

Coaches take on a mentoring stance during the Coaching Behaviors approach, providing teachers with resources, suggestions, and ideas, that may inadvertently lead to the disempowerment of the teacher if not done carefully and intentionally. To mitigate this risk, coaches should stay in this role only as long as it takes to provide teachers some ideas to work from. Additionally, the approach should only be used when teachers are truly out of resources, and it should be used in a manner that supports an immediate shift away from Coaching Behaviors as teachers perfect their ability to use new strategies and techniques. This chapter includes tools and strategies for making this shift as well as for using the approach in the most empowering way possible.

Techniques for Coaching Behaviors

Techniques for Coaching Behaviors help coaches provide suggestions, resources, and support while maintaining a teacher's agency and autonomy. Additionally, they are designed to set the coach up to shift to another approach as soon as possible. These strategies include Elicit-Provide-Elicit, Co-Planning, Brainstorming Technique, and Using Past Experiences (Figure 9.3).

Elicit-Provide-Elicit

The elicit-provide-elicit technique (Rollnick et al., 2008; Miller & Rollnick, 2013) (Figure 9.4) is another Motivational Interviewing tool and is used to ensure that teachers are ready to hear information coaches have to offer in support of their work. In addition, the technique helps a coach

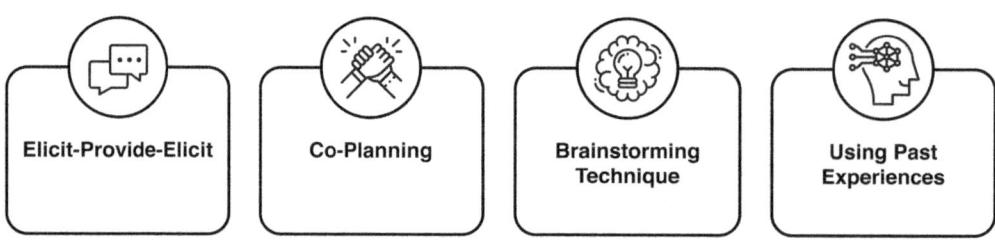

Figure 9.3 Techniques for Coaching Behaviors

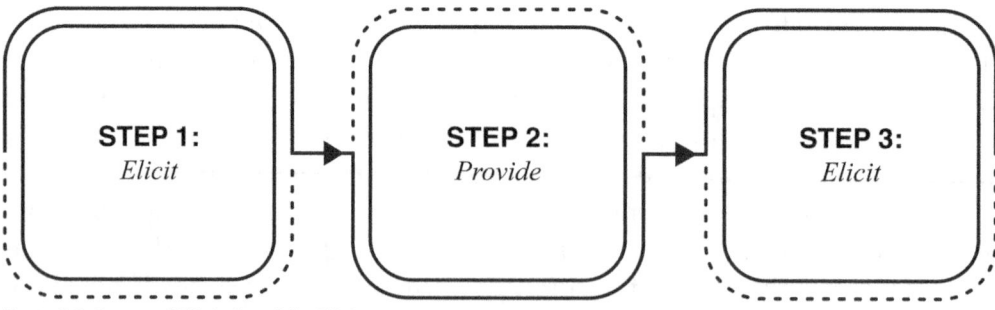

Figure 9.4 Steps of Elicit-Provide-Elicit

identify gaps in a teacher's knowledge in order to better provide appropriate support. Whenever a coach provides support in the form of specific resources or suggestions, they should always first explore what the teacher already knows and understands before offering additional resources and strategies.

Step 1: Elicit

The coach asks the teacher what they already know about a topic they are discussing. Examples include the following:

- Would you be willing to share with me what you know about PBL?
- What do you already understand about PBL?
- What resources have you used to help you learn about PBL?
- What questions do you have about PBL?
- What more would you like to know about PBL?

Not only does this opening empower a teacher by assuming that they know at least something about the topic, but it also ensures that a coach does not waste time by providing information that the teacher already knows. Additionally, the initial elicit allows a coach to listen for specific gaps in understanding and misconceptions. Armed with a clear awareness of what a teacher knows, doesn't know, and may be confused by, a coach can implement a more targeted approach by providing information, including resources, that fit a teacher's needs. Because a teacher may not share everything they know at the first invitation, a coach should be prepared to elicit additional knowledge with follow-up questions and statements like the following:

- And what else do you know?
- Tell me more about what you know.
- What else do you think is important to say about this topic?

Step 2: Provide

After ensuring that a teacher's knowledge has been completely tapped, the coach asks permission to provide resources. Asking permission situates the teacher as the final decision-maker. If the teacher gives permission, the coach moves forward.

- Would it be okay for me to share some resources with you?
- Are you willing to review some resources that I have that might add to your understanding?
- Are you ready for some suggestions?

After receiving permission, a coach provides multiple resources or strategies. For example, in the case of Ms. Shah, Jonathon might provide two or three resources that might add to her understanding of PBL. Or, if a teacher would like to incorporate more literacy in their classroom, a coach might provide three or four options for literacy strategies the teacher might try. Offering options places the coach, who has just assumed a mentor stance by providing suggestions and resources, in a position to quickly return to a coaching stance by asking which of the options would be most suitable for the teacher given their context.

Step 3: Elicit

After providing options to the teacher, the coach now elicits the teacher's reaction to the information provided. Questions at this point of the conversation might include the following:

- What do you think about these resources? Does one stand out to you more than the others?
- Which of the strategies would you like to try?
- Would you like additional information about any of these options?
- Which of these do you think would best support your goals?
- Which of these would work best with your students?
- How might you modify one of these to meet your needs?
- After hearing these options, what other ideas do you have?
- Have you ever tried something like this before? What was the outcome?

Here's how elicit-provide-elicit worked with Ms. Shah:

> **Elicit.** To start coaching, Jonathon asked Ms. Shah if she would be willing to share with him the materials that she had received at the conference and to tell him anything else she knew about PBL. There were a few rounds of, "What else can you tell me?" before Ms. Shah was out of ideas and information.
> **Provide.** Next, Jonathon asked Ms. Shah if it would be okay if he shared a few additional PBL resources with her that might fill in some additional details. Based on her understanding, Jonathon chose a few resources to share with her to read before his next visit and asked her to consider some standards and/or units that might lend themselves to PBL.
> **Elicit.** On his next coaching visit, Jonathon asked Ms. Shah to respond to the resources he had provided. She shared some thoughts about the new information as well as some additional knowledge she had picked up over the week by talking to other teachers. Based on her current understanding of PBL, Ms. Shah and Jonathon decided to move forward with co-planning a unit.

Co-Planning

Co-planning is a powerful tool for a Coaching Behaviors approach. During co-planning, a coach and a teacher work together as partners who each bring essential information to the planning activity. While the coach is the expert of the tools, strategies, or approach being studied, the teacher is always the expert of their own content and their own context. Context includes the teacher's knowledge of their own classroom, including knowledge of their students; knowledge of their school, district, and community; and knowledge of themselves as a teacher.

During her PBL co-planning sessions with Jonathon, for example, Ms. Shah was the science expert. She also knew her students, her own approach to teaching, and her community best and, therefore, made all the final decisions. Jonathon was able to use his knowledge of PBL to guide Ms. Shah's planning through questioning and additional resources. They planned over the course of a few coaching sessions, and Ms. Shah asked Jonathon to create several of the resources for the unit.

When Ms. Shah implemented her PBL unit, Jonathon continued the coaching partnership by shifting his strategy from co-planning to engaging Ms. Shah in reflective thinking. He was no longer the expert of the tools because Ms. Shah could now see them in action and reflect on how, when, and why they worked or didn't work for her students, her context, and her subject. As soon as Ms. Shah had what she needed to move forward, Jonathon shifted to Coaching Thinking.

Brainstorming Technique

Sometimes teachers don't know what they know and coaches find themselves working with teachers who just want their coaches to provide them with answers. Often, teachers who respond in this way lack the confidence to trust their own thinking. How can coaches encourage them, empower them, and increase their sense of self-efficacy while also meeting the need for support?

The brainstorming technique is one way to do all of these things. To use this technique, the coach simply asks, "Would you be willing to brainstorm some ideas together?" If the teacher is seeking answers, they will likely respond in the affirmative. With permission to brainstorm together, the coach next asks the teacher to start the brainstorming.

By asking the teacher to begin, the coach positions the teacher as the leader of their work. At the same time, the coach positions themselves in a support role through which they can still provide ideas.

Using Past Experiences

Even when teachers are learning something completely new, experiences they have had in the past can inform their thinking and support their implementation. In Coaching Behaviors, a coach should not only explore a teacher's understanding of a particular approach, but they might also want to use questions that ask how the teacher's prior experience might impact the current learning. The coach might ask a teacher about past experiences with the following questions:

- Have you tried a completely new approach in the past? How did it turn out for you? What made it successful/unsuccessful?
- Have you tried something similar to this new approach in the past? What worked well for you?
- What do you know from past experiences that might help you in this new approach?

Using past experiences can often build a teacher's confidence and encourage them to try something new even when it might seem risky to do so.

Considerations for Early-Career and Alternative-Entry Teachers

Teachers with limited experience in schools—beginning teachers or alternative-entry teachers, for example—may need more "expert" support from coaches than other teachers who have more experiences to draw from. These teachers will, at times, need to be given resources to support their instructional goals. Yes, it is okay to offer teachers suggestions, and coaches should feel comfortable providing options for these teachers as soon as they are needed with the goal to shift from a mentoring stance back to a coaching stance as quickly as possible.

Boxes 9.2 through 9.4 explore further considerations for Coaching Behaviors.

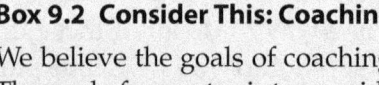

Box 9.2 Consider This: Coaching vs. Mentoring

We believe the goals of coaching and mentoring are very different. The goal of a mentor is to provide a teacher with the knowledge and tools they need to be successful right away. Mentors give information to a teacher, whereas coaches elicit information from a teacher. A coach's role is to draw knowledge from a teacher and help them build on that knowledge using their own internal capacity. When a coach uses a Coaching Behaviors approach, they briefly assume the stance of a mentor but always maintains the role of a coach. Even while a coach gives a teacher resources, they do so in a way that allows the teacher to use their own ideas to engage in reflective thinking on the resources and adapt them to their own needs.

>
> **Box 9.3 Quick Tip: Providing Resources**
>
> The keys to providing resources in a Coaching Behaviors approach include the following:
>
> 1. Ensure that a teacher's knowledge has been fully tapped and they do not have the resources on their own to move forward.
> 2. Always ask if the teacher is ready to receive suggestions.
> 3. Provide multiple evidence-based *options* for the teacher. Providing one strategy positions the coach as the expert with *the one best choice* while providing multiple options *empowers* the teacher to make the best choice for them and their classroom.
> 4. Quickly move back to a coaching stance by eliciting the teacher's reaction to the information or strategies provided.

>
> **Box 9.4 On Your Own: Making Connections**
> - How does the Coaching Behaviors approach align with the approaches, models, and theories presented in Chapter 3?
> - How do specific strategies presented in this chapter align with the approaches, models, and theories?
> - What other strategies do you use in coaching that might support a focus on Coaching Behaviors?

Addressing Equity through Coaching Behaviors

To address equity while using a Coaching Behaviors approach, a coach should seek out strategies that support equitable outcomes for all students every time a teacher requests resources and information. For example, if a teacher requests support for meeting the needs of students who are identified as academically or intellectually gifted, a coach should provide a menu of techniques that promote equitable differentiation strategies and techniques in the classroom (i.e., not allow the use of more work to equate with increased cognitive demand) and options for how the classroom conditions may impact the teacher's academically or intellectually gifted students. If a teacher needs strategies for scaffolding, a coach should provide strategies that scaffold instruction for a variety of learner needs. If a teacher requests help identifying student resources for a lesson, a coach should find resources that depict multiple cultures and different perspectives. When a coach provides support aligned with equitable outcomes, he takes a first step toward ensuring that equity is addressed in a classroom.

Conclusion

While coaches should always prioritize teacher agency, there are times when teachers simply do not have the resources to do the thinking on their own. In these cases, coaches provide resources and information by briefly shifting to a mentoring role with the intention of returning to a coaching role as quickly as possible.

Box 9.5 will help you reflect on the contents of your teaching toolbox, and Box 9.6 offers further tips for Coaching Behaviors.

Box 9.5 On Your Own: Analyze Your Teaching Toolbox

Consider your toolbox of instructional practices. Where are your resources limited? Where do you need to add resources in order to be able to provide options for teachers?

Box 9.6 Tips for Coaching Behaviors

- Teachers and coaches both have expertise. As a coach, know when and how to share information as necessary. Provide resources only when a teacher cannot move forward on their own without them.
- Balance the partnership during co-planning. You may be the expert of strategies, but the teacher is the expert of their context and how strategies will be implemented within that context.
- Be wary of suggestions! Teachers with limited resources may ask for suggestions. If they do, provide multiple options, not just one.
- Shift quickly from Coaching Behaviors to Coaching Thinking as soon as the teacher is ready to move forward with a particular strategy.

10

Integration of Approaches

Priority Approaches

Until now, we have discussed the four approaches to coaching—Coaching Values, Coaching Beliefs, Coaching Thinking, and Coaching Behaviors—as four discrete approaches. Our intention was to clearly define and differentiate the purpose, goals, and tools of each. Now that they have been described individually and separately, however, it is important to understand that these are not actually discrete approaches used in isolation from one another. Instead, each is a priority approach that helps a coach determine where to start. *After a priority approach has been identified and coaching has begun, these approaches should be used together as a coach moves through coaching cycles and responds flexibly to the needs of a teacher.* Before we discuss and practice integration of the approaches, let's take one final look at how to apply the priority approaches individually to coaching scenarios (Box 10.1).

166 ◆ Integration of Approaches

After a priority approach has been identified and coaching has begun, these approaches should be used in concert with one another as a coach moves through coaching cycles and responds flexibly to the needs of a teacher.

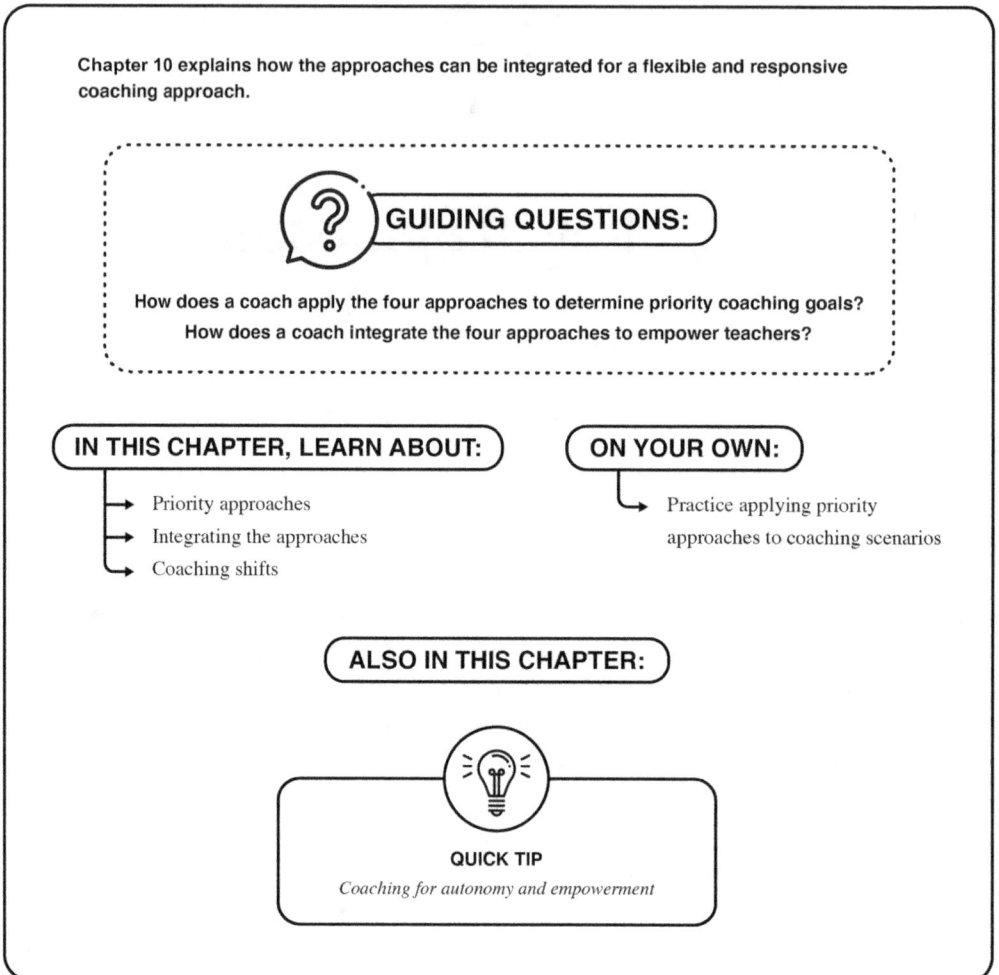

Figure 10.1 Chapter 10 Overview

> **Box 10.1 On Your Own: Scenario Review**
> Review each of the scenarios in this section. Identify key characteristics of the scenario that would help you determine where to begin. Select a priority approach for each teacher.

Ms. West

Ms. West

Ms. West is a new teacher who thinks that teacher-centered, lecture-based instruction is the most effective teaching strategy for all students, but she complains because her students are not engaged. During lectures, instead of taking notes, they put their heads down and sleep or play on their phones. Ms. West has recently returned from a post-observation conference with her principal. The principal told her she needed to be less "teacher-centric" and increase student collaboration. She is determined to make some changes because her job is important to her, so she has reluctantly come to you for support, but she does not think that collaboration is the answer. During her student teaching, she saw other teachers implement collaborative group work, but when she observed, it seemed that one student was always doing most of the work while everyone else sat around. She says that when she was growing up, teachers just gave kids information and expected them to learn it. She and her friends did fine. Nowadays, though, students expect to have "fun" during learning. Learning isn't supposed to be fun, she thinks. It is supposed to be hard and students are supposed to just do the work.

What is your priority approach and why?

Ms. Torres

Ms. Torres

Ms. Torres began teaching twenty years ago. She reached out to you to request coaching support. During your first meeting, she states that she would really like to improve her use of collaboration strategies. She says that when she began her career, lecture-based teaching was the standard, and collaborative groups were rare, and she has never received training in using collaboration strategies. She does have some go-to strategies she has tried to use like think-pair-share, consensus census, and jigsaw, but aren't working well. She is eager to learn and willing to take risks in her classroom, and she invites you to visit and see her collaboration in action. When you visit, she is implementing the jigsaw strategy. Structurally, she implements the strategy correctly. Students begin in home groups to divide the learning material and then move to expert groups to become experts on their sections. They return to their home groups as experts to share information and teach their peers. Ms. Torres becomes more and more frustrated throughout the activity because instead of working collaboratively, students are copying from one another. Ms. Torres repeatedly redirects students and reminds them that they are supposed to be teaching one another instead of copying, but the students are confused. The information they are supposed to be "teaching" their peers is not complex; it is simply recall-level answers like dates, names, and definitions from a reading assigned in their textbook. "Teaching" seems to just mean reading their answers out loud. Students know they could just as easily and quickly have completed the work independently.

What is your priority approach and why?

Mr. King

Mr. King

Mr. King has been teaching for ten years. When he began teaching, he used innovative approaches to teaching that emphasized collaboration in the classroom. He regularly used project-based and service-based learning and emphasized group goal-setting, student accountability to peers, and self-assessment. Over the years, his emphasis on collaboration skills and his use of innovative practices have waned. Most of the time when you stop by his classroom, students are sitting in rows reading from a textbook or listening and taking notes while he lectures. You have had a couple of conversations with him in the hallways that concern you. Mr. King says that he used to love teaching, but these days students just do not care about their learning and he does not have time to do any of the things he used to enjoy. Rather than creating relevant units that emphasize real-life skills and critical thinking, Mr. King says that all he has time to do now is get through the content. With the emphasis on testing these days, he needs to be sure his students memorize the facts and can answer the multiple-choice questions. When you try to engage him in discussions about bringing more collaboration to the classroom, he says that he knows how important it is for his students but as long as the state does not see value in 21st-century skills, he just cannot worry about it.

What is your priority approach and why?

Mr. Bell

Mr. Bell

Mr. Bell is a lateral-entry teacher, and it is the beginning of his first semester. He has been told during his onboarding that the district values collaboration, and he understands why collaborative learning is important. He jumps right in and uses group activities on a regular basis, but he is not really sure he is doing it right. When he hears you are available to help, he invites you to his classroom right away. When you arrive, he is giving students instructions for their collaborative task. Students will work in groups of four or five to create a skit that explains one stage of the life cycle. Mr. Bell tells students they have 15 minutes to complete the task. When time is up, they will need to be ready to share a 1- to 3-minute skit with their peers. He tells them to find groups and get started. Students quickly find their own groups and then socialize for a while before getting to work. About 10 minutes in, Mr. Bell tells students that they will begin skits in 10 minutes so it is time to focus. At this point, three of the seven groups are working together to plan. In two of the groups, one student is writing out the script on their own while others are checking cell phones, socializing, and wandering around the room. The final two groups have not yet started. After about 25 minutes, Mr. Bell tells students it is time to start the skits. When you debrief the visit with Mr. Bell, he says that he was disappointed in the end results and was not really sure students collaborated much. None of the skits lasted more than 30 seconds, and none of them showed a sophisticated or complex understanding of the material.

What is your priority approach and why?

Reflection

How did you do? Were you able to identify a different priority approach for each scenario? If not, go back and take another look. The details of each scenario should lead you to identify a different priority approach for each teacher.

Putting It All Together: Integrating the Approaches

Although we have introduced each approach as a separate entity, even when a coach prioritizes one coaching approach, they will likely integrate multiple approaches as they respond flexibly to each teacher's needs. Coaches may even use multiple approaches—or all four!—within a single coaching conversation.

For example, a coaching relationship that prioritizes Coaching Behaviors may quickly move into Coaching Values if a teacher becomes frustrated or overwhelmed as they tackle a behavior that does not come naturally or easily. They may need to be reminded why they chose to make this change, why the change is important to them, and why they should persevere through their challenges. A coaching relationship that prioritizes Coaching Beliefs may quickly move into Coaching Thinking, because a disorienting dilemma causes a major shift in a teacher's beliefs about student capability, for example, and motivates them to change their practice. Figure 10.2 provides an illustration of the integrated framework.

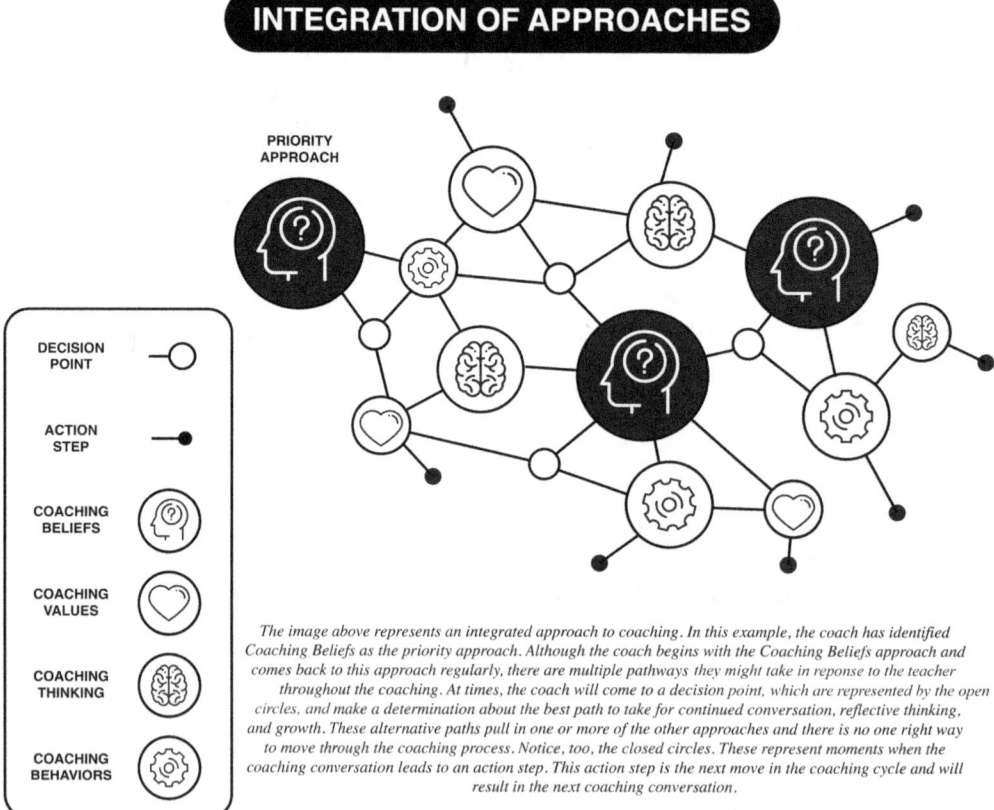

The image above represents an integrated approach to coaching. In this example, the coach has identified Coaching Beliefs as the priority approach. Although the coach begins with the Coaching Beliefs approach and comes back to this approach regularly, there are multiple pathways they might take in reponse to the teacher throughout the coaching. At times, the coach will come to a decision point, which are represented by the open circles, and make a determination about the best path to take for continued conversation, reflective thinking, and growth. These alternative paths pull in one or more of the other approaches and there is no one right way to move through the coaching process. Notice, too, the closed circles. These represent moments when the coaching conversation leads to an action step. This action step is the next move in the coaching cycle and will result in the next coaching conversation.

Figure 10.2 Integrated Framework

Let's start with the examples in Box 10.1 and consider how and why a coach might shift from one approach to another within a coaching cycle.

Ms. West—Priority Approach: Coaching Beliefs

Ms. West has some strongly defined beliefs about herself, her students, and teaching in general. These beliefs—that students should all learn simply by listening and working hard, that collaboration is an ineffective teaching strategy, and that she is the gatekeeper for all the knowledge in the classroom as evidenced by her lecture-based approach—do not reflect best or equitable learning practices for students. Given this scenario, her coach should focus on changing Ms. West's beliefs.

Ms. West

Other approaches may come into play like this:

Values: Although Ms. West is willing to make some changes because her job is valuable to her and her administration requires those changes, she will be more likely to persevere and to succeed if she finds value in the changes she attempts to make. If she does not find her own value in the changes, she will simply comply with a top-down directive, which may lead to resentment rather than engagement. To increase and support internal motivation, her coach should explore Ms. West's values and help her find a way to connect her values to her work to integrate collaboration strategies in her classroom.

Thinking: Ms. West has observed ineffective implementation of collaboration strategies during which not all students were held accountable for the work or the learning. Because this is what she saw, she will be likely to reproduce the same implementation mistakes she observed. When Ms. West is ready to try implementation in her classroom, her coach will need to provide planning support. Additionally, her coach should facilitate a follow-up reflective conversation to help Ms. West consider the difference between what she has seen in other classrooms and what happened in her own classroom.

Behavior: Because Ms. West is a new teacher and has prioritized lecture-based, teacher-centered strategies until now, she may not have a variety of collaboration tools and strategies from which to choose. When she is ready, her coach should be prepared to share resources and allow Ms. West to choose which tool or strategy she'd like to try.

Ms. Torres—Priority Approach: Coaching Thinking

Ms. Torres

Ms. Torres wants to become more intentional and more effective when implementing the jigsaw strategy. Therefore, improving her practice through Coaching Thinking is her coach's priority for this scenario.

Other approaches may come into play like this:

Values: Ms. Torres is frustrated by the results of her attempts at facilitating collaboration. Although the overall goal here is to emphasize her thinking about how to implement the jigsaw strategy and other collaboration strategies more effectively, she may benefit from a values-based discussion when she faces challenges to remind her why she chose this goal and to help her maintain persistence towards her goal.

Beliefs: Because Ms. Torres is frustrated and has had bad experiences so far with the jigsaw strategy, she may begin to believe that her students are incapable of collaboration or that she herself does not have the teaching style or capacity to use collaborative strategies effectively in her classroom. Her coach should listen for beliefs like these in all coaching conversations, and if and when limiting beliefs arise, the coach should use beliefs-based strategies as necessary.

Behavior: Perhaps Ms. Torres decides she would like to try a strategy other than jigsaw to start because she is already frustrated with this strategy. Although Ms. Torres says she has a few go-to strategies, this could be a time for her coach to ask if she would like some additional strategy suggestions. Of course, her coach should provide multiple options, ask which suggestion Ms. Torres would like to try first, and then move back into Coaching Thinking. Another good time for Coaching Behaviors in this scenario is at the end of a microcoaching cycle. Perhaps Ms. Torres does start with jigsaw and after a few rounds of coaching, she effectively implements the strategy. It is time now to move either to a new goal or to a new strategy within this goal. If Ms. Torres does not have additional strategies to try but wants to stick with her overall goal, the coach may shift briefly into Coaching Behaviors to provide additional strategies for her to choose from.

Integration of Approaches ◆ 173

Mr. King—Priority Approach: Coaching Values

Mr. King

Mr. King exhibits signs of stress and burnout, and needs to work to realign his practice with his values to ensure that he continues to be an engaged teacher.

Other approaches may come into play like this:

Beliefs: Because Mr. King is burned out, the first priority of the coach is to reengage him in his classroom; however, we can see in this vignette that his burnout is impacting beliefs about his students. He has already said that students do not care about learning anymore. What other beliefs might he be harboring about his students or about himself? Although his coach should prioritize Coaching Values in this scenario, they may need to simultaneously address some of his beliefs.

Thinking: Although Mr. King may not need support with implementing specific strategies, he may benefit from engaging in an action research project with his coach. Sparking his curiosity and developing a research plan may provide him the additional challenge he needs to reengage. When Mr. King is ready, his coach might consider ways that they can partner with him to affect learning for both Mr. King and for themselves.

Behavior: As a highly experienced teacher, Mr. King may not need the kind of resources a new or lateral-entry teacher may need; however, as earlier, reigniting his curiosity and interest is one way to help Mr. King reengage. Perhaps there is a strategy or approach he has always wanted to try but simply has not had time. In this case, his coach can become a valuable research partner to gather information and resources.

Mr. Bell—Priority Approach: Coaching Behaviors

Mr. Bell

As a new teacher, Mr. Bell's engagement is high as is his awareness of his needs. He does not have a knowledge bank of resources to draw from to implement effective collaborative group work. He needs to become more intentional and to fill his toolbox with techniques and strategies that would support more effective implementation.

Other approaches may come into play like this:

Values: Mr. Bell knows that student collaboration is a district value and although he understands the need, he may not feel that collaboration aligns with what is *most* important to him in his classroom. If this is the case, he may be attempting to implement collaboration in his classroom in response to a top-down directive, like Ms. West. When things get difficult or do not work as planned, he may not have the internal motivation to draw on to support his continued perseverance. To increase the chance of success, his coach may need to activate Mr. Bell's internal motivation by connecting collaboration to his values. A values conversation may reveal, for example, that Mr. Bell became a teacher because he believes in the power of teaching to prepare students to be successful professionals. He may value this preparation for the professional world above all other aspects of teaching. Tying his use of collaboration strategies to student preparation for the professional world will increase his internal motivation.
Beliefs: As a lateral-entry teacher, Mr. Bell may lack confidence in himself and his abilities to manage collaborative groups effectively. His coach should listen for beliefs about himself as well as his students that may inhibit his progress or impact equitable teaching and learning in his classroom and should shift into Coaching Beliefs as necessary.
Thinking: As soon as his coach has provided Mr. Bell with options for collaboration, they will shift into a Coaching Thinking approach to help him implement one of these approaches. Perhaps Mr. Bell chooses to use group roles the next time he asks his students to create content-based skits. His coach can help him think about what kinds of roles would be most effective to support group structure as well as different types of thinking for more complex understanding of the content. Furthermore, his coach can guide him in reflective thinking after implementation to determine whether his roles worked and what evidence he has to support his thinking.

Flexible and Responsive Coaching

Clearly, even when a coach has identified a priority approach for coaching, they should be prepared to use the other approaches of coaching as the need arises. A coach must always be flexible and shift from one set of tools to another in response to a teacher's needs in the moment. Even within one coaching session, a coach may find themselves moving into and out of different approaches.

Remembering Mr. Parsons

Mr. Parsons

Remember Mr. Parsons, way back in Chapter 4? Mr. Parsons was the first teacher for whom Jolie collected data and the one who caught Jolie off guard by asking her how his lesson went immediately after it ended. How might Jolie have approached Mr. Parsons differently using foundations of coaching and the CoachED framework we have described?

After efficiently side-stepping his request for evaluative feedback, Jolie's next step would have been to plan for the upcoming reflective conversation about the data without Mr. Parsons. While a timely follow-up is essential, a coach should also take time for their own thinking and planning prior to a coaching conversation. Although a conversation may not necessarily go as planned, beginning with a plan will help a coach keep priorities in mind so that they can adjust to the needs of the teacher while maintaining a track toward the overall coaching goal.

Here's what Jolie knew about Mr. Parsons from their initial encounters: His engagement and awareness were high since he had already chosen a goal for growth related to more effective facilitation of collaborative group work. In addition, Jolie had just facilitated a professional learning session at his school related to collaborative group work strategies, so she knew that his knowledge was high. On the other hand, what Jolie had observed in Mr. Parsons's classroom showed that his application was low. Given this profile—high knowledge, engagement, and awareness with low application—Jolie would have prioritized a Coaching Thinking approach for her follow-up conversation; however, with the knowledge and understanding that other approaches might also come into play, she is prepared to switch between approaches as necessary.

As you read the following transcript, see if you can identify shifts in coaching approaches that inform Jolie's coaching "moves," and specific techniques.

Jolie: Hi, Mr. Parsons! Thanks again for letting me visit your classroom earlier today. Have you had a chance to review the data I left with you?
Mr. Parsons: Yes, I took a look over lunch. What did you think? How did it go?
Jolie: That's just what I was going to ask you! What did you think? How did it go?

Mr. Parsons: Well, I'm not really sure. I was really hoping that I would see more students talking to each other. They didn't really talk to each other, did they?

Jolie: Okay, so you didn't see the students talking much to one another. Let's start with what went well, though. Is there anything that you feel went well or that you are proud of?

Mr. Parsons: I'm a little proud of myself for trying something new. It feels a little scary to let kids do the learning on their own when I don't usually let them do that.

Jolie: Yes, sometimes it is scary to turn learning over to students. Can you tell me a little more about why it was important to you to focus on student collaboration this year?

Mr. Parsons: I know I haven't been teaching for very long, but I see in the world outside school how important it is for people to be able to work together. Most importantly, I see how important it is for people to have empathy for one another and to be able to disagree with one another respectfully. There's so little real conversation these days.

Jolie: So even though it's scary, you really want to help your students learn to work together, disagree with one another, and have empathy for people who might not be exactly like them.

Mr. Parsons: Exactly. I feel some of those skills get missed in other classes, and I have the opportunity in my class to address them.

Jolie: Let's go back to the data. You said that you were disappointed that more students didn't interact with one another. Looking at the data, does anything specifically surprise you?

Mr. Parsons: Not really. The students with the most interactions are really my top students. I'd expect them to be doing the work, and they already have really good collaboration skills.

Jolie: What about the students who didn't interact with others? Does anything surprise you?

Mr. Parsons: No, these students don't have it in them to collaborate. I don't know what to do with them. I don't think they'll ever be able to successfully navigate the world of work. They are disagreeable and lazy.

Jolie: They don't have it in them. Let's focus on specifics for a minute and talk about Joey. He didn't interact with his classmates during this lesson. Have you ever seen him working well with others?

Mr. Parsons: Oh, sure. He collaborates in sports and other activities outside the classroom all the time.

Jolie: What do you think makes him successful with collaboration in those activities?

Mr. Parsons: Well, he enjoys those things. He doesn't enjoy my class.

Jolie: His engagement with outside activities is higher than his engagement in your class. What else can you tell me about Joey?

Mr. Parsons: Well, he's also really competitive and enjoys a challenge. It's amazing to see how hard he works on some things when I never see that kind of perseverance in the classroom. I guess he's not really one of the lazy ones. Just lazy in my class.

Jolie: Okay, let's keep Joey in mind as we continue our conversation about collaboration. What do you know about what makes effective collaboration strategies?

Mr. Parsons: Just what you said in professional learning last week. I know it is important for every student to have something to do and that I should keep the groups small.

Jolie: And how did you plan to meet those criteria in this lesson?

Mr. Parsons: Well, I kept the groups to no more than four and gave them roles, and I thought the assignment was big enough to keep everyone busy. They had to find resources, read and collect information, and create a presentation. That should've kept them all busy.

Jolie: Can you tell me more about what you mean when you describe the assignment as "big"?

Mr. Parsons: Well, enough to keep them busy. There was enough to do.

Jolie: Talk to me about the relationship between a "big" assignment and a rigorous assignment.

Mr. Parsons: Hmmmm, well, I guess I haven't thought much about rigor in creating collaborative assignments. I just want to keep the kids busy.

Jolie: Your goal in creating collaborative assignments is to keep the students busy.

Mr. Parsons: Yes, but I guess that's more of a management strategy now that I think about it. I'm trying to keep the kids under control. I don't want them to run out of things to do and start playing *Fortnite* or *Halo* on their computers or making Snapchat and TikTok videos on their phones.

Jolie: Let's return to the data for a minute. What would the data look like in your ideal scenario? If the students had collaborated as you intended?

Mr. Parsons: Well, I would've liked for them to talk to each other to grapple with and process their research. The data would've showed students sharing information with each other and making connections to create something new from all the research.

Jolie: And how might you have planned differently to make that happen?

Mr. Parsons: Maybe if I had given them more challenging roles. I mean, with the roles I gave them, one student could just read the texts and send them to the PowerPoint creator. The presenter didn't really have to do anything until the whole thing was completed. Maybe I need to rethink my roles the next time I plan for a collaborative activity. If I can rethink my roles and give all of the students a more challenging piece of the assignment, they might have to work together a little bit more to get it done.

Jolie: And what about Joey? Do you think this plan would have any impact on him?

Mr. Parsons: Well, I don't know for sure, but as I said, I know he likes a challenge. Maybe if he had more of a challenge in my class he might like it more. Maybe he'd be more engaged.

Jolie: Well, it sounds like we might have a plan for moving forward. You'd like to use different roles with your next collaborative activity. How can I support you in that work?

Mr. Parsons: Well, I don't really know what kinds of roles to use. Do you think you can help me with considering new roles and using them in a new activity?

Jolie: Of course! Would it be okay if I send you a few resources to review before my next visit and then the next time I come, we can discuss those resources and start co-planning?

Mr. Parsons: That sounds great!

Coaching Shifts

Did you notice the shifts? Jolie began with her priority approach—Coaching Thinking—by returning Mr. Parsons's question about how the lesson went back on him. Rather than responding to his question as an expert, she asked him to reflect on his own experience of the class to determine how the lesson went for himself. And then, Jolie shifted approaches throughout the conversation in response to Mr. Parsons:

- **Shift #1.** Jolie shifts from Coaching Thinking to Coaching Values when Mr. Parsons reveals that it feels a little scary to turn the ownership of learning over to his students. By focusing on why it is important to Mr. Parsons to do so, Jolie activates his internal motivation to make this change despite challenges.
- **Shift #2.** Jolie returns to her priority approach—Coaching Thinking—by referencing the data and asking for Mr. Parsons to reflect on his understanding of the data.
- **Shift #3.** Jolie shifts from Coaching Thinking to Coaching Beliefs when Mr. Parsons makes specific statements about his students that reveal beliefs that may get in the way of equitable instruction in his classroom. Mr. Parsons states that certain students in his classroom "don't have it in them" to collaborate. Jolie uses the Focus on Specifics strategy to challenge Mr. Parsons's beliefs.

- **Shift #4.** Jolie briefly addresses Coaching Behaviors by asking Mr. Parsons what he knows about effective collaboration.
- **Shift #5.** Jolie returns to her priority approach—Coaching Thinking—by asking Mr. Parsons how he used his understanding of effective collaboration in his lesson plan. She deepens his thinking by exploring his language, specifically his use of the word "big," returning again to the data, and asking Mr. Parsons about how he might plan more intentionally for effective collaboration in his classroom.

While most of this coaching conversation emphasizes a Coaching Thinking approach, Jolie weaves in Coaching Values, Coaching Beliefs, and Coaching Behaviors as opportunities arise in the conversation. Shifting to these approaches, even briefly, helps Mr. Parsons maintain internal motivation and focus on equity in his classroom. Box 10.2 shows how this conversation can be used to coach for autonomy and empowerment.

> **Box 10.2 Quick Tip: Coaching for Autonomy and Empowerment**
>
> Remember that coaches can add to or have a deeper understanding of a teacher's needs within their chosen goal. In the case of Mr. Parsons, Jolie knew from her observation that one of the elements of teaching and learning impacting his ability to implement effective collaboration was a lack of rigor in the classroom; however, because Jolie works from a framework of autonomy and empowerment, she found a way to weave rigor into Mr. Parsons's goals for collaborative group work rather than suggesting he change his goal. Notice in the transcript ways Jolie addresses rigor within the collaborative group work goal.

Although coaches will not always use all approaches in every coaching conversation and although they certainly will not use every tool presented in this text, understanding the approaches individually and recognizing the tools and techniques that can be effective within each approach helps coaches respond flexibly to teachers.

Conclusion

Coaching is a complex exchange between two people, and coaches must engage with teachers and follow their lead using whichever tools are most likely to cause a shift in practice that improves student outcomes. Ultimately, the flexible use of these approaches cultivates a relationship between teacher and coach that is humanizing, professional, and centered on student learning.

The CoachED framework is designed with the belief that coaching is one avenue toward improving and maintaining the well-being of teachers. *No matter the approach used within our framework (Coaching Values, Beliefs, Thinking, or Behaviors), the coach must always hold the empowerment of the teacher at the center of their work.* When we empower individuals like teachers, we strengthen both classrooms and whole school communities.

11

Getting Started

Identifying a Priority Approach

Coaching is complex work and should be intentionally planned. As we have seen in coaches' dilemmas throughout this book, there are times when a coach will find that teachers who request support for a new strategy may need additional coaching around the values and beliefs that underlie how they work in their classrooms. Coaches must address these additional coaching needs in a subtle and empowering way, not only to maintain a trusting relationship with a teacher but also to protect the teacher's autonomy and self-efficacy. Throughout this book, we have presented research that guides coaching, foundational coaching techniques for all coaching relationships, the CoachED framework for making decisions about how to approach coaching with individual teachers, and strategies for navigating coaching experiences and conversations within those approaches. We have provided tips and techniques, vignettes and transcripts, and many examples from our own coaching practices. But how does a coach begin identifying a priority approach in the first place?

A priority approach is based on a conversation or series of conversations that provides insight into a teacher's individual context, including their values and beliefs. These insights provide clues for a coach about what is important to the teacher and how their values play out in their classroom. When a coach listens well, these insights tell them if the teacher's beliefs are aligned with their values and practices and whether they are intentionally planning lessons and activities and analyzing the results to ensure equitable, positive academic

DOI: 10.4324/9701003186045-13

Coaching is complex work and should be intentionally planned.

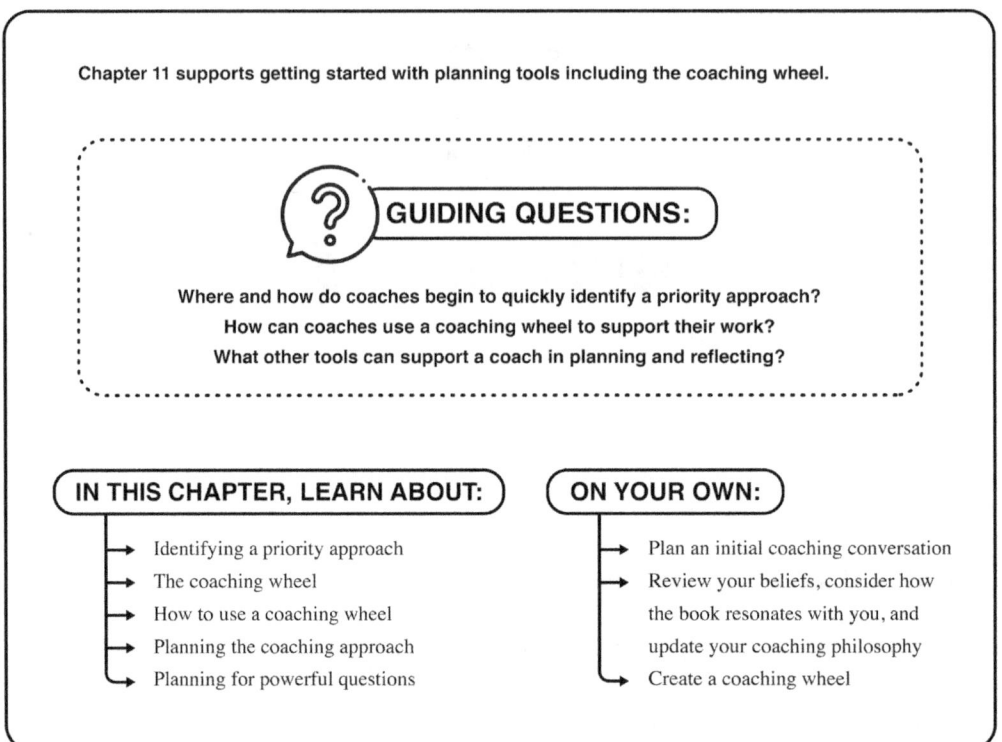

Figure 11.1 Chapter 11 Overview

and social and emotional outcomes for their students. Answers to these questions will inform their coach and help the coach determine if they will prioritize values, beliefs, thinking, or behaviors in their work with the teacher.

Identifying a priority approach is not always simple or clear, and a coach may need tools to support initial conversations that will help reveal deep and personal insights about a teacher. Walking into a teacher's classroom, making an introduction, and asking the teacher how they would like to begin is not typically enough to help a coach launch a coaching cycle with an intentional priority approach. When a teacher is willing and even eager to work with a coach, they still may not know where they want to start. Even if the teacher does know where to start, there may be deeper, underlying values and beliefs conflicts they are unaware of that must be coached alongside their own goals.

So, how does a coach structure initial conversations to gain insight into a teacher's context and begin to develop an understanding of their priority approach while developing a relationship with a new teacher? We will share a tool that we initially encountered through a health coaching model and now use to help guide our initial conversations with teachers.

The Coaching Wheel

We encountered the idea of a coaching wheel through the Personalized Health Inventory used by the U.S. Department of Veterans Affairs' Office of Patient Centered Care and Cultural Transformation (2019), but coaching wheels are used in many approaches to and traditions of coaching. A simple Google search will reveal wheels related to health and wellness coaching, business coaching, financial coaching, and life coaching, among others. The wheel allows a coach to begin a coaching partnership by prioritizing the teacher's own self-assessment.

The Personal Health Inventory is designed to allow patients to see a holistic view of their health and make individual decisions about health and wellness goals. The wheel is divided into sections with a different aspect of health in each section. Patients consider the wheel and rate the personal importance of the topic represented in each section.

In education, overall goals for improvement are often mandated based on school-wide or district-wide improvement goals. The wheel for instructional coaching, then, is often designed to support a teacher in identifying areas of growth *within a given context*. Although ideally a coaching wheel would be filled with topics important to an individual teacher, instructional coaches will often begin with a wheel adapted to a particular school or district goal.

The key to creating the wheel is to populate the sections of the wheel with elements of teaching and learning related to a larger initiative within which a teacher can choose a particular element. The wheel provides a concrete way to make meaning of and act on the teacher's goal.

Here are some examples:

Scenario 1: A district has decided to focus on social and emotional learning by integrating SEL into academic content across disciplines. They have adopted Yoder's ten instructional practices for promoting SEL (Yoder, 2014) to help their teachers learn to incorporate SEL into their academic instruction on a daily basis. The sections of the wheel indicate the ten instructional practices (Figure 11.2).
Scenario 2: A district has asked their coaches to work with beginning teachers on foundational classroom instruction using RTI International's High Quality Teaching and Learning Framework. The sections of the wheel indicate the six practices identified by the RTI framework.

184 ◆ Getting Started

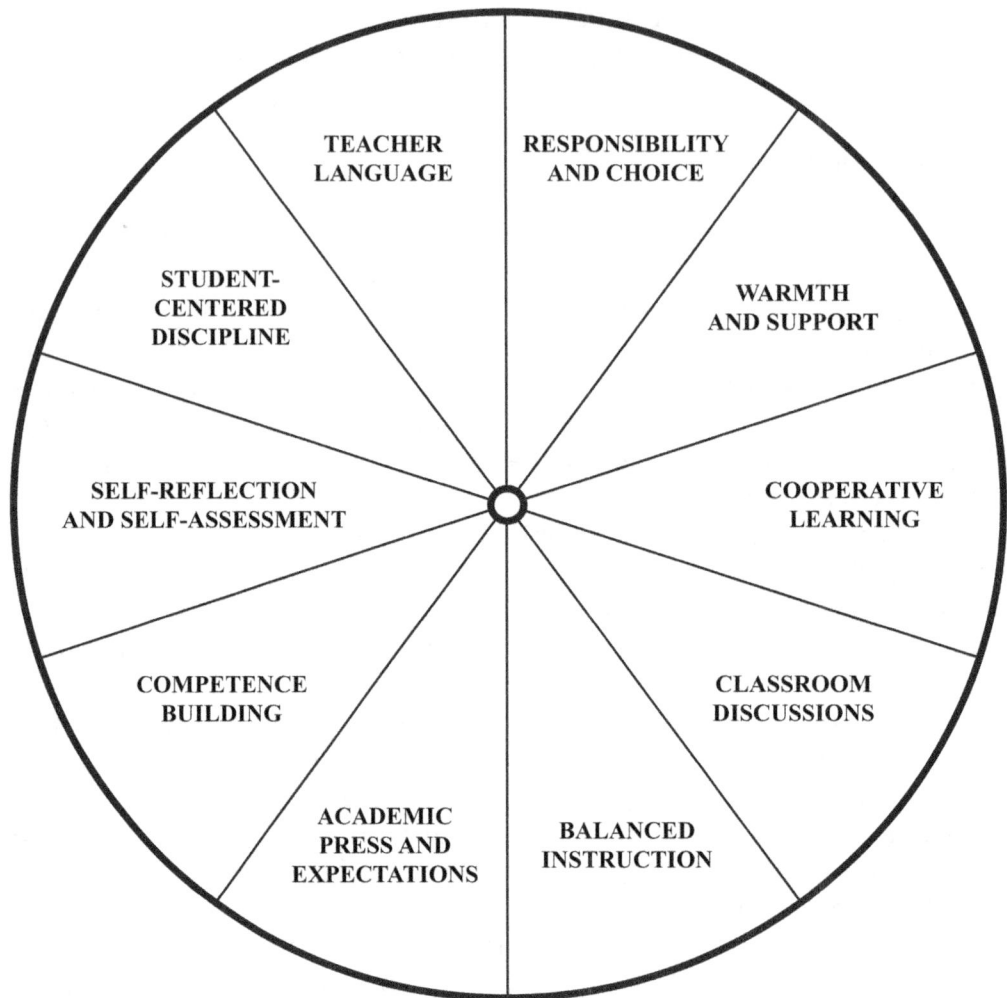

Figure 11.2 The Coaching Wheel

Scenario 3: A school is preparing to implement Project-Based Learning. As a foundational step, they are asking all teachers to focus on creating a classroom culture conducive to PBL using RTI's PBL Culture rubric (*RTI's Approach to Supporting High-Quality Project-Based Learning in Schools*, n.d.). The sections of the wheel would indicate the six elements of the rubric.

Using Scenario 1, if a coach is working with teachers on a school-wide or district-wide SEL initiative to improve supports for students' social and emotional needs in the classroom, he might complete the wheel with Yoder's (2014) ten research-based instructional strategies. Notice that each instructional strategy is a wedge of the wheel, with each wedge the same in size so no wedge seems more important than another. For example wheels related to Scenarios 2 and 3, see Appendix A.

Importantly, the wheel should also be accompanied by a document that describes the details of each item represented in the wedges. In this case, the coach would provide a teacher with the wheel and a document that describes each of Yoder's practices. For descriptions of Yoder's practices, see *Teaching the Whole Child: Instructional Practices That Support Social-Emotional Learning in Three Teacher Evaluation Frameworks* (Yoder, 2014).

The coaching wheel is adaptable to any coaching context and can be used during the initial stages of a coaching relationship as well as when a teacher is ready to move to a new macrocoaching goal. In any circumstance, the wheel helps a coach explore issues of motivation, confidence, and ability regarding a teacher's goal or action toward change.

No matter the sections of the wheel, the tool ensures that a coach begins with a teacher's own self-assessment and goals for growth and learning. Other tools that can be used for the same purpose include professional development or teacher evaluation rubrics, national education organization standards such as the National Board of Professional Teaching Standards, or the International Society for Technology in Education (ISTE) Standards. In keeping with adult learning and self-determination theories, starting from a self-assessment will lead to increased motivation and buy-in for achieving goals.

How to Use a Coaching Wheel

The coaching wheel is used during initial conversations about focus areas for improvement or change. A coach shares the tool with a teacher and allows time for reflective thinking. If possible, it is best to leave the tool with the teacher to give them time and space to complete it intentionally instead of asking them to complete it during a coaching session. However, if the teacher is unlikely to complete the tool on their own, completion of the tool may become a part of a coaching session. In this situation, the coach should allow 10–15 minutes for the teacher to complete the self-assessment and should allow for privacy during this time. This may mean that the coach steps out and returns to complete the coaching session after 10–15 minutes have passed.

To use the wheel, a teacher first considers each section of the wheel and uses rulers with scaling questions (see Chapters 6 and 7) to rate each one. Depending on the coaching context, the coach might begin with the following prompt: **On a scale of 1 to 10, how would you rate your ability to implement each teaching practice?**

After the teacher has self-assessed using the sections of the wheel, the self-assessment is used to guide follow-up coaching conversations. We describe these conversations as stages rather than steps because each may involve

Figure 11.3 Steps of the Coaching Wheel

more than one coaching conversation. The time it takes to explore a teacher's self-assessment will depend on the individual teacher, the relationship between the teacher and the coach, and other factors. Taking the time to have these conversations, though, will help to build a trusting partnership and ensure that once more active coaching begins it is focused on the right goals for each teacher.

Figure 11.3 shows the steps to using the coaching wheel.

Stage 1: Explore the Self-Assessment

Questions to guide the first stage of the conversation might include the following:

- How did it feel to complete this self-assessment?
- Where did you notice strengths?
- Where are your opportunities for growth?
- What would growth look like in any one area that you identified?
- If you were to improve in this area [the area that the teacher chose], what do you feel your classroom/your teaching/your life as a teacher would look like in 3–5 years?
- Of all the sections, including those we didn't specifically focus on today, where do you feel a change would make the most impact for you and/or your students?

Stage 2: Examine the Ratings

Additional conversation can focus on individual ratings for any specific indicator and might include the following questions (assuming the teacher rated themselves a 6 on the selected indicator):

- Of these elements, which would you like to discuss first?
- What does a 6 look like for you in this particular area?

- Why not a 5?
- What would it take to be a 7?

Stage 3: Focus on Values and Beliefs

Additional questions should help the teacher determine their energy and confidence for change in any selected area. Follow-up conversation might start with one or both of the following questions and these questions might be applied to one or more of the wedges:

- On a scale of 1 to 10, how important is it to you to make a change in this area?
- On a scale of 1 to 10, how confident are you that you can make a change in this area?

As a teacher shares their self-assessment and thinking based on the wheel, their coach listens actively and focuses on the teacher's assets and preferences for change. The coach should avoid telling the teacher what they should work on or how they should begin to grow in their practice.

Boxes 11.1 and 11.2 offer further practice with and tips for using the Coaching Wheel.

Box 11.1 On Your Own: Create a Coaching Wheel

Create a coaching wheel for an initiative your school or district is implementing. Whether this initiative is inquiry-based learning, culturally relevant pedagogy, trauma-informed instruction, or something else, identify components of the initiative and fill in the wedges.

If there is already a description of each of the components, include them on your wheel document. If there is not already a description of each competent, write your own. It is important that teachers have something to reference as they consider their practice and rate their interest and confidence for each wedge.

Box 11.2 Consider This: Using a Wheel to Narrow a Teacher's Personal Interests

Coaches sometimes encounter teachers who have many different ideas for making changes to their practice. These teachers are constantly seeking out new ideas and may have so many ideas that they don't know where to start. Coaches can use a coaching wheel to focus

> conversations with teacher like this. Ask the teacher to create a wheel with all of their ideas for change and then use the Importance and Confidence Rulers to decide where to start.

Planning the Coaching Approach

After an initial conversation, or perhaps conversations, with a teacher using the wheel, a coach can begin planning their priority approach and anticipating opportunities to engage other approaches as necessary. Having a plan helps coaches stay focused on a teacher's goals while also managing the change process. Coaches can return to the tool periodically to determine if a change in priority approach is necessary. Coaches should also keep in mind that although it is helpful to have a plan, a coach's work must be nimble. Ironically, a plan often helps coaches prepare to be flexible as changes to the plan become necessary.

Figure 11.4 shows the two steps for planning a coaching approach using the CoachED framework.

Planning Step 1: Plan the Priority Approach

Coaches should begin by using what they know about a coaching context to determine a priority approach. Using evidence in the form of key details about a teacher, their classroom, their students, their practice, and the indicators that make up their CoachED profile will help a coach intentionally choose a priority approach for getting started.

Planning Step 2: Consider and Explore Additional Approaches

After identifying and planning for the priority approach, a coach should spend time anticipating opportunities and needs for other possible approaches.

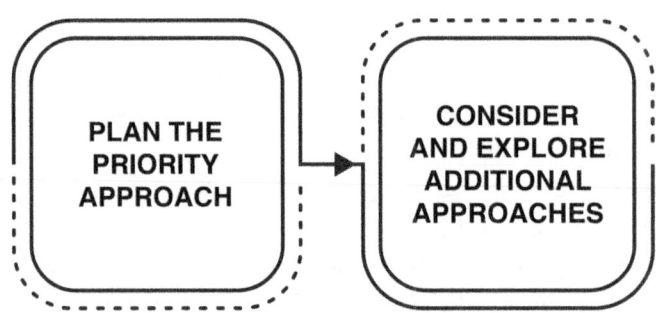

Figure 11.4 Steps for Planning the Coaching Approach

Again, they should consider key details about the teacher, their students, and their context to inform their own thinking.

See Appendix A for a step-by-step tool that coaches can use to reflect on initial conversations with teachers, including conversations that use the wheel, and to create a coaching plan.

Planning for Powerful Questions

Just as it is useful to plan for an intentional approach to coaching with each teacher, it is useful to plan for each coaching conversation. Planning for a coaching conversation includes identifying a goal for the conversation and anticipating powerful questions that will support the goal while also empowering the teacher.

There are many sources that provide guidance on asking powerful questions (Cardon, n.d.; Co-active Training Institute, 2019; Costa & Garmston, 2016; Kimsey-House, Kimsey-House, Sandhal, & Whitworth, 2018; Stoltzfus, 2008). From these sources, we have found seven question types to be most effective in planning for coaching conversations in our practice (Figure 11.5). These types are: beliefs and feelings, past experiences, hypothetical situations, comparisons, perspectives, and reflections.

Figure 11.5 Seven Question Types That Are Most Effective in Planning for Coaching Conversations

Hypothetical Situations

Hypothetical situations ask teachers to consider their practice in a different context than the reality in which they currently find themselves. Removing or changing constraints and context can heighten awareness of how decisions might be tied to personal values and beliefs. For example, if the constraints of a prescribed curriculum are gone, the teacher can tap into her own values to determine what she would teach without parameters, thereby helping her identify what is most important to her in terms of curriculum. If funding constraints are gone, the teacher again gets to determine decisions based on what she believes is most essential for her students. Although hypothetical questions can be used to explore values, they do not always have to be tied to values or beliefs. Hypothetical questions can be used in other contexts to help a teacher see a different perspective. Here are some more examples:

- If students had engaged in effective lab experiments today, what would that have looked like?
- Let's imagine you were doing this assignment with seniors instead of freshmen (or adults instead of students). How might the collaboration have looked different?
- If you taught the class for an entire year, would you do things the same?

Perspectives

Just as hypothetical situations allow teachers to consider their practice within new contexts or confined by new constraints, asking teachers to consider someone else's perspective may help them consider the relationship between their values, beliefs, and practices. Here are some other examples of perspective questions:

- What might a veteran teacher say to you about students owning their own learning during today's lesson?
- What would an administrator have seen if they came in during that lesson?
- How do you think your students would describe owning their learning during today's lesson?
- What would your first-year teacher self say to you about that lesson?

Beliefs and Feelings

These questions explicitly ask teachers to consider their beliefs and their feelings, which can be a result of their beliefs; for example, the feeling of frustration that may occur when a teacher *believes* students do not care about their learning. Here are some examples of questions about beliefs and feelings:

- What types of learning environments do you believe help your students learn best?
- How do you feel when you think students have disengaged from an assignment?

Past Experiences

Past experiences often influence teachers' beliefs and lead them to assumptions. Asking about past experiences can uncover ways that they have influenced a teacher's current thinking. Perhaps a teacher thinks about a past experience and realizes that they once thought differently. Past experiences are also helpful in applying lessons learned to new goals and action steps. Here are some examples of questions based on past experiences:

- When you taught this objective last year, what was different about your classroom context and how you chose to teach it?
- Have you been successful in the past in creating lessons that provided different supports for different students? What worked for you?

Comparisons

Questions that ask about comparisons help teachers to clarify and differentiate their thinking to avoid overgeneralizations or single perspectives. These questions can help teachers think about their ideal scenarios compared with their current reality. They might ask teachers to speculate on their judgments and can even surface teachers' values as they compare experiences, people, emotions, or points of view. Comparison questions may also involve other questioning types. A question might include both past experiences and comparisons. For example, a coach might ask, "How was this group work similar to and/or different from group work students engaged in last week?" Here are some additional examples of comparison questions:

- What would have been different about this lesson if authentic texts weren't included?
- How was your planning for this lesson different from your planning when the same activity has been more successful?
- Would you rather work on designing student tasks with higher cognitive demand or explore opportunities to increase student engagement?

Reflections

Asking teachers to explore the teaching and learning process through reflective thinking provides the time and space that teachers need to consider their practice intentionally. Coaching conversations build upon teachers' reflective thinking by moving to action. This allows a teacher to pursue actions that may follow from their reflective thinking. For example, in asking a teacher to reflect on data that a coach has collected, the coach might ask, "What do you notice about your paraphrasing of students' responses in class today?" The teacher may respond that they notice their paraphrase was the exact paraphrasing of the student's language. The coach might ask, "How does today's paraphrasing relate to your goal of students' use of academic language?" and wrap up by asking, "Based on your reflective thinking, what are your next steps for action?"

Here are some examples:

- What worked well today to support students' use of academic vocabulary?
- What would you like to do differently next time you engage students in collaboration?
- What would you like to do differently when reteaching the lesson on two-digit addition?
- What do you think contributed to your expectations for classroom talk during today's lesson?

Box 11.3 offers practice planning an initial coaching conversation.

> **Box 11.3 On Your Own: Plan an Initial Coaching Conversation**
>
> Plan an initial coaching conversation with a specific teacher in mind. Imagine that the teacher has decided they would like to improve their implementation of an instructional practice that the school or district has adopted. How would you plan the conversation so that it empowers and inspires the teacher to draw upon their own assets in identifying a focus for their growth and learning and beginning to implement the change they imagine?
> See Appendix A for a tool to support planning for a coaching conversation.

Conclusion

Coaching should not be implemented aimlessly. There should be careful planning about how a coach initiates a coaching relationship with a teacher as well as how ongoing coaching conversations proceed. A coach should be thoughtful, empathetic, and focused on student learning. They should be mindful of the teacher's needs and goals. Throughout this book, we have stressed the importance of giving voice and autonomy to teachers while navigating through coaching approaches with intent. We encourage coaches to practice using specific techniques and the coaching wheel, as we also continue to do.

> **Box 11.4 On Your Own: Review and Reflection**
>
> Now that we have put everything together, review your beliefs about teaching and learning, your beliefs about teachers and students, and the theories, models, and approaches on which our model relies.
>
> 1. What resonates with you? What does not?
> 2. Return to your own coaching philosophy, which we asked you to consider on page 11. Have your values and beliefs changed through reading this book? If so, how?
> 3. How do your own beliefs and values show up when you coach?

The CoachED framework is built on the foundation of empowerment. We hope that you feel empowered to coach in a meaningful and purposeful way that meets the needs of the teachers you serve and their students. Additionally, we hope that you and your teachers strive to build equitable learning environments where all students can experience joy and are prepared for their postsecondary endeavors and for life. We invite you to reflect on what you have read, consider what has resonated with you and what has not, and return to your coaching philosophies to continue revising and refining them. Box 11.4 will help you to do so. We wish you well in your journey and look forward to hearing of your experiences along the way!

Appendix A. Tools for Coaching

Appendix A provides tools to support coaches in getting started with teachers, planning for and reflecting on coaching cycles and coaching conversations, and collecting classroom data (Figure A.1).

The Coaching Wheel

Coaching Wheel: High Quality Teaching and Learning
The Center for Education Services at RTI International proposes a High Quality Teaching and Learning framework that is designed to communicate the many complex components of effective K-12 instruction. The framework assumes that the goal of education is to facilitate learning for students so that they become confident and competent in engaging with others and their environment in college, careers, and life. The components of the framework can be used in a coaching wheel when working with teachers to improve general instruction in classrooms and schools (Figure A.2). For more information on the framework, visit https://educationservices.rti.org/.

Coaching Wheel: Culture of Project-Based Learning
The Center for Education Services at RTI International has also created tools for implementation of project-based learning. One of these tools is a rubric for examining classroom culture. Elements of the rubric represent characteristics

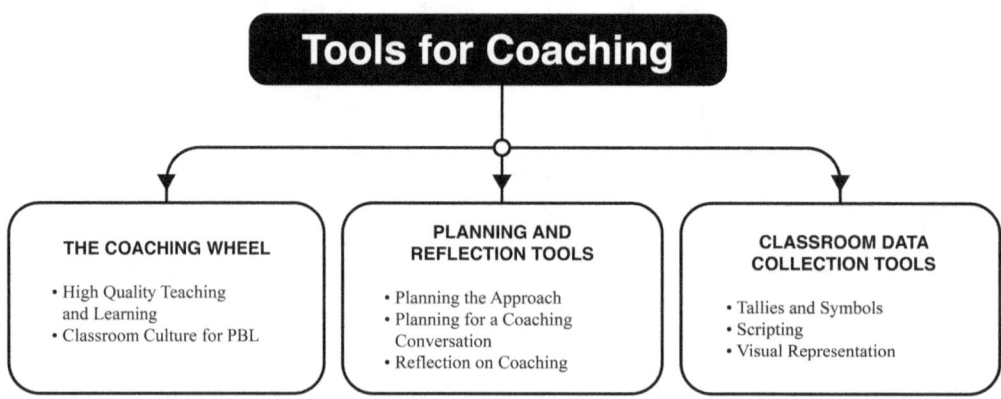

Figure A.1 Overview of Tools for Coaching

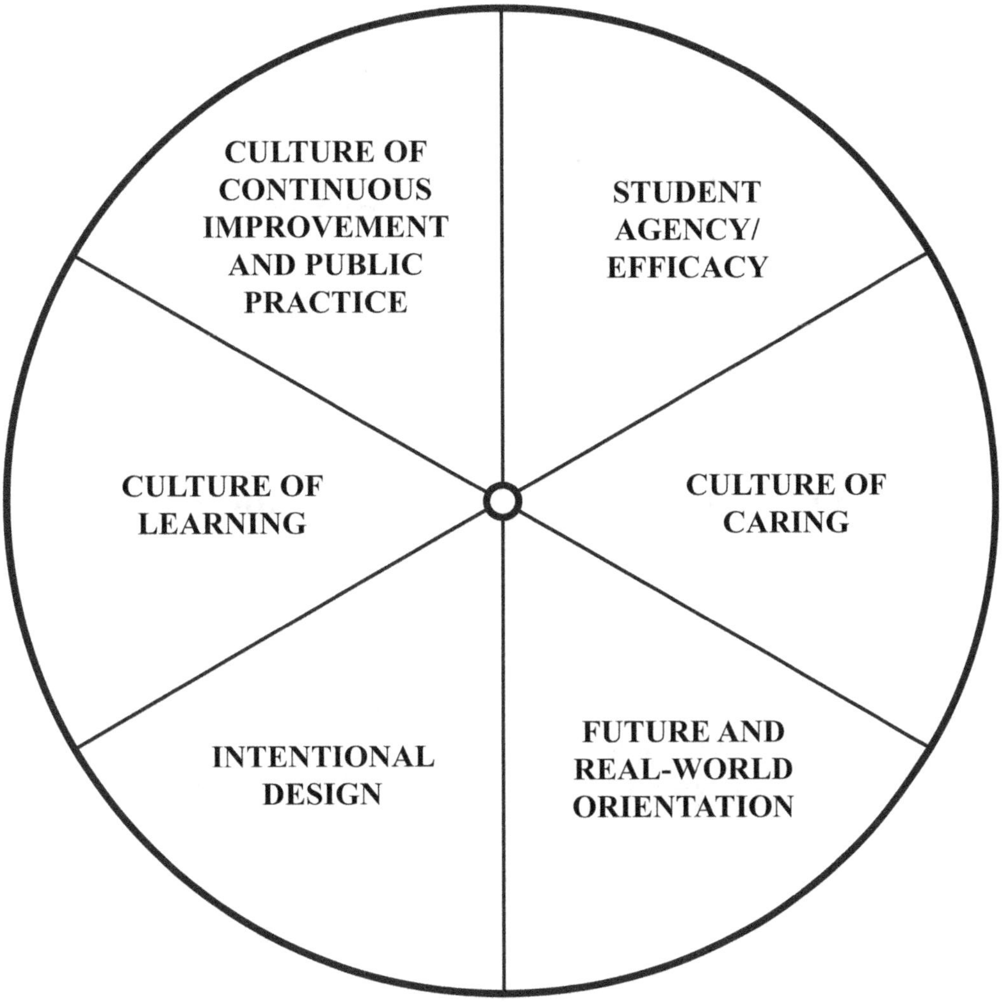

Figure A.2 Coaching Wheel for High Quality Teaching and Learning

of a classroom that is conducive to project-based learning. These elements can be used in a coaching wheel to support a teacher in considering and making changes to their own classroom culture (Figure A.3).

Planning and Reflection Tools

Planning the Approach

Although coaching conversations rarely go exactly as planned, having a plan can help a coach focus the conversation and keep the overall work on track. Use the tool in Box A.1 for planning how to approach coaching with a specific teacher.

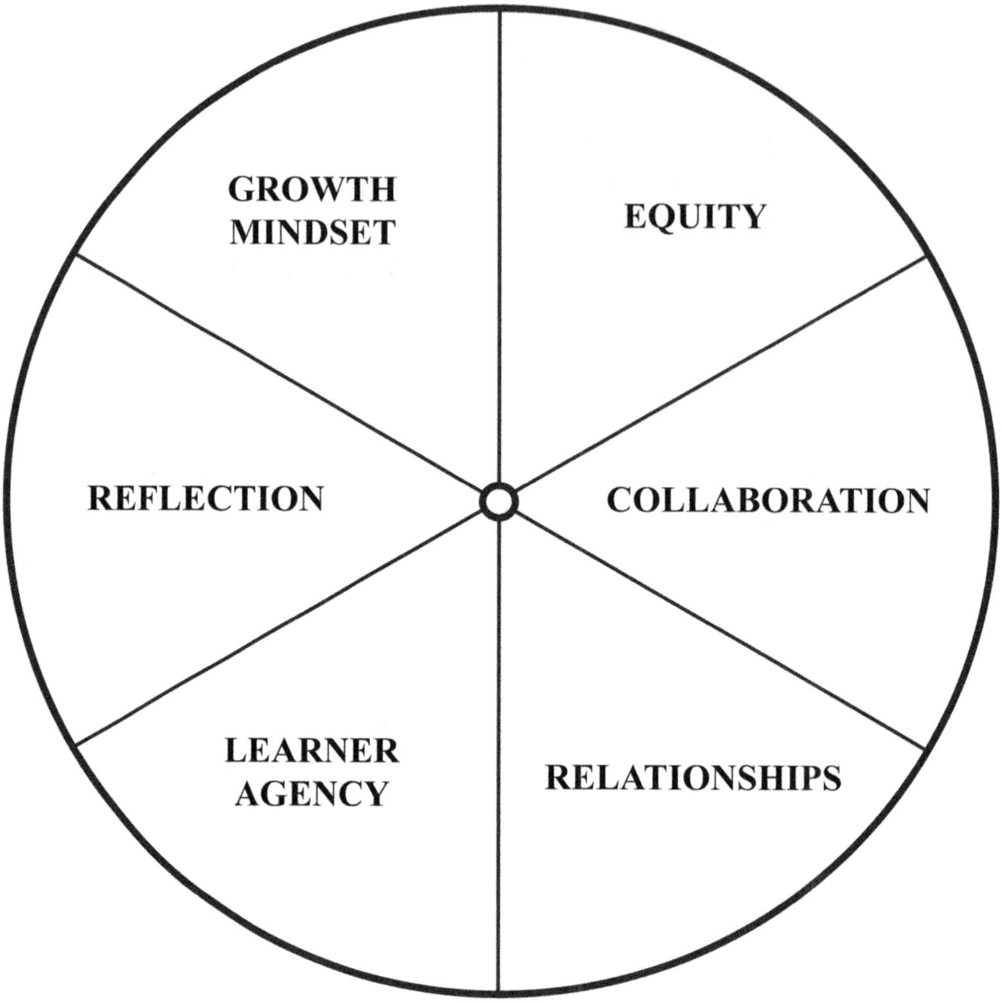

Figure A.3 Coaching Wheel for Culture of Project-Based Learning

Wheel sections: GROWTH MINDSET, EQUITY, REFLECTION, COLLABORATION, LEARNER AGENCY, RELATIONSHIPS

Box A.1 Planning the Priority Approach

Teacher:
Date and place of visit:
Teacher's current macrogoal:
Description of the coaching microcycle (including microcycle goal and action steps):

Planning the Priority Approach

What is your priority approach *at this time* in this coaching cycle?
What key details led to your decision?

Given your priority approach, what are some experiences, tools, and/or techniques that you might use?

Planning to Incorporate Additional Approaches	
Additional Approaches What other approaches might you need to use and why?	**Brainstorming and Planning** What are some strategies for these approaches and how might you use them in this coaching cycle?

Planning for a Coaching Conversation

Box A.2 provides a tool for planning the phases of conversation.

Box A.3 provides an example of what this guide might look like using the classroom data in Figure 4.8.

Box A.2 Planning the Phases of Conversation

What is the teacher's current state? (Consider stages of change and learning as well as current energy and engagement, relationship with coach, etc.)
Priority approach *at this time*:
Goal of *this* conversation:

Phase of the Conversation	Asset-Based Probing Questions (Hypothetical, Perspectives, Beliefs and Feelings, Past Experiences, Comparisons, Reflections)
Relationship Building/General Check-In	
Objective	
Reflective	
Interpretive	
Decisional	

Box A.3 Planning the Phase of Conversation

Phase of the Conversation	Asset-Based Probing Questions (Hypothetical, Perspectives, Beliefs and Feelings, Past Experiences, Comparisons, Reflections)
Relationship Building/General Check-In	• How are you feeling about your lesson today? • What went well for you today? • What did you expect your data to look like? Does it meet your expectations? • What surprises you about these data?
Objective	• How many students interacted in class today? • Of the interactions, how many were initiated by the students and how many were initiated by you? • How many of the interactions were student-to-student interactions? • What percentage of the class interacted? What percentage of the class did not interact?
Reflective	• How do you feel about the percentages and numbers we just discussed? • Do these results match your vision for your classroom?
Interpretive	• Why do you think the data look the way they do? • What about your lesson plan for today might have impacted the data collected? • What can you tell me about the students who interacted with you the most, the students who interacted with each other the most, and the students who did not interact at all? • How does what you know about your students explain the data results?
Decisional	• Based on what we collected today, what might be a goal for the next time we collect data? • How might you meet that goal? What steps will you take?

Reflecting on Coaching

Just as it is important for a teacher to engage in reflective thinking about their work, it is important for a coach to engage in reflective thinking about their own work as well. Keeping records will also help a coach to track the progress of their coaching work with individual teachers. Use the tool in Box A.4 to record your coaching sessions and reflect on your own strengths and opportunities for growth.

Box A.4 Reflection Tool

Teacher:
Date and place of visit:
Teacher's current macrogoal:
Description of the coaching microcycle (including goal and action steps):

Summary of the coaching session (include required follow-up)	
Potential next steps	
My strengths as a coach during this session	
My opportunities for growth as a coach based on this session	

Data Tools

Data tools ensure a consistent approach to collecting data in the classroom and can help a coach and teacher quickly identify a process for gathering information about students and student learning. In this section are some typical data tools a coach might use.

Data Tool 1: Tallies and Symbols

Tallies and symbols can be used for a variety of student learning data collection questions. Two examples are provided that show how to use tallies and symbols to record student and teacher voice in the classroom. The key to using tallies and symbols rests in the details. When using tallies, coaches and teachers need to agree how long each time increment should be and what specifically defines the looked-for behavior for student learning. When using symbols, coaches and teachers need to agree on what specifically defines the looked-for behavior, what symbol(s) represent that behavior, and how many forms that behavior may take.

Student/Teacher Voice. Collecting data on student/teacher voice can support a transition to a more student-centered classroom.

To collect data on student/teacher voice, the coach can create a table with columns for student(s), teacher, both, and none (silence). Each row in the column represents 1 minute, and each tally in the row indicates one sixth of a minute. Paying careful attention to a stopwatch, the coach should mark a tally at each 10-second increment to indicate who was speaking at that moment (see Figure A.4).

It is important to keep in mind that context of the class matters. As you look at the sample data, remember that the column "Both" should not be interpreted negatively because both does not necessarily mean a student is talking over a teacher. Perhaps students were in small groups and the teacher was helping one small group while other small groups continued their work together. We point this out simply to illustrate that context matters and the coach and teacher should be on the same page regarding what data are collected, how they are collected, and how they will be interpreted.

Data-collection Question: Whose Voice Is Heard?

Another more specific option for collecting data regarding student voice emphasizes the individual students in the classroom. In this case, rather than focusing on the whole class, the coach focuses on individual contributions. Using a seating chart that might indicate student names, gender, race, etc., depending on the teacher's goals, the coach records student contributions to the class (Figure A.5, as seen first in Chapter 4). Contributions may all be treated the same and indicated by a checkmark, or the coach and teacher together may decide to collect more specific data indicating what kind of contribution the student made. Types of contributions might include the following: asking a question, making a statement, connecting to another student, etc. Another option might be to indicate whether a student voluntarily contributed to class or was called on (Figure A.5). No matter what specific data are collected, the coach and teacher should create a clear key to indicate the various types of contribution to be collected and should clearly define each type together.

Notice in Figure A.5 that the coach was able to indicate student names for some students based on the teacher's direct interaction with those students using their names. Imagine the conversation the coach might be able to have with the teacher about student belonging based on these supplementary data. This is one way a coach could begin conversations aligned to but outside the scope of the teacher's immediate goal.

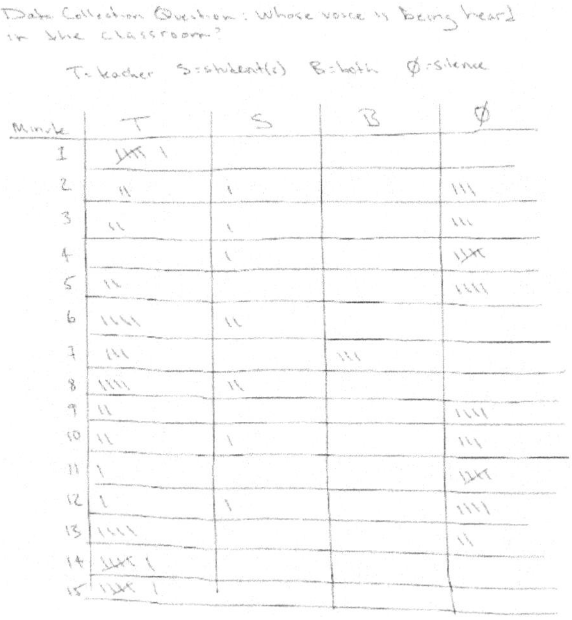

Figure A.4 Keeping Tallies

Figure A.5 Tracking Individual Classroom Contributions

Box A.5 provides an answer key for the effective feedback exercise in Box 4.8.

Box A.5 Revisiting Classroom Discussion Data: Answer Key to Effective Feedback

The feedback statements listed here are examples based on the "On Your Own" activity in Box 4.8.

Objective:
- There are 7 male students and 10 female students in the class.
- 11 students spoke at least once.
- 5 students spoke 4 or more times.
- 21 of 45 comments were made by male students; 24 of 45 comments were made by female students.
- 5 students did not participate in the conversation including 2 students who were called on but did not respond to the teacher's invitation to participate.

Subjective Interpretive:
- 5 students were not interested in the lesson.
- Male students felt more comfortable participating in the lesson than female students.
- The students who did not participate did not understand the discussion.

Subjective Evaluative:
- The teacher did an excellent job of engaging male students (positive value).
- The teacher did a bad job of engaging the female students so it was not a very good discussion (negative value).
- The students who did not participate were lazy (negative value).

Data Tool 2: Scripting

Often, data collection requires the coach to script exactly what students are saying during a class based on a specific student learning data-collection question. Scripting might focus, for example, on all of the questions students ask during a time period. Or, it might focus on everything students say that involves academic vocabulary. Other options might be to script evidence related to how students are working to support one another, how they are

ts What happens here in the nucleus?
ts What's that called?
ss Did you write down what he gave you?
ss How am I going to do them?
ss I'm supposed to do the other one, too - the d-RNA?
ss So, I transcribe it?
ss Does it look right?
ss Is that what you got?
ss Are they all in one group?
ss Which one are you looking for?
ss So, it ends there?
ss This is supposed to be U, right?
ss Are you sure?
ss What is it supposed to be?
ts What number did you have first?
st Is this right?
ss Who wants to go next?
st I just pick one?
ss So, we need UAA?
ss Now we switch people, right?
ss Do we arrange it?
ss Why?
ss Are we done now?
ss Did you do this right?

Ms. Lyles
November 15
7th period
1:50 - 2:00

Figure A.6 Example of Scripting

connecting with each other, or how they are making connections between class concepts. No matter the focus of the question, the process is simple. The coach records verbatim everything students say that relates directly to the focus question. Keep in mind that this type of tool works best when students are working in small groups. It may be difficult to keep up with the pace of student conversation, so the coach should record as much of the conversation as possible.

The data-collection question for the scripting tool in Figure A.6 was, "What questions are being asked in class, and who is doing the asking?" Notice that understanding not only what questions were being asked but also to whom and by whom they were being asked (ts = teacher to student, st = student to teacher, ss = student to students) was an important part of this teacher's learning goal.

Data Tool 3: Visual Representation

Visual data can be a powerful tool for conversations with teachers as well. Take a look at the data in Figure A.7. First, notice the teacher at the bottom of the page. Each "S" represents one student as they are seated in the classroom. The broken lines with open arrows represent student-to-student interactions

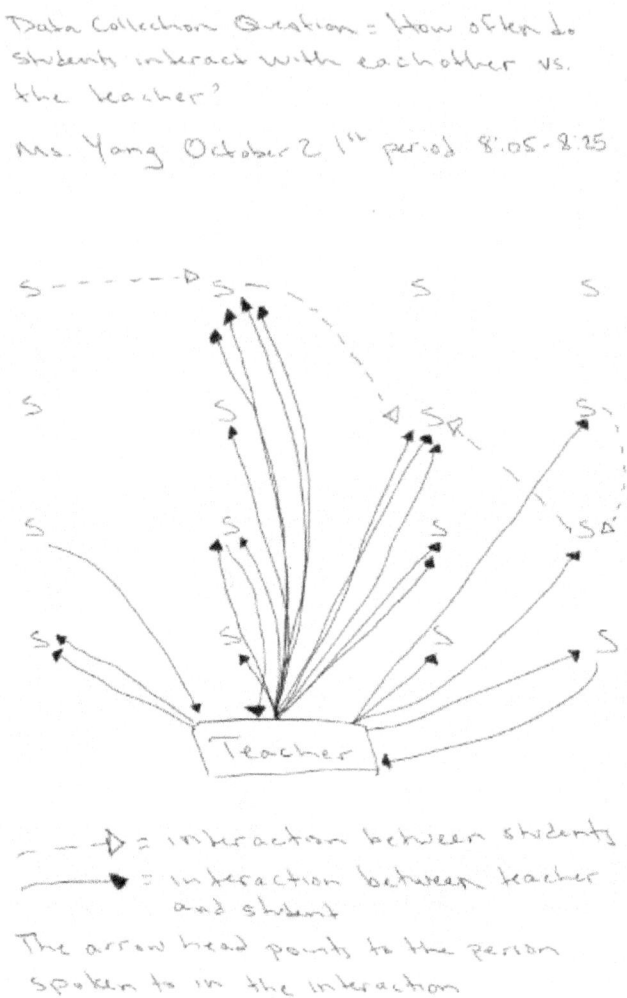

Figure A.7 Example of Visual Representation

while the unbroken lines with filled arrows represent teacher-to-student or student-to-teacher interactions. What stands out to you? What questions might you include given that the teacher's goal was to move toward a more student-centered classroom? What question might you ask if the teacher's goal were to involve all students in a discussion? What questions might you ask if the teacher's goal were to increase student-to-student interaction? How might you use these data to infuse equity into the conversation?

Remember, again, that context matters. There may be very good reasons why the few students who did not interact were silent during this lesson. The coach's questions should always come from a place of nonjudgment and curiosity and should support the teacher's personal reflective thinking.

Box A.6 provides the answer to the best coaching approach, based on the On Your Own activity in Box 5.4.

Box A.6 An Approach to Coaching for Ms. Varghese

So, what was the answer?

An approach to coaching for Ms. Varghese (see Box 5.4)

Based on the CoachED framework, we would choose to prioritize a Coaching Beliefs approach for Ms. Varghese. Ms. Varghese values the importance of math for her students and believes that all students could be successful *if they put their minds to it*. Her beliefs about students' motivation (or lack of motivation) for learning, her beliefs about what makes content rigorous, and her inattention to an understanding about student engagement are impacting her instruction as a teacher and thereby her students' learning. Rather than emphasizing her own role in planning for engagement and making content accessible for all students through scaffolding, she makes assumptions about her students and her content. Ms. Varghese first needs coaching to help her identify and evaluate her beliefs about her students, her content, and her own role in the classroom.

Appendix B. Coaching Transcripts

Appendix B provides transcripts to help coaches "hear" what specific conversations and strategies sound like. Transcripts provided include:

Transcript 1: Coaching Values—Exploring Values
Transcript 2: Coaching Beliefs—The Confidence Ruler
Transcript 3: Coaching Thinking—Problem Solving Technique
Transcript 4: Coaching Behavior—Elicit-Provide-Elicit

Transcript 1: Coaching Values—Exploring Values

In this transcript, Jolie works with Mr. Martinez to explore his values and ensure that they are aligned with his classroom practice.

Jolie: Mr. Martinez, thanks for making time to meet with me today. Let's start by just checking in. Maybe take a couple deep breaths. How are you feeling?
Mr. Martinez: [Takes several deep breaths] If I'm honest, I'm feeling tired. I feel exhausted. I have no energy for my students and that makes me really sad.
Jolie: Sounds like you are a little low and feeling bad about how that trickles down to your students.
Mr. Martinez: Yes. I used to have so much energy for my students. I loved to create new lessons that would be exciting and engaging, and I loved to have lunch with them. It was a time we could all relax and get to know one another. It made everything in the classroom so much more fun. Now I feel like I don't know much about them. I don't have time to get to know them anymore. I can barely keep up with the curriculum as it is and testing just makes time for anything extra impossible.
Jolie: Testing seems to be getting in the way of your true passion for teaching.
Mr. Martinez: Yes, maybe it's time to retire.
Jolie: Yikes! Before you make that decision, would it be okay if we explored some of your values around teaching?
Mr. Martinez: I guess so.
Jolie: Okay. Tell me what matters most to you in teaching.
Mr. Martinez: Well, it used to be the students. Now I feel like it's just test scores.

Jolie: You feel like test scores matter to you now more than the students do.

Mr. Martinez: Well, when you put it that way, they don't matter more to me, but they matter more to the principal and to everyone else, so I guess they have to matter to me, too.

Jolie: You obviously feel an external pressure to value testing. But what really matters to you?

Mr. Martinez: The students matter to me. I became a teacher for the students.

Jolie: For the students.

Mr. Martinez: Yes, it has always been about the students for me. They are more important to me than tests and grades and English.

Jolie: And when you became a teacher, what was your vision for your students and your classroom?

Mr. Martinez: I wanted to teach my students a love of literature and writing, but I also wanted to teach them resiliency and teamwork.

Jolie: On one hand, the content was important to you, and on the other hand, some of those skills we now call "soft skills" or "21st-century skills" were just as important to you.

Mr. Martinez: Yes, content is definitely important to me because I love reading and writing, and I want my students to love reading and writing, too. But, at the same time, there are skills just as important as reading and writing and the way our world is changing, I have to teach more than just my content. Those skills are so important to get along in the world.

Jolie: As a teacher, you feel you need to prepare students for the real world.

Mr. Martinez: Yes, and that means addressing things like how to get along with others and how to negotiate conflict and how to organize and manage collaboration. I feel like testing is such a small piece of education for the real world, and there's so much emphasis placed on it that everything else gets shoved to the background.

Jolie: You are frustrated that testing has pushed aside life skills and the social and emotional well-being of students.

Mr. Martinez: Yes, and sometimes that frustration just makes me want to quit.

Jolie: Well, I'd like to see if we can find a way to keep you in the classroom and also ensure that you can do what feels important to you. Are you willing to explore this more next week?

Mr. Martinez: Okay. I don't really want to leave the classroom yet. I just know something has to change if I'm going to stay.

Jolie: Great! Let's set a time to meet next week. I look forward to exploring and making that change with you.

This values-based conversation shows how Mr. Martinez has been living in a chronic state of stress between his values and his practice. His ideal values of emphasizing social and emotional learning in his classroom and addressing the personal needs of his students have been subsumed by his desire to keep his principal happy with his performance. The chronic stress caused by this conflict has led to burnout.

In this conversation, Jolie partnered with Mr. Martinez to explore his values and in preparation for identifying ways that he can better align his classroom practice to his ideal values.

Transcript 2: Coaching Beliefs—The Confidence Ruler

Ms. Daniels is struggling with classroom management. Her coach has been working with her on classroom management for a few months now and is beginning to get frustrated because there has been no change in Ms. Daniels's behavior and, therefore, no change in the behavior of students. The teacher has multiple tools for classroom management and knows how to use them, and this is a change she has self-selected and is invested in. Let's look at what a coaching conversation using values, beliefs, and scaling questions might look like with this teacher.

Jonathon: Thanks for taking the time to meet with me today. I know we've been working on classroom management for a long time. How are you feeling about this?

Ms. Daniels: I don't know. I know I should make some changes and when you leave every week, I feel like I can and like I have an action plan for moving forward and I feel energized, but then I come to work the next day and get overwhelmed all over again, and I haven't done anything we said I would do.

Jonathon: Let's spend some time exploring that if that's okay with you. We might discover some interesting things if we slow down and take a few minutes to talk more about your vision for your classroom and your values around classroom management. Would that be okay?

Ms. Daniels: I'm willing to try anything at this point. These kids are driving me crazy!

Jonathon: I'm glad to hear you're willing to explore your vision. Let's get started. First, when you think about your classroom and your role as a teacher, what matters to you most?

Ms. Daniels: Right now, it feels like peace matters to me. I want my classroom to be a peaceful and calm place. I want my students to come to class and learn, and they just can't do that with everything so crazy right now.

Jonathon: Peace. What does that word mean to you?

Ms. Daniels: Peace means calm and relaxing. No conflict.

Jonathon: And what is important to you about the idea of calm and relaxing and no conflict?

Ms. Daniels: I feel like I can't do my best work when there's conflict. I want my students, the parents, the administration—me—everyone to be on the same page working toward the same goals. The most important thing is student learning, and when there is conflict in the classroom or in the school that just can't happen.

Jonathon: So, you can do your best work when there isn't conflict in the classroom. I'm guessing you feel your students can do their best work in that environment as well.

Ms. Daniels: Exactly.

Jonathon: Well, on a scale of 1 to 10, with 1 being not at all motivated and 10 being very motivated, how motivated are you to create a peaceful classroom without conflict?

Ms. Daniels: A 10 for sure. It's the most important change I want to make right now.

Jonathon: And on a scale of 1 to 10—again, 1 is low and 10 is high—how confident are you that you can make this change?

Ms. Daniels: On a scale of 1 to 10, I'm probably at a 2.

Jonathon: Okay, well let's take a closer look at that 2. What does that 2 mean to you?

Ms. Daniels: I just haven't been able to make a change. No matter how important it is to me or how motivated I feel, it hasn't happened. I don't see that changing.

Jonathon: If that's the case, why didn't you say a 1 or even a zero?

Ms. Daniels: Well, I know I have the skills to make the change. I'm totally capable of it, and I have the resources. It's not like I'm totally clueless. I'm definitely aware of the need to make the change. If I said a zero, I think that would mean I didn't even know it was important or didn't have any resources.

Jonathon: Okay, great. You have resources and skills. That's definitely a start! What would it take for you to be at a 3 or even a 4?

Ms. Daniels: I don't know. Some of the supports I think I'm missing are from the parents and my administrators. I'm afraid that if I implement a classroom management plan with follow-through then I'm going to have to start sending kids out of class. Not forever but at least at the beginning to set an example and show that I'm serious about my boundaries. That has been the problem all along. I just keep asking kids to behave, but I'm not showing them my boundaries or providing consequences when the boundaries are crossed. To do this, I have to provide consequences for kids, and I'm afraid parents will get upset and my administrator will think I can't control my class, and then he'll start getting complaints from parents and then the whole thing will turn into a big mess.

Jonathon: You are afraid that there will be a snowball effect if you implement this change, but the support of parents and your administrator might help.

Ms. Daniels: Maybe. I definitely know that I'm afraid of the consequences from the parents and administration if I implement this plan.

Jonathon: What would help you to implement the plan without fear?

Ms. Daniels: I guess I could communicate in advance with parents and administrators. If they knew what was about to happen and were prepared for it then I wouldn't be so worried about their response.

Jonathon: If you made this change and prepared parents and administration in advance, how would that change your confidence level? On a scale of 1 to 10 how confident would you be after preparing parents and administrators?

Ms. Daniels: That would definitely help a lot. I feel like my confidence level would be at least a 6 or a 7 if I took that first step.

Jonathon: What ideas do you have for communicating with parents and administrators?

Ms. Daniels: Well, I send out a weekly newsletter to my parents. I could include information there, and maybe I should call a few parents in advance. I can e-mail my principal and request a meeting to sit down with her. Maybe she would even have some ideas about how I might communicate with parents.

Jonathon: What are you willing to do between now and next week?

Ms. Daniels: I will set up a meeting with the principal. Hopefully I'll even be able to meet with her before next week but if not, I'll at least have a meeting set up.

Jonathon: That sounds like a great first step. What are you taking away from our time together today?

Ms. Daniels: I hadn't realized how communication with others was holding me back. I was just getting so frustrated with myself for not making progress but now I realize that I was afraid of the consequences. I feel much more confident with this plan now.

In this conversation between the coach and the teacher, the coach used scaling questions to help the teacher identify the root cause of her inaction: a lack of confidence. This is significant because it changes the coach's approach to supporting the teacher. If the coach had instead assumed that the lack of follow-through was due to a lack of engagement, he would have missed an opportunity to build the teacher's efficacy and provide a strong foundation for the change.

Transcript 3: Coaching Thinking—Problem-Solving Technique

In the following transcript, Jonathon uses a Coaching Thinking approach to help Dr. Durham solve her own problem.

Dr. Durham: Good morning!
Jonathon: Good morning, Dr. Durham. How are you feeling?
Dr. Durham: I'm good, but you know how I said last week that I wanted to empower students to do more? I am having trouble with thinking about how to do that.
Jonathon: Is there another word that you would use to describe the trouble you feel? For example, responsive, concerned, stuck, disappointed?
Dr. Durham: Oh! I would say that I am stuck and . . . hmmm . . . probably overwhelmed. I have so many ideas about what I'd like to do.
Jonathon: Ideas about empowering students?
Dr. Durham: Yes. I went to this professional learning, and they talked about culturally responsive teaching. I really think that is what I want to do. You know we have students from all over, and I think I can empower them by being culturally responsive.
Jonathon: You sound excited. After you went to the professional development, what did you think about the most in terms of empowering your students?
Dr. Durham: I thought that although we use common lessons for the most part here, I want to give students more voice and choice during our units.
Jonathon: Are there strategies that you have tried that provide students with more voice and choice?
Dr. Durham: I used to think that the turn-and-talk technique and putting them in groups was giving them voice. And we used to tell them to choose one of three different products for their assignment as their choice, but I'm not so sure that is culturally responsive.
Jonathon: Turn-and-talk and collaborative groups are strategies that I've seen you use. How would you describe an activity that was more culturally responsive?
Dr. Durham: At the training, they said that culturally responsive was more than a party for Cinco de Mayo or talking about Langston Hughes during

the poetry unit. It was about bringing in students' lives outside the classroom and how that was important. They also talked about student-centered instruction.

Jonathon: Okay. So, you became aware of culturally responsive instruction at a professional development and you want to empower your students more. How might using culturally responsive instruction allow students to feel empowered?

Dr. Durham: I think that my students are compliant, but they are not engaged. They will do what I ask them to do, but they are not excited about it. I also have so many different types of students from different places. I don't think I've created a space for them to take social and academic risks. When I say that, I mean they aren't comfortable sharing their opinions. There are certain groups in the classroom. I try to change up the groups every two weeks but that doesn't get them to where I need them to be to support and challenge one another.

Jonathon: I see. They are doing what you ask them to do but not engaging in dialogue with one another.

Dr. Durham: Exactly. I already use student-centered instruction, at least I think I do. They said that was a big part of culturally responsive teaching. So, I think that I am on the right track.

Jonathon: I want to circle back to what you said about your students being compliant, which limits their empowerment. You have strategies for student-centered instruction, and you have been implementing those strategies in your classroom. So, you deliberately plan and implement strategies that emphasize student-centered learning?

Dr. Durham: Yes, I just feel like I can be doing so much more.

Jonathon: How confident are you that you can do much more?

Dr. Durham: I'm pretty confident that I could if I knew what to do. We have a poetry unit coming up, and if I can plan to incorporate some culturally responsive instruction into that unit, I would be excited about that.

Jonathon: Let me ask you for some feedback on what I think I'm hearing based on your reflective thinking. Through the use of culturally relevant instruction, which includes student-centered instructional strategies and providing students with voice and choice, you can make more progress toward your goal of empowering your students. Is that a fair statement?

Dr. Durham: Yes, I think you've summarized our conversation correctly so far.

Jonathon: Great. So, let's see. You would like to strengthen your use of culturally responsive instruction with your poetry curriculum unit.

Dr. Durham: I'm going to revise the unit that we already have.

Jonathon: And culturally responsive instruction is one solution for you toward solving the problem of student empowerment.

Dr. Durham: Yes . . . I think that is right . . . I know there are other ways, but like I said, there are so many different types of students in here, and I want them to be ready to explore the world and be respectful of others.

Jonathon: Respect, communication, and collaboration with others in the world is important to you. It can prepare your students for anything.

Dr. Durham: That's exactly right! I don't want them to think that the world is only full of people like them. I don't want them to be so shocked when they leave this place that they aren't able to function.

Jonathon: I hear the excitement in your voice! You see this poetry unit as a valuable opportunity for introducing more elements of culturally responsive instruction.

Dr. Durham: I'm super excited. That professional development really got me excited.

Jonathon: Are you able to identify some of your needs around learning about, planning, or implementing culturally responsive instruction in your classroom?

Dr. Durham: I think that I need to understand . . . well, I have a few resources from the professional development, so I could read through those. Wait . . . are you familiar with culturally responsive instruction?

Jonathon: Yes, I am.

Dr. Durham: Okay. I'm so glad that you are! In that case, I would rather start with the planning process. Even if I read through these resources, I will need help in planning to determine if the activities that I am choosing are culturally responsive. I have no problem with implementation. You know earlier I said there is so much more I can do. I think that if I consider some of the activities that I've already done, I can probably be more intentional with those to help empower students. My next unit is on poetry.

Jonathon: Ok, so we can set a goal around planning and your single layer inquiry question could be, "How do I plan activities with specific strategies that empower my students during the poetry unit?"

Dr. Durham: Yes, that is I want to know! That is my question, I'm ready!

Even though Jonathon was familiar with culturally relevant instruction, he did not reveal his knowledge until he was asked. Rather, he supported Dr. Durham in solving her own problem through active listening, reflective listening statements, and reflective questions. Empowering Dr. Durham in this way and allowing her to choose her own path of learning shows her that he believes in her ability in the classroom. This likely prepared Dr. Durham to be more accepting of support in the next stages of coaching.

Transcript 4: Coaching Behavior—Elicit-Provide-Elicit

Elicit-Provide-Elicit is used when a teacher does not have the resources to move forward on their own. In this example Jonathon supports Mr. Finch, an engaged and willing teacher who has successfully worked with Jonathon in the past, by providing resources only when it becomes necessary and when he knows what Mr. Finch already understands about the topic.

Jonathon: I think we've made a lot of progress on your work with classroom discussions. You've implemented a few new strategies, and we've hit your goal of ensuring that at least 85% of students engage in whole-class discussions. Would you like to continue working on this strategy, or are you ready to turn to a new topic?

Mr. Finch: Well, I'm really pleased with classroom discussions and I want to continue to increase student voice in my classroom, but I think I'd like to try to increase student voice through another strategy. I really want my students working in small groups for more of the class period. I feel like that would give even more students the opportunity to talk and would make the learning more active. I know there has been a push to see more collaboration in the classroom, but I've been teaching for a long time and when I started, there was no expectation of group work. Students in all classrooms sat in rows. I keep trying group work, but I just get frustrated and the students don't do their work. I just don't feel like I really know how to do it well.

Jonathon: You've tried collaborative group work in your classroom, but it hasn't gone as you would've liked, and you'd like to focus your next goal on how to improve your use of collaboration in the classroom to give students more opportunities to speak and be engaged in the class.

Mr. Finch: Yes, I think this would be a good next step for me and will also support the kind of learning students are expected to do these days.

Jonathon: Okay, well let's start with you telling me how you have implemented group work in the past. What have you tried?

Mr. Finch: Well, I know you are supposed to give students roles so I tried to do that once but then students just did their one assigned task individually and still didn't collaborate with or talk to each other. They were sitting in groups, but there wasn't any talking.

Jonathon: What was the assignment and what roles did you use?

Mr. Finch: They were practicing math word problems, and each student was assigned different problems that they were supposed to solve and then teach to the group. So they started off working independently on their word problem and then during the teaching, one student was supposed to be the timer to keep them on track, one was supposed to be the note-taker to take notes about their conversation, and one was supposed to be the questioner who asked questions about the problem.

Jonathon: So, there were four students per group, and they each had a different problem to start. Then during the collaborative part, they each had a specific task to focus on.

Mr. Finch: Exactly, but what they did was solve their problems and then pass their papers around so everyone in the group could copy from one another. They didn't even talk to each other unless it was about something outside school.

Jonathon: Okay, we'll come back to that image and talk more about what you would've liked to happen in a bit, but let's keep working on what else you know about collaborative group work.

Mr. Finch: I really don't know much else. I know that when I have smaller groups, things tend to be better but not always. I know that administrators want to see students working in groups during their walk-throughs, and I know that everyone says collaboration is an important 21st-century skill, and I agree with that. I just don't know how to make it happen.

Jonathon: So, it's important to you to get better at it because it's an important skill for students.

Mr. Finch: Yes, do you have some strategies I could try?

Jonathon: Of course! Let's review a few things I have that might work.

[Jonathon and Mr. Finch review multiple strategies]

Jonathon: Of the strategies we just reviewed, which do you think would work best for you in your classroom right now?

In this transcript, Jonathon began by giving Mr. Finch the autonomy to choose how to continue his coaching work. After Mr. Finch chose to focus on collaborative group work as a strategy to increase student voice in the classroom, Jonathon asked questions to elicit his current understanding of collaborative group work and was careful not to provide any suggestions until Mr. Finch asked. When Mr. Finch was ready for him to share strategies, Jonathon provided multiple strategies and then quickly returned to a coaching stance by asking Mr. Finch which one would work best for him given his current context. Box B.1 offers an activity for analyzing your own coaching transcripts.

> **Box B.1 On Your Own: Reviewing and Analyzing Coaching Transcripts**
>
> Reviewing and analyzing coaching transcripts can be a useful way to become more aware of coaching approaches, strategies, and tools. Consider recording and transcribing (or at least listening to) one of your coaching sessions with a teacher. As you review the transcript or listen to the recording, consider the following questions:
>
> - What approaches do you notice?
> - When and why do you shift approaches?
> - What is the impact of each shift on the coaching conversation?
> - What techniques did you use?
> - What was the impact of each technique?

Appendix C. Key Terms

Approaches: The term approach indicates a specific, targeted type of coaching that uses an understanding of the CoachED framework to direct a focus for coaching.

Beliefs: Teacher beliefs include both internal beliefs (beliefs about themselves, their ability and their self-efficacy, beliefs about how others perceive them, etc.) and external beliefs (beliefs about their students, their context, the role of a teacher, education and learning, etc.).

Context: When we refer to a teacher's context, we are referring not only to their classroom context, including their physical space, their students, and their content and grade level but also to the culture of their school, district, and community. We also include in context what the teacher knows about themselves and what others observe—their values and beliefs, their style and ways of being, their habits, etc.

Levers: Levers are indicators we use to help determine the best approach for coaching a teacher given their unique profile. Levers that help a coach determine a priority coaching approach are knowledge, application, awareness, and engagement.

Macrocoaching: The macrocoaching phase of the coaching process includes visioning, goal-setting, and planning and focuses on big picture goals.

Microcoaching: The microcoaching phase of the coaching process includes planning, implementation, and reflective thinking. Microcoaching occurs in short cycles that focus on one aspect of the macrocoaching goal.

Priority Approach: We use the term priority approach to mean the high-leverage approach that will most target the specific profile of a teacher based on their knowledge, application, awareness, and engagement.

Reflective conversations: a *strategy* **a coach** uses to engage a teacher in purposeful conversation. Reflective conversations between teachers and coaches include reflective listening statements and powerful questions to facilitate reflective thinking.

Reflective listening statements (Rollnick et al., 2008; Miller & Rollnick, 2013): a *technique* a coach uses to support a teacher's thinking. Using reflective listening statements requires that a coach repeat what a teacher has said through parroting, paraphrasing, summarizing, etc.

Reflective thinking: a *process* both **the teacher and the coach** engage in to intentionally consider plans, implementation, and results.

Strategies: Strategies represent an overall coaching plan and include co-planning, coaching conversations, and model teaching. Multiple techniques are used to support a coaching strategy.

Techniques: Techniques are specific protocols and activities that support an overall coaching strategy. Techniques include questioning, active listening, scaling questions, providing feedback, etc.

Tools: Tools are templates that can be adapted and used repeatedly in working with teachers.

Values: Values represent underlying ideas about what is most important to a person. Conflict between a teacher's practice and their values is one cause of teacher burnout.

References

Adams, C., Ford, T., & Forsyth, P. (2015). *Next generation school accountability: A report commissioned by the Oklahoma state department of education.* The Oklahoma Center for Education Policy & the Center for Educational Research and Evaluation.

Adler, S. A. (1990, February). *The reflective practitioner and the curriculum of teacher education.* Paper presented at the Annual Meeting of the Association of Teacher Educators, Las Vegas, NV.

Adler, S. A. (1991). The reflective practitioner and the curriculum of teacher education. *Journal of Education for Teaching, 17*(2), 139–150. https://doi.org/10.1080/0260747910170203

Aguilar, E. (2013). *The art of coaching: Effective strategies for school transformation.* Jossey-Bass.

Aguilar, E. (2014). *Spheres of control.* https://blogs.edweek.org/teachers/coaching_teachers/2014/01/spheres_of_control.html

American Federation of Teachers. (2017). *2017 Educator quality of work life survey.* https://www.aft.org/sites/default/files/2017_eqwl_survey_web.pdf

Anderson, G., & Blase, J. (1995). *The micropolitics of educational leadership: From control to empowerment.* Teachers College Press.

Banaji, M., & Greenwald, A. (2016). *Blindspot: Hidden biases of good people.* Bantam Books.

Bandura, A. (1989). Human agency in social cognitive theory. *The American Psychologist, 44*(9), 1175–1184. https://doi.org/10.1037/0003-066X.44.9.1175

Bandura, A. (1997). *Self-efficacy: The exercise of control.* W.H. Freeman.

Bandura, A. (2001). Social cognitive theory: An agentic perspective. *Annual Review of Psychology, 52*(1), 1–26. https://doi.org/10.1146/annurev.psych.52.1.1

Berg, I. K., & de Shazer, S. (1993). *Making numbers talk: Language in therapy.* https://www.semanticscholar.org/paper/Making-Numbers-Talk%3A-Language-in-Therapy-Berg-Shazer/2ce14f10b195ab94d0c29bf62943e57256bf854d?p2df

Berry, B., Daughtrey, A., & Wieder, A. (2009). *Teaching effectiveness and the conditions that matter most in high-needs schools: A policy brief.* Center for Teacher Quality. https://files.eric.ed.gov/fulltext/ED508532.pdf

Blackburn, M. V., & Schultz, K. (2015). *Interrupting hate: Homophobia in schools and what literacy can do about it.* Teachers College Press.

Blankstein, A. M., Noguera, P., & Kelly, L. (2016). *Excellence through equity: Five principles of courageous leadership to guide achievement for every student.* ASCD.

Broadwell, M. M. (1969). Teaching for learning. *The Gospel Guardian, 20*(41), 1–3. https://www.wordsfitlyspoken.org/gospel_guardian/v20/v20n41p1-3a.html

Cardon, A. (n.d.). Powerful coaching questions. *Metasysteme.* https://www.metasysteme-coaching.eu/english/-powerful-coaching-questions/

Co-Active Training Institute. (2019). *Powerful questions.* https://learn.coactive.com/hubfs/2019%20Toolkit/Co-Active-Coaching-Toolkit-POWERFUL%20QUESTIONS.pdf

Costa, A. L., & Garmston, R. J. (2016). *Cognitive coaching: Developing self-directed leaders and learners.* Rowman and Littlefield.

Costa, A. L., Garmston, R. J., Anderson, R. H., & Glickman, C. D. (2002). *Cognitive coaching: A foundation for renaissance schools* (2nd ed.). Christopher-Gordan Publishers.

Covey, S. R. (2004). *The 7 habits of highly effective people: Powerful lessons in personal change.* Free Press.

Danielson, C. (1996). *Enhancing professional practice: A framework for teaching.* Association for Supervision and Curriculum Development.

Day, C., Kington, A., Stobart, G., & Sammons, P. (2006). The personal and professional selves of teachers: Stable and unstable identities. *British Educational Research Journal, 32*(4), 601–616. https://doi.org/10.1080/01411920600775316

Day, C., Sammons, P., & Gu, Q. (2007). *Teachers matter: Connecting work, lives and effectiveness.* McGraw-Hill and Open University Press.

Dewey, J. (1938). *Experience and education.* Touchstone.

Doran, G. T. (1981). There's a S.M.A.R.T way to write management's goals and objectives. *Management Review, 70*(11), 35. https://community.mis.temple.edu/mis0855002fall2015/files/2015/10/S.M.A.R.T-Way-Management-Review.pdf

Duffy, G., Miller, S., Parsons, S., & Meloth, M. (2009). Teachers as metacognitive professionals. In D. J. Hacker, J. Dunlosky, & A. C. Graesser (Eds.), *Handbook of metacognition in education* (pp. 240–256). Taylor & Francis.

Elmore, R. F. (2005). Agency, reciprocity, and accountability in democratic education. In S. Fuhrman & M. Lazerson (Eds.), *The institutions of American democracy: The public schools* (pp. 277–302). Oxford University Press.

Flavell, J. H. (1979). Metacognition and cognitive monitoring: A new area of cognitive developmental inquiry. *The American Psychologist, 34*(10), 906–911. https://doi.org/10.1037/0003-066X.34.10.906

Frank, R. (2018). *Caring about vs. caring for*. https://www.ct3education.com/2018/10/30/caring-about-vs-caring-for/

Freire, P. (1993). *Pedagogy of the oppressed: New revised 20th anniversary edition*. Continuum.

Fullan, M. (2007). *The new meaning of educational change* (4th ed.). Teachers College Press.

Gawande, A. (2011, September 26). Personal best. *The New Yorker*. https://www.newyorker.com/magazine/2011/10/03/personal-best

Gawande, A. (2017). *Want to get great at something? Get a coach* [Video file]. https://www.ted.com/talks/atul_gawande_want_to_get_great_at_something_get_a_coach/transcript?language=en

Gay, G. (2010). *Culturally responsive teaching: Theory, research, and practice* (2nd ed.). Teachers College Press.

Goleman, D. (2001). Emotional intelligence: Issues in paradigm building. In D. Goleman & C. Cherniss (Eds.), *The emotionally intelligent workplace: How to select for, measure, and improve emotional intelligence in individuals, groups, and organizations*. Jossey-Bass.

Green, A., & Hauser, J. (2020). *Tips for writing SMARTIE goals*. https://www.managementcenter.org/article/tips-for-writing-smartie-goals/

Hargreaves, A., & Fullan, M. (1996). *What's worth fighting for in your school?* Teachers College Press.

Harmer, J. (2001). *The practice of English language teaching*. Pearson Education Limited.

Health Resources and Services Administration. (2020, June). *Adverse childhood experiences*. https://mchb.hrsa.gov/sites/default/files/mchb/Data/NSCH/nsch-ace-databrief.pdf

Henderson, J. G. (1992). *Reflective teaching: Becoming an inquiring educator*. Palgrave Macmillan.

Hock, R. R. (1988). Professional burnout among public school teachers. *Public Personnel Management, 17*(2), 167–189. https://doi.org/10.1177/009102608801700207

Hughes, G. (2012). Teacher retention: Teacher characteristics, school characteristics, organizational characteristics, and teacher efficacy. *The Journal of Educational Research, 105*(4), 245–255. https://doi.org/10.1080/00220671.2011.584922

Jiang, Y., Ma, L., & Gao, L. (2016). Assessing teachers' metacognition in teaching: The teacher metacognition inventory. *Teaching and Teacher Education, 59*, 403–413. https://doi.org/10.1016/j.tate.2016.07.014

Joyce, B., & Showers, B. (2002). *Student achievement through staff development*. Association for Supervision and Curriculum Development.

Jung, L. A., Frey, N., Fisher, D., & Kroener, J. (2019). *Your students, my students, our students: Rethinking equitable and inclusive classrooms*. ASCD.

Kafka, J. (2011). *The history of "zero tolerance" in American public schooling*. Palgrave Macmillian. https://doi.org/10.1057/9781137001962

Killion, H., & Bryan, C. (2012). *Coaching matters*. Oxford, OH: Learning Forward.

Kimsey-House, H., Kimsey-House, K., Sandhal, P., & Whitworth, L. (2018). *Co-active coaching: The proven framework for transformative conversations at work and in life* (4th ed.). Nicholas Brealey.

Kise, J. A. G. (2006). *Differentiated coaching: A framework for helping teachers change*. Corwin.

Klusmann, U., Richter, D., & Lüdtke, O. (2016). Teachers' emotional exhaustion is negatively related to students' achievement: Evidence from a large-scale assessment study. *Journal of Educational Psychology, 108*(8), 1193–1203. https://doi.org/10.1037/edu0000125

Knight, J. (2007). *Instructional coaching: A partnership approach to improving instruction*. Corwin.

Knight, J. (2009). Coaching. *National Staff Development Council, 30*(1).

Knight, J. (2018). *The impact cycle*. Corwin.

Knowles, M. S. (1990). *The adult learner: A neglected species* (4th ed.). Gulf Publishing Company.

Knowles, M. S., Elwood, R., Holton, R., III, & Swanson, A. (1998). *The adult learner: The definitive classic in adult education and human resource development* (5th ed.). Heinemann.

Kolb, A. Y., & Kolb, D. A. (2005). Learning styles and learning spaces: Enhancing experiential learning in higher education. *Academy of Management Learning & Education, 4*(2), 193–212. https://doi.org/10.5465/amle.2005.17268566

Kolb, A. Y., & Kolb, D. A. (2009). The learning way: Meta-cognitive aspects of experiential learning. *Simulation & Gaming, 40*(3), 297–327. https://doi.org/10.1177/1046878108325713

Kozol, J. (1991). *Savage inequalities: Children in America's schools*. Crown Publishing Group.

Kraft, M. A., Blazar, D., & Hogan, D. (2018). The effect of teacher coaching on instruction and achievement: A meta-analysis of the causal evidence. *Review of Educational Research, 88*(4), 547–588.

Kraft, M. A., & Gilmour, A. (2016). Can principals promote teacher development as evaluators? A case study of principals' views and experiences. *Educational Administration Quarterly. EAQ, 52*(5), 711–753. https://doi.org/10.1177/0013161X16653445

Krathwohl, D. R. (2002). A revision of bloom's taxonomy: An overview. *Theory into Practice, 41*(4), 212–218. https://doi.org/10.1207/s15430421tip4104_2

Lai, E. (2005). *Mentoring for in-service teachers in a distance teacher education programme: Views of mentors, mentees and university teachers*. Paper presented at the Australian Association for Research in Education International Education Research Conference, Parramatta.

Lopez, S., & Louis, M. (2009). The principles of asset-based education. *Journal of College and Character, 10*(4), 1–8. https://doi.org/10.2202/1940-1639.1041

Luttenberg, J., Imants, J., & van Veen, K. (2013). Reform as ongoing positioning process: The positioning of a teacher in the context of reform. *Teachers and Teaching, 19*(3), 293–310. https://doi.org/10.1080/13540602.2012.754161

Manasia, L. (2015). *Creating A-HA moments in teaching practice. Routine versus adaptive metacognition behaviors in teachers*. Proceedings of the Scientific Conference AFASES, pp. 1255–1262.

Marzano, R. J., Boogren, T., Heflebower, T., Kanold-McIntyre, J., & Pickering, D. (2012). *Becoming a reflective teacher*. Marzano Resources.

Maslach, C. (1978). Clients and burnout. *The Journal of Social Issues, 34*(4), 111–124. https://doi.org/10.1111/j.1540-4560.1978.tb00778.x

Maslach, C. (2003). *Burnout: The cost of caring*. Malor Books.

Maslach, C., & Leiter, M. P. (2016). Understanding the burnout experience: Recent research and its implications for psychiatry. *World Psychiatry, 15*(2), 103–111. https://doi.org/10.1002/wps.20311

Meier, D. (2002). *In schools we trust: Creating communities of learning in an era of testing and standardization*. Beacon Press.

Mezirow, J. (1991). *Transformative dimensions of adult learning*. Jossey-Bass.

Mezirow, J. (1997). Transformative learning: Theory to practice. *New Directions for Adult and Continuing Education, 74*(74), 5–12. https://doi.org/10.1002/ace.7401

Mezirow, J. (2009). An overview on transformative learning. In K. Illeris (Ed.), *Contemporary theories of learning. Learning theorists . . . in their own words* (pp. 90–105). Routledge.

Mezirow, J., & Associates. (1990). *Fostering critical reflection in adulthood. A guide to transformative and emancipatory learning*. Jossey-Bass.

Miller, W. R., & Rollnick, S. (2013). *Motivational interviewing: Helping people change*. The Guilford Press.

Mind Tools Content Team. (n.d.). *The action priority matrix: Making the most of your opportunities*. https://www.mindtools.com/pages/article/newHTE_95.htm

National Child Traumatic Stress Network. (2020, August 3). *Secondary traumatic stress*. https://www.nctsn.org/trauma-informed-care/secondary-traumatic-stress

Noddings, N. (2002). *Educating moral people: A caring alternative to character education*. Teachers College Press.

Opper, I. (2019). *Teachers matter. Understanding teachers' impact on student achievement*. Rand Corporation. https://www.rand.org/education-and-labor/projects/measuring-teacher-effectiveness/teachers-matter.html

Prochaska, J. O., & DiClemente, C. (1982). Transtheoretical therapy: Toward a more integrative model of change. *Psychotherapy (Chicago, Ill.), 19*(3), 276–288. https://doi.org/10.1037/h0088437

Prochaska, J. O., & DiClemente, C. (1983). Stages and processes of self-change of smoking—Toward and integrative model of change. *Journal of Consulting and Clinical Psychology, 51*(3), 390–395. https://doi.org/10.1037/0022-006X.51.3.390

Prochaska, J. O., Redding, C. A., & Kerry, E. E. (2008). The transtheoretical model and stages of change. In K. Glanz, B. K. Rimer, & K. Viswanath (Eds.), *Health behavior and health education: Theory research and practice* (4th ed.). Jossey-Bass.

Prochaska, J. O., & Velicer, W. F. (1997). The transtheoretical model of health behavior change. *American Journal of Health Promotion, 12*(1), 38–48. https://doi.org/10.4278/0890-1171-12.1.38

Roegman, R., Allen, D., Leverett, L., Thompson, S., & Hatch, T. (2019). *Equity visits: A new approach to supporting equity-focused school and district leadership*. Corwin.

Rogers, C. R. (1961). *On becoming a person: A therapist's view of psychotherapy*. Houghton Mifflin.

Ryan, R., & Deci, E. (2000). Self-determination theory and the facilitation of intrinsic motivation, social development, and well-being. *The American Psychologist, 55*(1), 68–78. https://doi.org/10.1037/0003-066X.55.1.68

Ryan, S., von der Embse, N., Pendergast, L., Saeki, E., Segool, N., & Schwing, S. (2017). Leaving the teaching profession: The role of teacher stress and educational accountability policies on turnover intent. *Teaching and Teacher Education, 66*, 1–11. https://doi.org/10.1016/j.tate.2017.03.016

Rollnick, S., Miller, W. R., & Butler, C. C. (2008). *Motivational interviewing in health care: Helping patients change behavior*. The Guilford Press.

RTI's approach to supporting high-quality project-based learning in schools. (n.d.). https://www.rti.org/publication/rtis-approach-supporting-high-quality-project-based-learning-schools/fulltext.pdf

Sabzalian, L. (2019). *Indigenous children's survivance in public schools*. Routledge. https://doi.org/10.4324/9780429427503

Schon, D. A. (1983). *The reflective practitioner*. Basic Books.

Shirrell, M., Hopkins, M., & Spillane, J. (2019). Educational infrastructure, professional learning, and changes in teachers' instructional practices and beliefs. *Professional Development in Education, 45*(4), 599–613. https://doi.org/10.1080/19415257.2018.1452784

Short, P. M. (1992). *Dimensions of teacher empowerment*. https://files.eric.ed.gov/fulltext/ED368701.pdf

Singleton, G. E. (2012). *More courageous conversations about race*. Corwin.

Smith, J. M., & Kovacs, P. E. (2011). The impact of standards-based reform on teachers: The case of 'no child left behind'. *Teachers and Teaching, 17*(2), 201–225. https://doi.org/10.1080/13540602.2011.539802

Stephens, D., Morgan, D. N., Deford, D. E., Donnelly, A., Hamel, E., Keith, K. J., Brink, D. A., Johnson, R., Seaman, M., Young, J., Gallant, D. J., Hao, S., &. Leigh, S. R. (2011). The impact of literacy coaches on teacher's believes and practices. *Journal of Literacy Research, 43*(3), 215–249. https://doi.org/10.1177/1086296X11413716

Stoltzfus, T. (2008). *Coaching questions: A coach's guide to powerful asking skills*. Coach22 Bookstore, LLC.

Ting, S., & Scisco, P. (Eds.). (2006). *The CCL handbook of coaching: A guide for the leader coach*. John Wiley & Sons, Inc and Jossey-Bass.

Travis, J. W., & Ryan, R. S. (2004). *The wellness workbook* (3rd ed.). Penguin Random House.

Treatment and Services Adaptation Center. (2020, August 14). *Secondary traumatic stress*. https://traumaawareschools.org/secondaryStress

Tversky, A., & Kahneman, D. (1973). Judgment under uncertainty: Heuristics and biases. *Oregon Research Institute Research Bulletin, 13*(1).

U.S. Department of Veterans Affairs. (2019). *My story: Personal health inventory*. https://www.va.gov/PATIENTCENTEREDCARE/resources/personal-health-inventory.asp

West, L., & Cameron, A. (2013). *Agents of change: How content coaching transforms teaching & learning*. Heinemann.

Whole health coaching participant manual. (2018). Training materials prepared under contract to the Veterans Health Administration by Pacific Institute for Research and Evaluation.

Yoder, N. (2014). *Teaching the whole child: Instructional practices that support social-emotional learning in three teacher evaluation frameworks* (Rev. ed.). American Institutes for Research. https://gtlcenter.org/sites/default/files/TeachingtheWholeChild.pdf

Yoder, N., & Gurke, D. (2017). *Social and emotional learning coaching toolkit: Keeping SEL at the center*. SEL Solutions at the American Institute for

Research. https://www.air.org/sites/default/files/downloads/report/Social-and-Emotional-Learning-SEL-Coaching-Toolkit-August-2017.pdf

Young, A., & Fry, J. (2008). Metacognitive awareness and academic achievement in college students. *The Journal of Scholarship of Teaching and Learning, 8*(2), 1–10.

Zeichner, K. M., & Liston, D. P. (1996). *Reflective teaching: An introduction.* Lawrence Erlbaum Associates.

For Product Safety Concerns and Information please contact our EU
representative GPSR@taylorandfrancis.com
Taylor & Francis Verlag GmbH, Kaufingerstraße 24, 80331 München, Germany

www.ingramcontent.com/pod-product-compliance
Lightning Source LLC
Chambersburg PA
CBHW080924300426
44115CB00018B/2930